YOUR INFINITE INTIMATE EMBRACE

Dearest Barbara

moonlight floods The garden path

walking on clouds

footless

acres of love
eons of sky
I love you,
Nancy

YOUR INFINITE INTIMATE EMBRACE

you have never left

NANCY NEITHERCUT

ISBN-13: 9781975783914
ISBN-10: 1975783913

CHAPTERS

DEAR READER,

All my life I suppose I was a seeker, a seeker of ideas of love, a seeker of ideas of peace, a seeker of ideas like wonder and mystery, a seeker of other better more or next, but never a seeker of enlightenment. I had met seekers of enlightenment and they always seemed so serious, dressed in white, speaking in hushed voices, and mediating meditating meditating, like they were trying to be dead. It seemed like a lot of hard work! And like descriptions of heaven I'd heard as a kid, no fun. Where was the laughter? Where was the dancing, the sunlight the joy? Where was the bar?

Although I did my share of reading books, I had never really heard this profound permanent shift in perspective described. I am certain that if I had read my poems or the songs of some of my friends I would have hungered for this.

Yet I also mediated on and off, I liked the high, and as I used to dance and sing along with songs like, 'I gotta lose this skin I've been livin' in' the goal was vague, but always in the future.

The light and love and magic I longed for was all around me, in me through me as me. It was only these ideas of what I was and what the light was and my desire to capture it that create this imaginary barrier between inside and out. The desire to transcend what is going on, to escape this skin, was what defined me. I was those very barriers I was trying to explode.

My songs and videos will not give the seeker of enlightenment any hope or encouragement, and they will not be popular, as they will not give succor by giving methods and practices that perpetuate the illusion of separation. However some may resonate if these words echo their own heart songs. I am not trying to convince you of anything as awakening is not a belief, and I cannot give you anything. Or nothing. Yet without a listener there is no song, and there is no singer.

Knowing there is no me nor you nor love, here are the love songs that flow through me, simply life playing amongst its own echoes, dancing as the tree tops playing in the summer breeze.

Sometimes poetry or ambiguous words can leave the mind with no where to go, nothing to grasp, suspend the belief in belief, and leave the mind hanging, as what is going on cannot be figured out and is indeed ambiguous. However the objectifying brain and it's thought stream of this and that seem to split apart what's going on into separate bits and then seems to put what was never separate back together into some kind of place of rest or understanding. Awakening is not about your getting something or reaching a place of understanding. It's beyond belief or understanding, just like life.

Most mistake description for understanding, for example some say, "It's all nothing, or energy vibration, frequency, or emptiness or a mystery" They believe they have nailed it and search endlessly for examples to prove this. What's energy? What's emptiness?

We see a flower and recognize it as a flower even though many flowers appear quite different. That is the brain objectifying the perceptual input into things and categories of things. It is truly marvelous how the thought steam paints the dream of separation with words ideas concepts. However no one knows what a flower is, no matter how many books they might read about botany and ecology and chemistry, or how many days and nights they may watch and touch and taste them, or put them under their pillow at night, to try to dream of being a yellow flower.

What is yellow?
What is a what?
What is not a what?

What is love?

Only with imaginary separation can we marvel at the wonder of awe and love and the mystery and majesty of life, and only with the objectifying brain is this possible.

The feeling of there being nothing actually substantial underneath the swirling thought dream and the belief that there is a controller or a doer or a feeler or a thinker or a conductor of life creates quite an imaginary distance and a painful one between you and a world of things. That tension is felt physically and psychologically and is that feeling of being a solid separate person around which the world swirls.

When the belief in separation is seen through there is a palpable release. Like a heavy load dropping to the ground. I truly felt that my body would collapse to the floor or I might pee my pants!

I thought how could life be going on without a me doing anything? I was and am still amazed that life does itself. I am simply the shimmering reflections of a hard white diamond that disappeared.

It's like time died.
The whirling center of the dream had exploded and imploded into a vast unknowable unknown and there was no one to look for safe harbor and no empty pockets left to hide in or a need to fill them. No reference points whatsoever were left. Yet this dream dance of love creates these feets that move to the heartbeat of existence. This and that the rhythm of love singing you singing me singing us as we sing.

All words and concepts spin around pin pointing to each other and never ever capture what seems to appear, yet the words and this thought dream as I sing are also what seems to appear
Utterly spontaneously
Life does itself
Totally naturally the dream paints itself
Like this

Love,
Nancy

APRIL SONGS

I remember as a kid as I walked to school I always avoided the cracks in the sidewalk. I would repeat the saying,"Step on a crack break your mothers back". One day after a perceived hurt from her I stepped on every crack I could that morning. At one point during the day it dawned on me... oh my!

What had I done? I wasn't sure what a broken back was, but it sounded bad!

I spent the rest of the day in utter terror, and ran home as fast as I could1 She was there, just fine. Even through I knew stepping on cracks was not harmful, and not stepping on them was not beneficial, I continued the practice for awhile until it was eventually forgotten.

It seems a lot of beliefs disappear like this. There's an initial seeing of their falseness, yet they still hang around for awhile.

For example, although I had had the profound permanent shift in perspective of knowing and feeling that there are no things, when faced with the utter devastatingly ravishingly beautiful emptiness of self, I called it, and was the idea of 'timeless awareness' for awhile, clinging really to air, to keep myself from falling totally. A beautiful new set of clothing, this belief that there is still something solid and unchanging and fixed.

There is truly not even nothing under our nakedness, not even pure consciousness or emptiness. Many seem to permanently retreat into the fetal position of hope and fear, and I can't blame them. This isn't about feeling better, and very few fall the whole way.

Ripples flow over and through each other
A shadow dances with its own reflection on the waves
There is no shore on this sea of dreams
Just the dance
A clear perfect unending always ending sourceless tone reverberates on a delicate flowing membrane of reflections that appears to create and define you with your unique coloration and overtones, syncing in a rhythmic vibe dancing as the dance primeval. When the words and rhythm are no longer searched for as a key to what has no lock, this magic floods the marrow out if your timeline and this unrehearsed symphony resounds ...centerless edgeless location-less.
Yet without you, there is no music. You are the symphony of life singing itself through your very lips.

You are the window through which life sees its own beauty and majesty

Love sings
Like this
And calls your name
Oh
Here you are
I love you
I am you

How long did we wait for our lives to begin? Believing that everything had to be 'just right', so we could finally relax
When you least expect it, when all hope is gone, when you realize that tale will never get pinned on the donkey, when you realize that all the ladders in the world will never reach the moon, when you're tired of trying to catch the wind, kiss your reflection in the moonlit pond, that it was simply a misconception that you were in charge of the stage door, and had to turn the crank on the merry-go- round, you find infinite permutations of a butterfly kiss, and a beautiful intimacy of life slipping through your fingers as you slip through the lines, losing yourself and finding yourself awash in iridescent awe.

No more regrets. No more what if's. Simply absolute perfection and utter rest when it's known and felt deeply that this is indeed all there is. This edgeless seamless ever blooming ever wilting momentary.
Immediate and brilliant, burning, consuming itself as soon as it is recognized. The ashes of memory leave our footprints in sky like a trail of winged shadows so we can recognize our reflection in our lovers eyes. No one is a stranger, as we know we are each other. All and everything utterly familiar and yet ever new and sparkling, life kissing you deeply as you kiss it. No middle no sides, nothing more or less than what seems to appear, beyond intimate, beyond infinite, beyond the reaches of every love song, beyond the hearts of a million kisses. All I ever wanted, always on, always this.
I reach out my hand to touch the blue and it is sky and space and my hand in an edgeless brilliant transparent bejeweled light stream singing swirling pouring through me as me. This ecstatic love dance of one of two of many of none. Such a tender delicate fragrance of this, that has no words yet includes all words, twists and twines into a lush rich dreamscape, ever spiraling, ever expanding, ever collapsing, ever arising, ever dying. A magnificent shooting star consumed by its own love dissolves into itself.
The warmth of a thousand suns in the kiss of midnight.

I see you feel this magic, I recognize it in the beauty of your shining eyes. For what is the wetness of tears, no one can say. What is this warmth of love or pain of sorrow or the splendid incomprehensibility of wonder itself? Unspeakably marvelous that you cannot

2

touch life yet everywhere you point inside or out, anguish or awe, you are not separate from it, or the pointing.

Sunrise bathes your tender face as last night's kisses run down your heart into this sea of dreams where you dance. No safe harbor to arrive at and hide. You soar as wetness in water, where sky has collapsed into sea and sea into sky, awash, adrift with no rudder or sail or direction or path to an imaginary future, or a wake or trace of an imaginary past. There is no center or edge yet you remain as this centerless jewel, the dream spinning around you creating infinite facets that all reflect your beautiful face.

There is no path to where you have never left, there is no key to unlock a door that never was. It was only your footsteps that formed themselves that seemed to create direction and purpose, and imprints of time upon your multicolored shadow as you danced in star-light, showering the spark of love's beauty back into the skies.

Blue sky spills across the canyon, pools as silent slumber in shadows deep embrace. Soft lights gaze as wordless wonder sings a shimmering ripple casting dreams into an edge-less sea. Splashing rainbows caress your tenderness as wind paints an empty heart to hold your beautiful tears. Infinite prisms skip colors across your doorstep awaiting your magical adornment of this sea of love.

You have never left this magic that we share in our aloneness, together. It calls you beck-ons you, 'hello goodbye hello'. You cannot hide forever from this magic that you are, as even hiding from it or trying to grasp it reflects love's beauty in your eyes. You have never left home as you are emptiness overflowing in every direction without direction. You have never been nor will ever be, yet here you are, such unspeakable beauty, wrapped in your own infinite intimate embrace...

What is that ache inside your chest?
What is that sound that keeps you awake at night?
It is the roar of the universe ripping your heart open and wings of love taking flight.
Unraveled from the fetal position your toes stretch into the light ....
Naked and unafraid awash in moon glow...

We are simply and most beautifully sourceless shimmering reflections, loves empty shad-ows dancing, lit with echoes of each others love light, memories sing our phantom sil-houette in sky.

This is so simple it cannot be grasped, it is mind boggling unbelievable that life does itself and has no separate parts nor edge.

All this! spontaneously appearing. How magical! Truly the magic you seek is already right here right now, and there is no here nor there nor now nor then or next. Have you ever found a next? Or better or more or anything other than this as it seems to appear? There are no separate things yet all and everything seem to arise, don't they? All perception, sight sound tactile sensation taste bodily sensation feeling thought self arising and self releasing as soon as the symphony of perception is recognized. The zing of this brilliant immediacy looking and feeling like anything at all. Truly you know that life is a precious miracle. You are awareness aware of being aware through this streaming flowing dream of separation. The magic, always on, is you.

So many believe their ultimate perfection lies beyond beliefs, preferences and opinions. But self is composed of these. They paint the color in the sunset. Under the swirling random water color thought dream that you are, there is not even nothing.
You, just as you think you are, are unutterably beautiful. I love your emptiness and your fullness, your unique window dressing. You cannot see this, nor can I see my own beauty, but as we exist only as echo'd reflections in each other's I's, we can swoon into and through ourselves in this amazing love dance of one of two of many of none.
Knowing there is no you nor me nor love, the passion play continues. This is not the end of love. An uncontrived unconditional love arises knowing no one is the instigator of thought feeling belief or action. Such beautiful humanness flowing as us, painted empty, multifaceted bejeweled woven and tattered tapestries soaring fleeting love letters in the wind.

You don't have to hide, you cannot hide. I see your heart ache, your tenderness, your tears, your joy, your vulnerable delicate humanness. I know that deep infinite emptiness you fear, and your longing. Our meeting is always nakedly intimate, yet we need flowing colors to see each other as there is no dancing without a costume, there is not even nothing under these swirling mirrored gypsy skirts. There is no one dancing and there is never truly another to meet or kiss.
Sunlight pours through an empty glass and sings of love and love lost and weeps the stories of birth and death into a paintbrush saturating the the canyon walls. Wind and water flow ripples into ripples, whirl pooling in infinite pirouettes, tumbling twirling blurring the edges of song. What cannot be articulated we all know deeply as a magic that seems to have eluded our grasp. Yet the grasping is magic, as is the song of silent wonder erupting daydream starlight singing ancient memories that pierce us in a profound recognition of the marvel of unknowing.
The passion play of what you never did what you never were and what will never be strums our heart strings that reverberate together as our melody seems different, the overtones and undertones are the same. The same notes and the same back-beat of

this and that thrum thrum thrum on the naked desert floor and starlight dances in waves of joy and sorrow in a dance where your feet always know where to go, going nowhere, echoing everywhere, finding their rhythm in my feet in your feet in the footless footfalls that crumbled as soon as you thought you touched the ground.

Are we not and have not we always been loves dance in each others eyes?

her eyes bedecked with starlight pouring through loves beautiful reflection

We are this beautiful ocean
we have never been separate
and yet songs flow through us and write our imaginary lines
erased with tears
sung with rainbows
A painted desert
a painted dream
Dissolving into and through itself
Un-capturable amorphous
Beyond beautiful
It paints itself

Laughing winds ripple your name in the vastness and find no place where your song is not. A caress of a hush like a lullaby swinging in the boughs of sky billows ever outwards and kisses you from within. Reaching out to touch the flowing dream your touch dissolves in wonder, for it is always your own eyes that you see smiling laughing weeping love's beautiful reflection in your intimate infinite embrace. Leaving no trace your footfalls never hid the ground, your face always shimmered sky. Spaciousness so vast no tears can be counted as it dissolves into itself through your kiss.

And all that was left was an all encompassing sound. The hum of the universe that she had sought was everywhere and nowhere. It was the all pervading knowingness that life had always done itself, looking and feeling like anything at all.
I love you. It's all light and you are it. Illumined from the inside and the outside, and it feels like love. Your beautiful humanness and love light shining irrevocably just as all you seem to be. Every hitch in yer get-a-long is a beautiful rhythm never wavering from the walk the trot the gallop of love kissing itself through your beautiful beautiful lips.
You have never left your intimate infinite embrace. The heaviness of light astounds me. The weight of nothing blinds me. Your all pervading love light is me.

The gift you seek was never yours to give away or keep. It was never found nor lost. Hand-less hands appeared to hold a seamless embrace of paper dolls around an ocean of tears, of every tear dried up and rolled into a paper cup folded into an origami fan tale sky blooming unfolding always the magnificent fairy tale story of love.

It is love that sings my lines.
Words fail yet they stream through my fingertips. No longer do I look to find my finger-print in sky.
Years and years of tears and fears erased my cloud shadow sparkling in the sun as all my empty footfalls were simply echoes in the sand while my world crumbled to the sea.
All the scaffolding that seemed to hold up the sky fell, and under the blue there was not even naked sky. Ropes of air untied the knots that held my heart in a sling and the sea crashed through the sky and smashed all my ideas of love into smithereens and there was no one left to glue back together the shards of mirrored blue.
Yet it is love that gathers the ashes into a shadow bird that soars and dances in and as the wind in love as love through love life kisses itself through our beautiful lips.
Waves crashing into themselves sing a song like this
Soaring without nakedness
Skimming across the sea of dreams
How many tears to wash the tears away?

What is the shape of blue?
Where is the outside to love?
Only a made up place to rest in your beautiful beautiful heart
Under the blue not even sky

Lassos of words kiss a patch of blue and the edges create and pierce your heart. Starlight illuminates the solar winds and swirls a phantom flowing picture of time. The pulse of this and that is the heartbeat of existence. Life breathes you and it is so stunningly beautiful it takes your breath away simultaneously.

Words soar and scatter through these empty pages weaving a passion play of gusts and shadows through pillared halls of moonbeams dancing in a wind ballet. Oceans of light pour through waves of prism'd jewels of light shimmering into and through this dance. Cleansed by tears the painted day washes off revealing a stark emptiness as you real-ize you had been caressing a future that has never arrived. It is your own love that rips you apart from the inside and out until a sideless glance reveals the seamless ease of life doing itself. How beautifully life swishes through your toes and writes your name in puddles of wonderment. The edges of your footprints collapse as the roots were imaginary that held you in sky's grasp. You fall until you are the falling falling through itself, and an essence of sweetness subsumes the wakeless wake of dreams. Wetness, the liquidity of home, embraces your nakedness.

And where was the song of the meadow lark that you heard yesterday eve echoing in the distant canyon? Where was her path on the evening breeze? Where did your love go when you were not?

The dream was ripped wide open. An empty swing softy moved in the evening breeze, and nakedness ran through the open fields.

What is that ache inside your chest?
What is that sound that keeps you awake at night?
It is the roar of the universe ripping your heart open and wings of love taking flight.
Unraveled from the fetal position your toes stretch into the light ....
Naked and unafraid awash in moon glow....

Words fall through the window they paint and dissolve in seamless sky. Night time, another shadow, races across the great unknown, erasing all certitude of hope and fear of tomorrow. Lost in the grip of the terror of unknowing the great maw of desire consumes your reaching out for love in a flood of the starkness of no one left to love or be loved. This great all consuming utter blankness creeps into the night time and the day time dream like forgotten melodies weaving their heartache into the brightest day. A melancholy tune that cannot be erased by any thought or action it calls you, beckons you to announce your nakedness. And who would be revealed under that cloak of hope and fear? Your unadorned neck waits for the hot breath of the tiger that is your own love. Morning arises unseen under the canopy of storm, thunder and lightning draw us deeper into our warm blankets listening to the heavy rain drops on the roof of the van. Soon, raggedy rain clouds part and sun kisses the mountains and valleys with shine and shadow. Bejeweled leaves shimmer in the late morning light as winds sweep down from the peaks, and where does the mountain end and the valley begin? I take off my sweater, and where does my wrist end and my forearm begin? Where does my hand end and the sky begin? Without words there are no mountains or wind to toss the long Meadow grasses into a sparkling dance. There are no fingers to point to the beauty of sky. There is no seamless blue or clouds. There is no this and that to waltz or tango without imaginary separation.

As soon as you began to learn the names of things your world began to be shattered. The vast unknowable edgeless unknown began to be split and divided into things that were you and things that were not you. The word 'tree' seems to stop and hold a bit of the seamless fluid stream of perception into all that is 'tree' and all that is not 'tree', including you. All qualities and characteristics, all time dimension, all measurement is made up. The known, or conceptual world, is mentally fabricated. A dream of separation, a virtual reality, a hologram, a pseudo reality of this and that, outside and inside, trees mountains wind and you. Somewhere deep inside there is an intuited knowing of the seamlessness of life, but it is a frightening place to go, as if there are no things, what would that mean about you? Yet, simultaneously, there is a longing to return to that knowing, but you can never grasp or have this seamless ease, as you are not separate from the magic you seek.

Indeed, you have never left your infinite intimate embrace. There is no outside to what is going on, no more no other nor better nor next. There are no things inside it, as there is no inside, yet all and everything is included. All perception, including sight sound taste touch sensation, all thought of this and that, memories of past and thoughts of the morrow are happening as this uncontainable vibrant momentary. How rich and lush this aliveness that you are!

All you can truly know is this utterly obvious brilliant aliveness that appears as the stream of perception and the recognition of it. The worded description that seems to capture it never does, yet that is what seems to make it 'knowable'. It is truly never known or grasped as there is no one separate from it to know it. Are you separate from the symphony of perception? Are you separate from the recognition of it? Are you separate from the thought stream that describes it? Is there an inside (you) or outside (not you) without thought? As there is truly no inside or outside there is no other better more or next, is there? If there truly is no next, what will you do? What could you do? The end of belief in next is the end of belief in you.

Most live on a teeter totter of hope and fear of a never arising next, yet with the gnawing feeling that this is indeed it, and that dissonance creates a painful tension that is felt always. Like a tight fist gripping your heart. I cannot convince you that this ever emerging ever blooming ever wilting immediacy is all there is, as it is not a belief or understanding, yet I know you know this deeply. This all encompassing momentary has no edges, no beginning or ending, as it is always beginning and ending simultaneously, without time or non time. Have you ever found a beginning or end to a moment? Are there indeed separate moments? Is there someone separate from this atemporal flowing who could capture it or stop it or change it? How could there be movement or non movement when there are no separate things to be stable or flowing? How could there be perfection or imperfection if there are no things to be put together into an idea of perfection? There is no outside or other to what's going on, so nothing can be added or taken away. Where would it come from? Where would it go? Life is all of a piece, of itself so. It is seamless perfection always. Even the feeling that it is not arises naturally and is perfect.

Nothing has any more or less meaning than the play of shimmering waters on your laughing hand. For what is the meaning of things or events when there are no separate things or moments? Who could hold meaning or purpose when there is no one separate from the flowing?

Rolling thunder echoes across the rocky peaks and the dog looks anxious. We pet her and reassure her. But there is no dog or anxious feeling or thunder echoing on tall naked mountain peaks and no one to know this until my brain paints this beautiful story. The physical world exists yet it has no separate characteristics without names.

We exist only as this flowing dreamscape. Bodies are real yet there are no 'things' called bodies until named. Selves are entirely imaginary. How amazing that your brain paints a flowing movie of things and events and creates a star of the movie! Through this made up steaming thought dream of this and that, awareness is aware of being aware. Through the miracle of this two step, the universe can see touch and feel it's own aliveness. Through the magic that you are life kisses itself.

Love waltzes in and says, 'I love you. I am you!', when it's truly realized that there is no next, there is no more, there is no better. There is no other. You are sublimely bittersweetly alone. Yet in the dream here we are living and loving. How wondrous!

Truly when it's known deeply always that there are no things nor non things nor you, life feels like an ecstatic love dance, a constant union of what was never separate. An Intense and dream-like surreal passion play of one of two of many of none. You are life dancing as life dances you.

Words sing silent rivers of rain on rain, wet on wet, moon on moon, time and smiles and tears magically appear out of not even nothing. And you, a reflection without source or shadow, dance.

Late afternoon light shimmers on the lake, sun dancing rippling wetness, a few fishermen stand, they have weathered the tempest. Some of us have survived the tsunami of sea crashing headlong into sky and found we could breathe underwater. None of us was brave or special in any way. There were no special thoughts or feelings or dreams or actions to take for enlightenment to happen. We have not arrived anyplace special, nor have we attained a magical prize. We have no special powers. We have nothing the seeker lacks. Merely our brains no longer believe the dream it paints. This is an empty prize for no one. The price was everything and nothing. As this vast emptiness lacks even emptiness, no one can choose to pay this priceless price, and there is no path to nowhere. This is it always, just as it seems to appear. Simple as that.

Sometimes the walking wounded return to the battlefield where oceans of blood and tears have been spilt and watch the flowers grow. We marvel at the sun sliding across the vault of sky, and weep at the beauty of our beautiful humanness. We hear the screams of those trying to escape the only world they can ever know. And we sing.

Night embraces the mountains and the day is done. You are but a brief brief window, an aperture, an I through which life catches a glimpse of its own majesty. How wondrous! Marvelous and Superb!

Pure brilliant spaciousness consumes itself in this vast emptiness where not even nothing exists.

Not even a shadow of an echo reverberates until it's name is called.

How ease-fully the wind slips through the long summer grasses waving tender stalks of greens and blues and tips of flowering yellows, dancing ripples on waters kissed by sun sparkling diamonds. How tenderly it caresses your delicate face and envelops you in its coolness. How intimately your thought streaming describes this scene, this feeling of all encompassing beauty, seemingly bringing it inside you in a flowering dreamscape of wonder.

Where is the outside of this intimate caress? Are the sensations separate from you? Is the sound of the leave's softly rippling wind dance outside of you? Is not the sensation of water jewelry what you are? Is there someone watching the play of light and shadow who is outside the dancing winds? How could there be a separate watcher without the flowing sight and sound and feeling of this mountain song? How magnificent this naturally arising self releasing uninterrupted indivisible symphony of perception!

Morning paints the sky behind the tall pines and releases them from the grip of night. Bird songs soar down the canyon, cascading waters echo on the canyon walls, wind and light play on the water, and all of this is evenly and equally instantly spontaneously recognized.

There is no separate observer or awareness of this streaming flow of perception, you are not separate from it. It's not even an it, as it has no edges or outside to it. Without this rush of life there is no you, and there is no you separate from this utterly obvious dance of life. All of this unspeakably wondrous vibrancy we call life simply most marvelously happens all by itself.

For many it is easy to feel this seamless ease when they are in the natural world of oceans lakes mountains and desert, but difficult to see that the passion play of thought and emotion are as well indeed simply life happening all by itself. They have been taught that certain feelings or thoughts or actions are bad, and spend a lifetime trying to change the natural flow of life. But it's all natural, and trying to change it happens naturally also. Trying to accept or reject or surrender to it is the flowing. For certainly if they could change thought and emotion they would, and if they were truly the conductor of their lives perhaps life would not look and feel as it does! Feeling out of control most seek comfort in the illusion that SOMEONE HAS GOT TO KNOW! Looking for meaning and understanding in philosophy, psychology, religion or spirituality.

There arises a great tension with the deep intuited knowing that life does itself, and the illusion of someone doing life that can be exceedingly painful. Many try to 'relax' into their feelings, especially those believed to be painful, or surrender to or accept what's going on, aching for an ease of being that they imagine lies in going with the flow, not realizing that it is all the flow.

All trying or trying to not try perpetuate the painful illusion of a separate do-er. It is unimaginable that life as it seems to appear does itself and that there simply are no sepa-rate parts. No separate feelings or thoughts or actions. No separate thinker or feeler or do-er. No past or future or now, no separate moments.

The stream of perceptual input is far too simple and rich and lush that it cannot be 'known' until it is artificially divided into this and that by the use of shared leaned words. The thought stream seems to throw lassos around that which is not a that or this, and creates imaginary separate things like wind and light and happiness and mountains. Most painfully it seems to create a separate feeler of wind and light and happiness and a seer of mountains. When the thought stream ceases for just a moment all 'things' including you disappear. There is no knowing that there has been a thought free state until thought returns!

The silence of which I sing is not a thought free state, or a perpetual state of happiness. It is the deeply integrated apprehension that all this 'thingness' is made up. Truly many have glimpses of this whilst watching a beautiful sunset or strolling through the forest, or falling in love. As the seamlessness of what is going on is always the case, and you are not separate from it, there is nothing you can do or not do to realize this or fabricate it. You are an imaginary piece of what cannot be divided, like a mirrored slice of sky. When imaginary separation is believed in, it feels like infinite shards of blue are piercing your heart.

The feeling of unicity or wholeness, of all encompassing natural perfection cannot be contrived, yet many spend a lifetime trying to achieve this, to reach a goal called awaken-ing that can never be attained. Enlightenment is an empty prize for no one. There is no here nor there nor next nor anyone to go there.

Have you ever found an edge or outside to what is going on? There is no next or other, ever notice? This is it coyote. Your one and only Precious ever emerging ever dissolving miraculous momentary, and it's not even yours. Life happening all by itself looking and feeling like anything at all. There is no one or thing outside of life making it happen. Life occurs seamlessly and effortlessly as even the feeling of effort arises effortlessly!

Mirrored reflections dance and play upon the water, and there is no grasping the shifting clouds or their shadows, or your beautiful reflection shimmering on the ripples. You are as substantial as a lovers kiss in last night's dream. Like towering cloud castles before the storm, you cannot walk the pillared hallways. You cannot dance across the echoes of nautilus song that reverberate tales of moonlight in those forgotten sea shells you wistfully collected, like all the hopes and fears and dreams of yesterdays held onto by non existent tomorrows. You are a shadow illuminated by dreams, by drifting waves of memories, sung by the thought stream. Fleeting description whispers your name and like a sigh in the wind it traces your footprints in sky.

This fantastical infinitely faceted sound and light show magically paints itself through the thought stream beginning with one word. Like a lightening bolt the razor of thought seems to separate the sky into uncountable shards of blue. Creating color and form and all imaginary division, all this and that seem to appear. Yet what is going on is never actually divided. It cannot, as it is not a thing nor a non thing and has no edges or center or reference point. You are an imaginary reference point around which the dream of separation, the worded world, the virtual reality swirls.

How utterly unspeakably amazing that this life magically appears! Without any effort or non effort this spontaneous symphony of perception arises and is simultaneously inseparably recognized. They are not two things, awareness and perception, the observed and the observer, nor one. As there is no outside to life, you are not separate from it and you cannot grasp it. All trying to understand or grasp life simply is part of the swirling, like trying to capture the moon's reflection in a lake.

You are indeed the magic you long for, you cannot capture it. Trying to grasp it is magical. You cannot escape this vibrant aliveness you feel or gain it. This marvelous aliveness that is utterly obvious always, as the symphony of perception and the recognition of it, is all a complete confirmation of your infinite perfection. You are a precious jewel, utterly empty, yet overflowing. You are the aperture through which love and beauty enter the universe. For without the imaginary separation your brain paints, there is no sky nor sun to slide across it, no horizon and no one to hold each other's hand and say, 'oh my! How beautiful! I love you'. We can wonder at the wonder of life, be in love with love, and delight in our delightedness. Realizing that all separation, all thingness, including love is made up is not the end of love, however. The dream continues to paint itself, all super saturated with awe.

The realization that all thingness, including yourself is essentially empty, is devastating. This profound shift in perspective is most often preceded by a personal Armageddon that can be a huge conflagration or a slow burn. Some have a free glimpse of this and rush to find ideas to fill in this vast emptiness. It is the ravishingly beautiful shredding and ripping apart of all that you have held to be true about yourself and the world including all ideas of truth and the idea that there is anyone to have a world. It hurt more than I thought I could hurt without actually dying. It indeed feels like dying, but it is realized that no one ever existed. In the end there is not even nothing left. More empty than a vast barren desert, not even one tiny wisp of hope remains, yet this is also the end of fear. When I was small I read a book about the aftermath of a nuclear war, when an entire continent knew they had only two years to live. I wondered how they could build homes, fall in love, have children and live quite normally. Now I know that living, knowing there is no next, is more marvelous than any living I could have ever imagined or wished for.

Her fingers could not grasp her nakedness. The rhythm of the rhythmless sound punctuates the dream with tides
And tears

Thrum thrum the night swings. Already no me nor you yet these words create an imaginary line that cannot be crossed and when they disappear so do we. Vibrant aliveness sings overtones of unbearable beauty as it swoons into itself through your beautiful beautiful eyes. Silhouettes of whispers dance

Are you in the music or is the music in you? This pulsating rhythm of life, your footfalls dancing, your breath, your very lips kissing the words that kiss you, that sing this marvelous song of this and that, you and me, here and there, this and that, into this heart beat of existence. Does the song sing you or do you sing the song?
A shimmering flowing carpet of light and shadow reveals an uninterrupted seamless symphony of touch taste sight sound sensation thought and emotion. This obvious vibrant aliveness, this bejeweled wonderland flows through you in you as you. No lines can be found between water and wetness, between your lips and the kiss, between your tears and your shining beautiful eyes, between you and what's looking, between you and the kaleidoscopic sound and light show. The feeling of solidity between inside and outside comes from the belief in words, every one seems to split up infinite spaciousness. Yet you cannot choose to not believe, as you are the belief in separation. You cannot untie the

imaginary lines but it can happen that they are no longer believed, and known and felt to be imaginary. That's all enlightenment really is.

You are like the beautiful swirling iridescence on the surface of a soap bubble, the space inside is the same as on the outside. Simply a prismatic interface between the unknown and the worded world. We exist only as this swirling thought dream, this water color passion play of time and dimension and measurement. But where is the beginning and end to a thought or feeling or moment? You arise as the symphony of all these and are not separate from this wondrous music, there are no separate moments, are there?

Where is your last breath, was there one outside of love's storybook of someone sailing out to sea? Where is your next breath, is there one? Where does the light come from in your dreams? Gazing out gazing in, where is time, where are the colors you sing? Where is the rainbow that pierced the stormy evening and your heart many moons ago? Where is all that love you were afraid to lose?

You are like flowing water in a mirage, transparent mirrored sun light dancing reflection, spinning twisting twirling whirl pooling rushing roaring silently singing multifaceted shimmering empty jewelry coming from nowhere going to nowhere timelessly pouring sun into sun.

How the ripples catch sunlight and darkness waving mountains and sky and your beautiful reflection into a breathtaking fluid fabric without beginning or end. A timeless tale unfolds of time, and joy and sorrow and deep kisses and laughter. No inside or out, these unfathomable songs reaching out reaching in finding no middle or edge. Never touched always touching, kissed from without kissed from within. Songs from nowhere songs from everywhere, simply this poem of unbearable marvel, this magic of life dancing a daydream without cause or direction or any place to rest.

This sublime and bittersweet alone-ness, knowing you can only touch your own heart has ravished you and left you dancing alone, in love as love through love. The longing to kiss knowing there are no others paints my silhouette in sky with sky. Under the blue there is not even nakedness. No one to be free or bound, no strings ever held up the clouds, there is nothing to be untied.

All that effort to repair the scaffolding you thought prevented the sky from crushing you falls away when you realize you have never been separate from vast endless sky. How it hurt so to try to remember to sign your name on every tear.

Love opened a skylight to madness, but you fell back through into an empty house, stripped of everything, of nothing, even your nakedness, even love. Yet love trembles and hums in these transparent walls and reveals your tender humanness unadorned with hope and fear and need of next.

Resplendent ease bathes the dream in an all encompassing exploding sun lit kiss. An ecstatic love dance a constant union of what was never apart, light kissing light, space kissing space, life kissing itself through your beautiful beautiful lips. Suspended as not even nothing as wide open awe and living and loving as the dream of you of me of we. Calliope sings of a better place, but there is no past or future or someplace in between. It's only the moon-glow on a shimmering lake that reveals the watercolor of your face. For what would you be without forgotten dreams of what may come or what has been? Flowing thought paints these rich and wondrous hues of love's tale written on a timeline between birth and death.

It's always only utterly intimate as there are no others to kiss. You may howl at that moon of your great alone-ness, and I will hear your bittersweet song. But it is always my song echoing across the vastness. The inside of a side-less kiss. This is the very deepest intimacy and as vast as limitless space. Between meaning and non meaning there is nothing to grasp and no empty hand. Beautiful source-less reverberating echoes rippling sky into sky. A soundless sound trembles and explodes in your heart and reveals that this was never your heart or your life. Always obvious this beautiful aliveness soaring pouring through you in you as you.

Are the trees reaching up to kiss the sun, or is the sun reaching down to caress the trees? Is the wind dancing in the tree tops or do the trees sway and leaves shimmer in the wind? It is only words that make that distinction, you know they are not separate, and that you are not separate from the perception of this dance. Without the lasso of words which have never captured the wind, there are no separate things like wind and trees and your lovers gentle caress. Nor a cheek nor lips to kiss nor a you underneath that mask of fear of unknowing.

You are like the memory of a footprint in sky, a wisp of a cloud that seems to form a hand reaching out to grasp the sun, dissolving. Sun kissed shadows ripple and flow and you cannot touch this magic of life as you are not separate from it. Is life in you or are you in life? Such obvious vibrant aliveness inside and out, all lines are imaginary, aren't they? In and out, here and there and of and through, all dream directions going nowhere going everywhere, you are a phantom in a magicians tale, a swirling thought dream vanishing just as it seems to appear.

Most story book characters seem to be on the roller coaster of hope and fear of a never arriving next, and that's not better or worse as there is no chooser of thought or feeling.

15

I have not won a prize of constant bliss, I'm just not here. Yet I seem to appear as shimmering reflections in your beautiful eyes. I will meet you knowing there is no you nor me except in this dream world of love and magic. You appear to me as unutterably beautiful just as you think you are. There is no special or right or wrong way to appear, no special way to be. Simply this, this unbearable beauty of life appearing all by itself, looking and feeling like anything at all.

And what can be said of all of the above? Just a bunch of zip zap nonsense words painting dream clouds in the sky. There are no things nor non things to be true or false. Simply all and everything and nothing at all self arising and simultaneously self releasing without meaning or non meaning. This is far too simple to grasp. Trying to grasp this creates an empty hand.

There never were any shards of blue, always only this sky like vastness. Knowing we are made up is like a Surreal dream and yet more vibrant and intense than could ever be articulated. Rich and lush beyond measure. Beyond joy or sorrow.

Silence sings through a day dream of un-paralleled wonder. How amazing that under your adornment of star light there is not even nakedness.

Self remains knowing it never existed. Mangoes remain knowing there are no things until named. Love remains knowing that there are no two to love. Knowing that there is no one who holds beliefs and opinions doesn't end them.

I exist as beliefs and opinions knowing I am made up. I love myself and I still love mangoes and I still love love.

Beyond beyond. More empty than pure unbound nothingness. This ravishingly beautiful emptiness extends everywhere and nowhere simultaneously without movement or non movement, without direction or non direction. Containing no things or non things yet including all and everything and nothing at all.

Love a glue that spins around an imaginary center and unleashes the fluid canvas of vast endless sky falling through sky as water color dream bows arch their backs into the sun.

Gaping cracks in the sea wall of fear burst into beautiful bloom as the dam of unknowing reared its terrifying head and ate all your sea dreams in an un-tethered ocean that time forgot. You had cast your ripples of loveliness across sun bathed echoes searching for an answer to the questions you can no longer remember.

Quite unexpectedly as if by magic, a nameless sound ripped open your heart, silently exploding and imploding into infinite intimate vast spaciousness. Winds rushed across the empty fields and ripples of forgotten dreams slid into echoes of a name no one wears.

There is no song not born of empty wings of desire plunging its tailspin into ricochets of wonder. Empty parentheses radiate spirals of overlapping underlapping waves of joy and sorrow tapping on a sunlit window, reaching through and kissing your beautiful face.

Waves silently weeping and laughing hang suspended as they crash into and through themselves, a tympani of awe roars through your speechless heart and sings of the lack of tomorrow's daydream as you soar into the folds of night.

Words soar and scatter through these empty pages weaving a passion play of gusts and shadows through pillared halls of moonbeams dancing in a wind ballet. Oceans of light pour through waves of prism'd jewels of light shimmering into and through this dance.

Cleansed by tears the painted day washes off revealing a stark emptiness as you realize you had been caressing a future that has never arrived. It is your own love that rips you apart from the inside and out until a sideless glance reveals the seamless ease of life doing itself. How beautifully life swishes through your toes and writes your name in pud-dles of wonderment. The edges of your footprints collapse as the roots were imaginary that held you in sky's grasp. You fall until you are the falling falling through itself, and an essence of sweetness subsumes the wakeless wake of dreams. Wetness, the liquidity of home, embraces your nakedness.

And where was the song of the meadow lark that you heard yesterday eve echoing in the distant canyon? Where was her path on the evening breeze? Where did your love go when you were not?

The dream was ripped wide open. An empty swing softy moved in the evening breeze, and nakedness ran through the open fields.

For many the spiritual search is all about feeling better, and often includes getting away from their precious humanity. So many have the misconception that after the shift we become selfless doormats. The self remains but it is transparent, a crystalline lens through which life catches a glimpse of itself.

A river needs its banks to flow
Life is desire
Wind without movement is not
glistening eyes ripen
tears fall
Love soars
and its medium is you

I am the rushing roaring thunderous silent still river singing me as I sing it. There is only this flow, there is no outside nor inside.

I breathe this supreme spaciousness as it breathes me. I drink this sublime liquidity as it drinks me. I bathe in brilliant clarity as the river bathes me in its ultimate intimate infinite embrace. I hear its silence roaring as it listens to itself through me. It kisses itself through my lips. Everyone I see, everywhere I look is the rivers shimmering reflection dancing. I fall madly in love with everyone I greet, my heart pierced forever with love's unspeakable majesty. This ecstatic love dance of what was never separate flowing into and through itself in this magnificent twisting twining eddying whirl pooling pirouetting winged water ballet.

I have never been separate from this liquidity of home as even the thought of escape or the belief in an outside lies within its heart song. This song that I sing is your song our song singing itself through our beautiful beautiful lips. I can only see my beauty and I can only know love through my reflection in your beautiful beautiful eyes.

Ahhhhhhhhh
This love of knowing there is no one or two or none. Knowing deeply that there is no you nor me, that we exist only in the shimmering reflections of mirrored kisses in each others eyes. Feeling always that we are not separate, that there are no separate things or moments. Without time or non time. Flowing as the river. Water in water. Wet in wet. Light falling through light. Space swooshing through space.

Falling in love as love. Is it pain or joy this sublime ache of our humanness. I am has been ripped apart and our hearts exploded and imploded into the vastness of we are.

Love like life is immeasurably vast and unknowable. This love that I feel always is really not like what I would have called love before as there is no hope or fear or need of more or next.

Life like love is insatiable, it will eat you alive., yet no one can prepare to be eaten. No one can throw themselves into the fire, yet burning happens. Out of the ashes as they are carried into the sun's setting orange-y reds a love song unlike any other pierces your heart deeply. It is your own voice singing, "I love you, welcome home, I've missed you"

Yet the slipstream of I am slides through the dream of we are... pointing to starlight dancing your words your finger dances as the reflection on your beautiful beautiful face.

This love light sun dancing brilliance is often so blindingly bright, as I swoon into your magnificent beauty your after image remains as part of my heart like a precious gem that will stay as part of my love song until I die.

There is no message. No one can point to nothing. No one can give you what you already are. No one can show you that you have never left home and that all there is is home, a vast vast emptiness extending infinitely everywhere and nowhere without moving or staying still. You cannot die as you were never born. You exist only as a flowing thought dream, and the story of you will end when that incessant undermutter ceases. Shhhhhhhh..... all those hopes and dreams and regrets and fears of what never happened and what will never come are your beautiful adornment, under which there is not even nakedness. This brilliant obvious aliveness that looks and feels like anything at all, is all you can know, and yet it is unknowable, as you are not separate from it.

Once truly seen this cannot be unseen as it is a shift in the brain that paints this dream of you that no longer believes in its own painting. It feels like an ecstatic reunion of that which was never apart. Always in timeless beingness, a most magnificent awe shimmers through the emptiness dawning as your new unfettered adornment, it feels like love.

Sun dances through swirling trembling bough and branches, waltzing kissing the quivering twirling leaves. It streams untraceable fluid patterns on the forest floor. They gently caress your sun dappled countenance in this shadow land ballet. You are the overwhelming enormity of this rippling shine and shadow flowing over and through you. This dance without end or beginning, without time, leaves no footfalls yet explodes in ecstatic rhythmic delight.
Your shadow beckons a pas de deux with itself and love songs are born as they die on Main Street. Echoes of echoes reverberate as soundless memories ricocheting between who you never were and who you will never be. For you have never had any substantiality you are like a magic show on an empty stage in a dream time music box that feels the wind kiss your cheek but there was never any skin or touch separate from the breeze.
Only in the telling of the tale does a story teller seem to emerge. Only in the singing does it seem like a singer appears. Only in the touching does it seem like there is a you and me rippling in each other's reflected light and shadow.

We are memories coalescing into bright fluid water color paintings, whirl pooling, slip sliding ephemeral pictures coming into and out of focus in infinite array. Seeing through the veil of tears, knowing the dream time story's ultimate emptiness, and your ultimate unreality we see the painting on the glass and the vast unknowable light. No scratching of the paint is required.

No contrived silence will lead you to this ultimate silence, which sings so loud, so explosively, once it has pierced your very being it can never be missed. It has nothing to do with sound or thought or the lack thereof, it is the deeply intuited knowing feeling that the picture show is made up. There is no more trying to grasp that glass of wine on the three D television screen and drink it. Watching the movie and being a character in the passion play, simultaneously real and unreal. It is magnificently vibrant and alive knowing there is no other and no next.

She was the warp and woof of the sound and light show, as it unraveled tattered bits of wind from her hair.
The push and pull of the tides wrote her name in sea foam dissolving. Sky kissed its reflection in her footsteps and became beautiful in her gaze.
Empty designs swing and swirl into a vibrant pattern exploding and imploding, expressing nothing more or less than a dream of incalculable wonder as it wove her reflection into endless pure rippling sky.

There are many descriptions for this seamless unicity and every one falls short by infinity as every word shatters the sky into countless shards of blue.

We are the rainbow river. Prisms of beauty flowing in us as us through us. Swirling rushing roaring silently singing a most unbearably wondrous chorus of one of two of none. Between everything and nothing love flows. Without imaginary others there is not even nothing, one half of a kiss does not exist.

How many decades did I wrap my arms so tightly around myself trying to not fly apart into a gazillion pieces, shutting out light and life and love. After my heart exploded and imploded simultaneously I realized that there were no pieces, no separate parts to this lovers kiss.

echoes singing reflections of echoes
hello goodbye hello
an ecstatic love dance seems to appear and create my breath and take it away simultaneously

this emptiness cannot be filled, yet it is always full

it is ravishingly devastatingly wondrous that there are no things nor non things yet all things are included

we exist only in the touching, and there is only your hand reaching... vast spacious emptiness sings a love song of one of two of none

This hyper awareness of being aware is the gem the jewel yet it only exists through the dream of separation.

From which no one awakens.

Life kissing itself through your lips as you sing it

It sings you

A beautiful thought dream is what we are

No thing that has thoughts, and no thing that we 'actually' are.

It is a common misconception even among those who are considered sages that there is something that has beliefs and opinions.

Under or prior to the flowing thought dream there is not even nakedness. As under or prior are thought.

Through the slip stream of crossing falls

Oceans laughing

torn and ragged half notes urged to fruition

Pause and jump into the underbelly of dawn

In the darkest hour he could hear a Robin song

but he could not read his handwriting as the pages had escaped

like the notes of the songbird they left no trace

Wings in the dark felt

he knew their tender beating hearts

He could feel the tides pushing and pulling continents away

he could feel the sun sliding on the other side of the rainbow

Here in tears of time

As it died

he could feel the sorrow of dreams abandoned

He could feel the anguish of love lost
The despair of abandonment
the joy of love remembered
and his heart exploded into infinite sorrow and joy
As they fell into and through each other into a deep currents of un-named un-owned emotion

And the dawn and wind and life soared through him
As him

This dance is not moving or non moving, it cannot kiss itself without your lips. Without your beautiful feet there are no steps.

Watching the thought stream, knowing you and all thingness arise in the streaming dream it paints, is like soaring as the wind whilst the wind soars through you. It's a reel time movie spinning a world of light and shadow. Flickering holographic images that almost seem to appear and disappear simultaneously without solidity or independent existence. Silhouettes of space kissed with love light. A shadow puppet dancing, a mirrored costume swirling with no puppet master and not even bare naked wonder under the twirling skirts.

I hear my heart song echoed from across the canyon born on winds desire and just a glance from your beautiful beautiful eyes and I swoon into your utter magnificence.

Suspended as nothingness as belief is suspended, like bright brilliant eyes looking through unparalleled amazement. Walking floating soaring streaming as a watercolor flowing free of its paper and boundaries. Your feet emerge to dance, your hand emerges to touch, your heart emerges to love. No thing ever touched or kissed yet the resonance of a kiss signs your name with tears.

We exist only as imaginary division as scintillating holographic images and can recognize our selves only through each others reflections shimmering in the imaginary spaces in between us.
Without imaginary selves there is no division. A space that does not exist cannot be crossed. We exist only in the touching, knowing that there are no two to dance.

I cannot find the past. It feels like time died. The richness and fullness of this un-owned edgeless heart ties and unties ribbons of moonbeams rippling through the laughing trees where I once hung my heart to gaze upon its beauty. Sky fell through the looking glass and eons of tears exploded as rainbows reached down to caress their reflection in my beautiful eyes.

How amazing! all I have ever wanted, all I have ever longed for right here right now, un-adulterated pure sweet brilliant magic. Un-contained unfettered untrammeled never graspable by the mind of this and that always on yet rarely recognized. Truly felt, but for some that aching feeling in the pit of their stomach of something so brilliant so magnificent so unbelievably wondrous that they fear this obliterating devastating wondrousness will blow them away. And it may

There is no prior to thought, as before and after are thought. Yet most long for that hush they remember vaguely. Like a song they dimly remember singing but have never heard the words, as there are no words to capture this feeling this undeniable suspicion they have deep deep down that they are made of thought stuff. That everything they know and everyone they love is a flowing thought dream.

So many long to cease thought to capture this silence they imagine exists only sometime. But this silence is always on. It is merely the recognition that all seemingly separate things and moments are made up. There is nothing a thought dream can do to recognize this. Yet it may happen that all ideas of this and that come crashing into each other as the brain sees that it is painting an imaginary tale. It is terrifying for the imaginary character to contemplate that they never existed, nor the past or future, as that means all dreams of better or enlightenment will crumble like sea foam castles in the sea. The fear of not knowing a wall that encompasses their heart may melt or not.

All trying or trying to not try perpetuate the painful illusion of separation. Yet as long as you feel separate you will try to erase it.

Can you imagine an edge to your world? Can you step outside of what's going on and grasp it? Can you step outside of yourself? Where are the thoughts you had this morning? Where is the morning except as this flowing thought? Are there indeed separate thoughts? Is there a day you can capture, except with the thought of day? Is the thought day really the day?
When does day turn into night?
The singing of this is what paints my flowing dreamscape. Days when I'm not, as yesterday in town, there is simply suspended as awe. Hollow echoes resonating through nameless brilliant flowing infinitely hued emptiness shimmering without direction or place. A waking dream falling into and through itself.

Self illumined wonder propels the dream as there is no one walking these feets, no one thinking or feeling or describing this timeless kiss.

It is a sleepless dream
....there is no purpose or rhyme and there is no looking for it
Time has lost its shadow.....
Wandering footless perpetually stunned

There is actually no perfection or imperfection, yet knowing this deeply everything seems unbearably perfect.

Many claim to know the unknowable.
Self is a wall of fear of unknowing. Beliefs glued together with hope and fear, and the belief that something can be done or not done in order to arrive at a place of peace or enlightenment. There is simply no next. No one to be asleep or awakened.

Truly, this is either known without a doubt or not, as it is completely inconceivable, that there are no things or non-things to know or to put together into some kind of place of rest or understanding, and no one separate from what's going on in order to do this.

Those who believe that inquiry can lead to the shift seem to believe that awakening happens to the person. There are many who say to look prior to thought but there is no prior as all before and after are thought created.

Awakening is not a belief or understanding or a philosophy or a set of rules to live by.

There is no urge to consider or hold the momentary knowing that even the ideas of separation and oneness are made up. Yet the dance continues, knowing it's a dream, that you're a made up flowing thought dream, and everyone you have ever known or loved is as well.

wind blows
Suns rise and set over imaginary lines where the sky kisses sea and earth
Tears fall
Bodies die
Thoughts cease
The story of you ends

This is it coyote.
Your one and only brilliant infinite instant
And it's all made up
Even love

Lights breathes it's own luminescence and ripples extend through the infinite vastness of light. All echoing the silence of your heart blooming tender petals of velvet tears. The sweet taste of taste is life delighting in itself sung by your lips as your lips are kissed with song. Endless facets of the centerless jewel that is you reflect not even nothing into unfathomable color, and wondering at the marvel of wonder itself life bursts into song. You can't hear it without a backbeat of a mirror shimmering almost into existence, but never more solid than a dream. How can you catch a star shadow as it flows down the stream? Its only existence is in its reflection, like your lovers kiss in last nights dream.

It feels like it is on the tip of your tongue, you can almost taste it, and the anticipation is killing you. The longing to burst into bloom, for some thing, for the final piece of the puzzle you have been trying to unravel for decades, for the ultimate secret to reveal itself, for a clarity of understanding of why of where of who you are and what this is all about. To shed this skin that feels so confining. To arrive at a place of ease.

You may hear the songs of others who seem to know. You may hear the songs of others who say that they have arrived at this unattainable place up high on the mountain. You may attempt to do or not do the things they recommend.
I never say don't do this or that. I simply say that there is no you to do or not do anything or nothing. There is no understanding what I am singing of and there is no one to understand. You exist as the prison you feel you are in. Outside the cage of words there is not even nothing. There is no outside, or inside. This is it coyote, the only world that you can ever know. There is no magic secret or key to the unlocking of a door that never existed. There is no path to unknowing.
You are already the flower blooming, the sunset looming, the song singing your story of years and years of rainbow tears. Nothing can be done, nothing need be done to realize this. It can be realized that the worded dream world is indeed made up. Yet that would mean that you are made up, and that would mean the end of you. There is no next and no one going there.

Clad in hanging lanterns of new born green the aspens arch over the trail reaching for light. Every leaf shimmers in ecstatic union with sky. Every arabesque of bough and trunk dances a slow rhythmic timeless waltz with the leaf covered hillside newly shedding the deep winter snow that clothed the undulating hills in a seamless brilliance. Alive and vibrant all things illumined with this articulate description, yet wordless wonder saturates the feeling of separate notes or singer in this symphony of perception.

Bathed in a silence a stillness a magic, it's like being submerged in a bottomless ocean, suspended as the very water that you drink and breathe. Rainbow reflections paint an iridescence that seem to form a line where sea kisses sky, but there is no gasping for breath for another moment for another kiss.

Love a silent day dream transfixed by its own reflection. The seamless fluid immediacy embraces your heart in ever widening circles of joy.

Every mournful cry and all joyful laughter paint a picture of love and love lost and birth and death always it is perfection singing.

The passion play, every turn of a leaf, every kiss, every glance, every ripple sliding across the dream of sighs is all thunderingly momentous yet it has no significance nor non meaning at all.

Starlight burns a hole in your heart that floods you with longing. A thirst that cannot be quenched with anothers dream. Transparent seamless beingness twisted itself into ropes of hope and fear, a longitude and latitude of hunger and called itself you. Only your own song will empty your cup to overflowing.

How I believed all the songs, that love would fulfill me, another would complete me. Looking everywhere for that other expanded into other ideas I heard about how to feel finally ....right. Not lacking. If I ever reached that place where I could stop searching, I could finally relax. The love I sought somehow turned around and kissed me full on the mouth and eviscerated me. The circle was complete, it had always been, but these lips were never mine or yours in this unending kiss.

It was such a faint memory an undefinable essence floating through me, like a sweet summers breeze that beckoned! A light in the dark I could not see directly, it was always just to the side of where ever I looked. I truly believed I could learn to look and tried every method and path I discovered. Searching high and low and inside and out for a way to measure the universe to capture it to know it to be it. This magic which I knew without a doubt to be true. This endless searching casting shadows of doubt across all ideas of certitude.

Everyone knows the magic of love, yet when it hears it's name it seems to hide on the in breath, like all of life no one can really say what it is. Like a bottomless ocean it's mysterious depths contain unseen mysteries that pull our hearts into a beautiful wordless song and looking to capture it hurts.

This vast spaciousness without name or non-name sometimes referred to as nothingness or emptiness is a concept. Like all named things. Made up like you. You are a conceptual being and you can only see concepts, or understand things. Can you take a glass and pour the wine out and remove the sides and the bottom and pour the emptiness out? What you want you cannot have as it is not something to get.

There is no path to nowhere. There is no goal to reach and nothing to attain. There's nothing to learn or unlearn. Nothing to know or not know as there is no one to know or learn or think or feel or believe. Or do. Or not do. Anything or nothing.

The longing to catch the wind to hold onto life, to grab the magic that you know is here cannot be quenched. It must dissolve on its own. Just like all of life, it happens all by itself. You are an imaginary character, the belief in other better more and next, and there is no other better more or next, is there?

You are the idea that there is a goal to reach, and yet all of your life you have been this reaching this longing this aching heart. All of your life your hand has grasped nothing more or less than not even nothing. As what is going on is not divided into this and that here and there. All separation is a dream. There are no things to be connected or separate.

One day without any effort, your time line brakes loose and the web of tears that had seemed to hold back the sun fell. You find you were the light the magic you had been longing for. It was simply an idea a painting on the window that seemed to create an inside and outside. That great emptiness that you were trying to fill cannot be filled. Or removed.

You are the un-findable space between your lips and a kiss, between breath and song, between sun and shadow. This is more intimate than your tongue in your mouth your breath, your heartbeat.

The shimmering iridescence playing on the surface of the rushing waters cannot be caught. It never could. Trying to iron out the waves of sorrow your heart sinks and you no longer believe in a dream of inside and out.

And the wind flies down the canyon and dances in the treetops. A ballet of light and shadow pirouettes on the sidewalk reflecting in the mountain stream. Sometimes I can hear your voice like a kiss in the night.

And a rush
Soaring
Floods through me
As we are swallowed in skies shadowlight

His shadow precedes him on this moonless night as island breezes wash through him. Where was his partner in this dance for no one? Where were the waves after they crashed on the rocks? Silently thunder sings of the storm. Where was the shipwreck that crashed all his dreams into the sea? Whose tears were sliding down his cheeks...

She yearned to stitch the the sun to the sky and hang it in her heart forever, but it sank like moonbeams in silence and swallowed her needlework, leaving an emptiness that not even nothing could fill. She could no longer find a pocket to put her heart in and the endless night rushed through her into an ever emerging dawn.

....and how can one know the storms up ahead ....when the ship looses its anchor and the rudder breaks off... when the waves tower over the ship and crash on your tenderness ....thunder can not tell of the lightening to come... it pierces you to the very core...
...and after the storm ...you look out at uncharted seas ...the ship has no where to go... waves lapping softly ....and the sun slides over the bow and illuminates your nakedness ....in the swirling ...there is no distance ...as I slide into and through you
It is a perfect fit when two empty pockets overflow with love ....whose tears slide down my cheeks. Rainbows explode as we are catapulted over the moon ...and fall with showering stars
Echoes of love precede themselves leaving sparks of rainbows scintillating....
And ....in the distance storms ignite
When it feels like a unitary seamless flowingness all ideas of karma or cause and effect seem like trifling ways of trying to describe what cannot be touched with words or ideas. Yet I can speak with others about this ....the cup is dropped and it hits the floor and breaks ....what caused the cup to be dropped ....it's endless speculation leading nowhere
The mind will never be satisfied
It is designed to search
And never find
It's all a unitary flowingness ...nothing pushes or pulls it
All attempt at describing it creates stories like billiard balls hitting each other
But it no longer feels like I'm a separate ball hit or reacting to seen or unseen forces .... there are no separate bits that need to be somehow connected ....like a connect the dots picture

I'm just watching the shadows play across the wall and ultra content and can't remember why I ever wanted more or better moments. Still the dream paints itself as indefinable edgeless awe. Rain on the windshield. Big drops siding. The world stretches and slides down the pain.
At first it feels like you're fighting the river trying to swim upstream. Then it's like you relax and are flying with the stream until you realize you are the stream. Needing it's imaginary banks to flow, watching so beautifully the dream slide through you. As you.
Moonlit shadows sang her steps into a dance where time leapt from the pages and place could not find itself. She could not look behind her as everwhere had fallen through

nowhere. Where was her breath where was the moon where was her shadow? Oh! It was dancing on a hint of a breeze in the tree tops shining in the golden dreams that had crashed. Toppled crystal castles left only memories of a shimmering echo.

She sang of moonbeams and she sang of shadows dissolving into each other, and she swam in the deep heart current where joy and sorrow merge, and she danced on silent stars shooting through endless skies. No amount of twisting will gather light into darkness. Songs merely seem to heighten the intensity of this amazing seamless blending of what is beyond understanding. This emerging submerging richness of nothing dancing. I sing of what can never be touched or captured with words concepts ideas. This is far more direct intimate and honest. Living without belief in description is wondrous beyond measure.

Birdsong flowing breath thoughts feelings untouched, time sleeping fire burns smoke rises clouds disperse, river rolling wind caress in steps softly padding. No one leads and no one follows in this dance of life waltzing with itself.

Dragon's shadow sweeps the ground with tears. Love is the lions roar that silences the world. This blazing light of simple knowing that words can never capture this fills you subsumes you, and you vanish in un-knowingness. as golden threads stitch your garment of awe together. Yet it never was apart as you are it. Falling into the dancing you can no longer find your feet. Your fear of dancing vanished as tears flow unnamed and uncounted and disappeared into the vastness where no one resides. Sweet music plays unrehearsed and deafens the mind with awe. A magical symphony of no one playing to itself.

Soaring skinless you are the wind and the wind blows through you. Kissing the sky you fall into the vastness. Swooning into what is, there is no thing left but this unknowable light dance flowing through light.

Love guided my dreams in the darkness and beckoned me through out the day. How I longed for this unnamed treasure deep within the darkness, unseen and hidden. For a magic key that would reveal all the secrets of the universe, the secrets of love. Like a light beneath my eyelids it burned my heart at night, and lured me ever onward during the day, Glimpsing the jewel I tried to hold it, but it always disappeared, burning my hand and heart. A stolen glimpse and my heart was pierced. A hint of a melody echoing in the canyon and I would swoon. Chasing its shadow, looking up I never saw it, but I knew it was there there there! Around the next corner over that hill hiding in the rainbows reflection, in the echoes of moonbeams. The dancing waters cried my name, and I longed to hear it to capture it to hold it to make it mine. My heart reached for the sun and burned, vaporized in its own brilliance. One day I saw its reflection in the mirror, and fell into and through myself and drowned.

And love put out its hand and pulled me back. It has never left. It kisses me awake in the morning and caresses me as I go to sleep. The delicious roar of aliveness in love with itself.

Nighthawks swoop and swirl in moonlight
Written on the wind
Tears reflect the flowing

All the whispers never drown the silence after you have lost yourself in the dancingness you cannot trace your steps. There was never anyone dancing. soaring as the vastness itself you no longer look for wings.

Our stories are written in endless skies. For a brief moment they sing and blend into the symphony of life, and they are swallowed in the unknowable vastness.

I am just as substantial as the beautiful castles and fairy tale kings and queens dancing in the cloud reflections in the puddles as they dry in the morning sun. Wind skims the dance and the passion play is painted in my mind stream. As it dries was there ever a puddle? Was there ever wetness? Is there wet or dry without the constant stream of thought?

What is this life but a brief cloud dance that disappears as soon as it seems to appear? Nothing and everything never existed yet all is clearly apparent. Obvious this brilliant aliveness that you feel, isn't it? The aliveness wholly complete always, a total confirmation through the symphony of perception and the recognition of it. Nothing can be added or removed ever as there is no outside to this dance, nor inside.

An unbelievable stunningly magical movie appearing center stage on your mind screen, neither moving nor still without sound or silence, an unbound symphony exploding and imploding into a dream of you and me and love. Utterly without perfection or flaw it is naturally spontaneously perfect. All happening by itself nothing has ever needed to be done or undone, as a cloud reflection has never moved the clouds.

You don't need fancy dancin' shoes to dance.
You don't need any magical incantations or drugs or any other eyes than your own beautiful liquid eyes to recognize the beauty dancing in you through you as you.

delighting in our own delight discovering we have always been our perfect lover

Trying to pin life down
Hurts
Like you're sticking those pins in yourself

There is not even nothing underneath your beautiful rainbow clothes. Swirling mirrored skirts shimmer your song in love as love through love. Echoes of your heartbeat vibrate the canyon winds into songs that dance and scatter myriad reflections of light soaring through light.

Where was the space that fell through space calling your name? In ancient photographs that smoldered and burst in the flames of your raging heart and crumbled into ashes blowing in waves around your empty foot falls. There were never enough tears to put out your fiery desire, to quench this thirst, to calm the tempest on your search for what you knew not.

Now the passion play continues but it happens for no one, to no one. It never needed a next. So many shadows dance, lit by a candle that will burn to the ground. Utter stillness floods through a song that used to bear the weight of a thousand suns, but has no name nor need to escape its own beautiful fire.

Seeing perfection reflected in your eyes I tried to drink you. I tried to write of this perfect love and my pen couldn't touch the paper. Yet I fell into the unsung words and fell into and through myself, and no words were necessary...

Twilight kisses the tattered remnants of storm, murmured rumblings fade, whispers dance across puddles where streetlights dance. My many petaled shadow precedes me and watches me swirling, suspended without time I look for traces of my story and find you loving me ....loving you. Only through love can I find my footprints in sky.

Absolutely transfixed enchanted by this indivisible openness, like an endlessly blooming flower ever wilting, slipping away from all sides and underneath, melting merging exploding into a seamless rainbow dance of color light sound and this roar of deafening silence. Brilliant emptiness reverberates creates dreamlike shimmering fleeting images that dance and sparkle and ripple through my mind stream. There is never any need to grasp to hold to capture this amazing display, as there is no feeling separate from the flowing. subsumed in utter peace, drenched in awe.

When the center of the cyclone disappears, it is simply a story unowned, spinning weaving itself with gossamer shreds of emptiness. Meaning nothing yet deeply felt.

Your heart explodes, Turning you inside out. No longer are there any secrets to conceal. living resplendent in loves infinite embrace, flowing through the ecstasy of life touching itself through you. cast adrift in sublime edgelessness there is no need to know why the stars fill you with awe as you recognize yourself.

I can say nothing really
this beauty wastes me
Shreds me

Reduces me to nothing but awe....
I'm like a breathing eyeball ....washed in loves essence. Licked clean of a life time of hope and fear. Life Kissing itself with the softness of unknowing. Truly astounding this beautiful beautiful life.

There is no thinker
There is no one having thought
There is nothing underneath or 'having' the thought dream that you are
There is no one to drop the illusion of thinker, as all separation is illusion.
Illusion is illusion

Sun dappled grasses flowing as clouds began to form in the mountains, sky gathering...
The storm he had been fearing his entire life began to blow and sun flew out the window. The tsunami of fear and hope crashed in thunderous waves lashing his tale his body his head his heart his dreams. His eyes illumined with the scent of storm as his foot steps fell through empty shadows. Lightening raging in his chest ripping out his heart. He fell through the earth as earth and sky plummeted through through his chest.
In the wake of storm and grassy seas and sky collapsing into and through each other there was left an empty calm. Shimmering
We all know this aliveness we feel so deeply, as it is apparent in and through this ongoing symphony of what we call perception that has no edges or separate parts. There are no words that can even touch that which we all know, and our feelings that have no edges yet can pierce us deeply. What would life be like without emotion? We call them fear and anger and love, yet without names they are simply a profound current where joy and sorrow merge. It pulls us into its mysterious grasp and drowns us and we can no longer find a feeler or a feeling but a unbound stillness where love and lover and loved are us.

How beautiful that we are random bits of swirling memories and flowing description of the symphony of perception and beautiful thought dreams of a never arriving next

Tears melt rainbows into glass and shatter your dreams of finding future perfection. piercing your tough exterior your own love heart magic eviscerates ravishes the very core of who you thought you were and renders you utterly bereft of hope and fear. Life and wind and light soaring through you as you are skinless soaring in the warm evening breeze. Waking amazed, standing utterly naked knowing there is not even nothing under your tender nakedness, the universe flowing through you as you. Sun slides across the sky from horizon to horizon loving the imaginary edges that touch the sky.

I never actually meet anyone. I just fall in love, story-less. No one is a stranger yet we can never know each other. We exist only in the imaginary spaces in between. On the surface we are lovers but really we are each other, there is no me nor you.

Love is an idea just like you as there were never two to merge. Yet the seamless ease of knowing and feeling always that there are no things nor holder of them is like love, but far beyond any idea we might have had about love, as there is no hope or fear. This love is unowned. your heart drops and love bleeds into the dream. I am explodes into we are. It was never your heart. it was never your love. We exist solely as this dream. There is knowing that we are and all thingness is made up yet living and loving as the dream of separation. Sliding rainbows shimmer and are seen only in their own reflections. We are an amalgam of learned shared words ideas and concepts. simply put, we are made up. It is in the imagined spaces between notes where the melody is born, a pure tone without overtones has no life no richness. It takes the illusion of twoness to know there are no two. Simply beyond logic or reason. The sweep of dawn erases the shadows of apparent duality. There is no place left to hide and no one left to hide. Pure light of clarity pierces you deeply there is no turning back, there is no back.

How amazing that all perception arises evenly and equally without any effort. this seamless beingness is always on yet rarely noticed, and all effort to recognize it seems to obscure it.

It is neither emptiness nor non-emptiness. Nor both nor neither. extending infinitely in every direction without direction or space subsuming all thingness indefinitely reaching everywhere and nowhere. Subsuming all things it is beyond all extremes yet includes them. A shoreless ocean waving crashing, a silent sonic boom. It is beyond freedom nor non-freedom when there is no one left to be free.

Erasing all notions of this and that
Burning subsuming all ideas of twoness
Shadows are but memory stories reflections Ungraspable shimmering on mists of unobscured brilliance
Your eyes licked clean by your own light
It is simply unbelievable unutterably wondrous as all extremes fall away time dies, yet this and that still move
in this perfect stillness.
Mists like many colored droplets shower through you and you sink. Your heart drops yet it still beats.
Passionate yet dispassionate.
Intimately played soundlessly felt and sung with utter abandon.

You are the dance it sings itself.

Marvelously so without any effort

Crystalline words appear and the two step begins. Obviously apparent yet having no separate existence thingness blooms like a many petaled rainbow and simultaneously weeps infinitely varied shadows dancing on the edge where colors die and run down your daydream and dissolve in the night. Dripping sensuousness into existence love radiates magnificently into itself. Walking on the edge of the vastness ocean crashing on unseen shores

glimmering moonlight peeks in a sigh of a place we used to hide.

Ah! The touch of nothing the consuming union of space and light. The play of echo and shadow. The continuity of completeness. Overwhelmed by the exquisite nature of all things and nothing at all. Irrevocably sublime. Naturally perfect. Only ever none other than this as it seems to appear. A cool breeze on a hot summers day. Stretching your toes as you lie in your comfy bed. All hearts desire answered. No more questions. Nothing to attain. Nothing to fulfill. Sublime quiescence. Natural perfection. The magnificence and mind blowing awe of. Simply this. Absolutely unavoidably

Yes

You are an uncapturable indefinable choiceless always new and fresh constantly changing never changing seamless flowing thought dream. A brilliant transparent centerless multifaceted jewel of crystalline magnificence through which the universe sees itself.

And that's sumpin'!

An imaginary self cannot do nor not do anything or nothing to see that it is made up

Trying to define what has no parts

to grasp what has no edges

Looking for the source of light when light is everywhere

The razor of thought cannot mend what was never separate. The assumption that it actually divides whats going on is the beginning of the shattering of the sublime feeling knowing of wholeness. As indivisibility cannot be conceived and is not a belief or understanding, it cannot be arrived at by looking for it or trying to relax into it, or by hypnotizing yourself into it. All attempts of doing or not doing merely substantiate the illusion of a doer.

If you find yourself in this magnificent conundrum, like between the jaws of a tiger, knowing truly that you cannot do nor not do anything, yet still wanting this not knowing what it is, but recognizing that it is there there there just beyond your grasp...

it has to be here here here
Where is there without here? All thought dreams,
Like you

Most people feel that what is going on is somehow not right. That gnawing sensation that life shouldn't hurt so much. The belief in being an individual autonomous person is always in conflict with the intuition that life does itself. So they try to fix the hurt to run or hide or ignore the pain as well as other thought or feeling they have been taught is 'bad'. Usually they look for answers in psychology or philosophy or self help or spirituality. Anything that might bring this ease they desire. Often they hear of a state of no self or enlightenment and that sounds good. 'Get me outta here!'

They may try methods or practices and whilst they may seem to work for awhile, the pain returns, and instead of blaming the practice they blame themselves. Meditate more or harder they think, or be in the now! So they find a teacher or guru that confirms this, that they are flawed, and who gives them even more methods or suggestions to relieve the pain of being human.

There is truly no special way to think or feel or act and no chooser of these things as there is no you separate from thought or feeling. My heart weeps when my friend tries so hard to eliminate various thought or action one of his gurus has told her is bad. One guru was telling her that complaining is bad. I just said, well, if someone is feeling pain it's natural that they are talking about it. What seems like complaining to you may just be your brain describing what's going on which happens utterly naturally. I couldn't say more as he wants confirmation and there is so much more to say. I usually just end with, I know you are utterly naturally perfect.

Awakening isn't about leaving your beautiful humanness. It's not the end of joy or sorrow or love. It's the end of feeling separate from life. Somehow joy and sorrow and love and awe are this same beautiful ache.

As soon as self is conceptualized it begins to be felt deeply that there is an autonomous isolated individual, solid and permanent and unchanging, battered about by unseen forces trying to do life and trying to make life happen. Yet deep down this is never quite believed, and like all beliefs is accompanied by hope and fear. So the lifelong quest begins to solidify itself so that it may never die. By grabbing more and more beliefs or ideas to concretize the wall of beliefs that is glued together with hope and fear.

And where it finds blank spots the fear of the unknown prevails and self will fill-in the blank spots with shared learned concepts like God or even nothingness or emptinessAll the pretty words from all the pretty people can never take you where you want to go. They may make you feel better, and point to a bright future, to a peace they describe.

You believe in love and your quest for freedom but the clinging to a path a method a word a pointer a hand a teacher, an answer has to go, as self is the clinging. It's the chasing your tale. that spinning that seems to create an imaginary center. Building a false front a wall of fear. The spinning has to unwind all by itself. Until inside is seen and felt to be the same as out. Being patient or impatient has nothing to do with it. It seems rather it is your own desire that rips the threads of the illusion, You, open.

All of these stories you tell yourself simply constantly re create the story of you. It is hypnotizing, the story of next. Have you ever found one? There is looking at what's simply going on through a haze of tales told about it and what it is supposed to be like. It is the looking to escape the pain of imaginary separation that drives the search, and perpetuates the illusion of next of other of more of better. Yet all looking for a key to unlock the magic of 'wholeness' or 'unicity', simply creates an imaginary door, a barrier between you and it. The mighty river longs to drown itself in the sea, and the juice of the fruit longs to spill into the earth in utter release. Yet the sea cannot drink itself, and as you long to swallow endless sky the sky cannot cut itself into pieces and place them on a plate for you to eat. You are indivisible vast flowing directionless unknowable untouchable uncaused, and not even a thing or non thing.
There's no other place and no other time and words may seem to point to this and perhaps you've glimpsed this, but the end of grasping must happen on its own as you are the grasping itself.
The imaginary line between inside and outside. Under the costume there is not even nothing there. Your entire world would come crashing down including any ideas that there is someone who has a world. Self is the very ideas or limits it is trying to transcend. It is the very looking for freedom that forms your imaginary lines, yet without them you are not. Somehow they are seen and felt to be imaginary.

After the shift the self remains, I remain beautifully human, feeling deeply, loving. I still love mangoes and sparkly things and love and hugs, and walking in nature, and singing with all my beautiful lovers, and love. If someone short changes me I ask for the money back, and if someone starts to cut off my leg I will try to get away. I still have desires, I still make plans, knowing there is no next. There's simply no weight to the passion play. There is no belief in belief or preferences or belief in disbelief. Life is impersonal yet felt deeply at the same time. The passion play continues much as it did before to write and erase itself, yet there is no feeling of solidity. Belief in thought creates a psychological and physical feeling of solidity of permanence. Who said this would be a walk in the park? How could it not hurt to die? The whole thing is like a giant sorrow machine, yet when life embraces itself through you your magnificence is revealed.

This is it coyote. Self is a beautiful phantom. It cannot be caught, it's a constantly shifting shadow, and it echoes it's wonder in starlight breezes. They softly caress the sunrise and color in our world. This is the ever emerging un-pinpoint-able edgeless momentary. We are description, a flowing thought dream. Like candy sprinkles on a shoreless ocean, sparkling iridescence rippling over under into and through itself. Knowing all thingness is made up, the dream continues.
Our beautiful humanness shared.
This magnificent singularity appearing as anything at all. Infinite shades of color shifting dancing sliding as liquid dreamscapes. You melt into the stream and swim and play. Rainbows stream through your body and you stretch everywhere yet can never touch an edge. You hear an echo in the depths, it is you calling yourself to join the song. Rubbing noses and joyfully playing in the roaring deafening scintillating brilliant river of love, as the sigh falls into and through the sigh, and softness falls through softness and light pours into light, space falls into space. And the empty cup, your empty heart that was never yours was found to be the treasure chest as light and love pour through you as you.

Every ounce of cricket song poured into this glass, simply meaningless reflections. Words that try to catch the essence of this sublime edgelessness, butterfly wings kiss their own iridescence flying on hearts with no strings to play this music of awe flooding basking bathing drowning into and through itself. Drenched in love, this is what I do. Singing to myself these beautiful songs of love. The mountain stream catches the cool air and brings it to the desert, and blue butterflies hover by the shallow pools glittering in the evening sun.

Chattering birds hidden in deep shadowy bushes punctuate the roaring waves, footfalls erased in sand, lovers under hanging cliffs baking in their own hotness. There is no path in this vastness there are no parts of sky. Shimmering streaming loose ends of my hair, ribbons in the wind, no inside no outside. A touch a glimmer a song of whatever appears in you as you through you, a cool evening breeze caressing your cheek, a slap in the face a tear a sob an echo singing life's beautiful melancholy, a rainbow awash in evening's breeze, shadows sliding into the light, flute songs coming from nowhere and everywhere, a kiss in the dark illuminating this wondrous mystery that feels like a gazillion petals endlessly unfolding into an unbearable tenderness, the bloom the blush of love reflecting in everyone's eyes, dreams of life and love smashed to smithereens on the cliffs where you fell, your beautiful wings like tattered sails catch the last rays of sun. Rudderless, cast adrift on this edgeless sea of dreams, yet dancing twirling singing living and loving weeping in the canyon between the world of things and no things. The memory of the battle hangs, colored by so much love and laughter and rivers of tears smiling, the warmth of home.

Life as a human being is filled with great sorrow and deep despair and unutterable joy. Didn't you ever put on a sad song because it felt so beautiful to cry? Truly it is the impermanence the fluidity that you fear that is life's beauty. You long to fall into the falling yet you long to be held. Yet you are the falling falling through the falling and simultaneously held in your tender wraparound tears.

Life has never been these ideas that were taught to you called fair or right or wrong. Life simply happens all by itself and looks and feels like anything at all. I love how deeply we feel each others pain. How beautiful is it that we can feel at all? There is no escaping your beautiful humanness, because under those swirling mirrored skirts there is not even nothing.

Knowing and feeling that you and the world were never broken and that there is no next is wondrous. All of life is your infinite intimate embrace. There is a sublime melancholy that colors this beautiful aloneness.

Every brush of watercolor tears paints a heartbreaking story of you melting into sunset. Your tears unmasked were never yours yet they wrote your heartsong in an endless stream on the river of life that never began yet is always beginning and ending. You spied the magic in the flowing fleeting rainbow and longed to grasp it, but you never could as all you could find was your own empty heart reflected in the center of your eyes. Trying to catch the storm before it crushed you threw you into the whirl pool and you broke into a gazillion pieces of sky, each one reflecting the tears you so feared, and the love you were terrified to feel too deeply as you knew somehow that this love this precious life was never yours and you would lose it. You held out your hands filled with tears and melted into your own reflection.

This unbearably wondrous magic of life that seems to sing you as every thought dreams you, your tears unsigned are beauty itself. A love letter written for no one for everyone for this dance of tears and laughter and echoes soaring across the canyon melting merging twining twirling in a wind ballet through your mind screen. You are the love the lover and the beloved in this dance without an other or a center of the cyclone. You can feel the magic of life streaming through you as you wrapped infinitely and most intimately in your own loving embrace.

Wind stirs in the aspens loosening late summer lanterns golden treasures flowing, skimming, cerulean waters rippling reflections of infinite winged sky. Blossoming morning swirls into a call and answer sing song of shine and shadow pirouetting into a breath of cloud. Of wind of rain of tears of smiles and that silent gasp of beauty recognizing itself, of a glance a touch an embrace, of voices across the lake echoing the music of songs of hate of love of passion in the night, of all songs that were never written and never sung yet heard and felt deeply, of my song of your song, of this song soaring blending merging effortlessly light into light.

Clearly seen in this infinite kiss deeply intimate yet never mine to hold to capture to grasp and plunge it into my heart so I may know the song of life that sings me. Knowing there are no songs to hold I always feel the magic of life, of death, of this fluidity of nothing of everything merging forever without dimension or time or any place where it is not, this obvious sublime miracle that feels like love swooning into love.

Suspended in a drift of memory, there are no steps to where I never left where I never was, where I missed my shadow one late evening staring into the empty brilliance I have always been yet never was. This magnificent unknowable mystery of life of love subsumed me and cast away all dreams of love yet love remained as a tattered tapestry of infinitely facetted jewels riding bare back across my mindstream.

The symphony is over, so many headlights going down canyon create a flowing river. My shadow precedes me and for awhile seems continuous, and then a hush. The stars sing of the vastness and weave my braids into the Milky Way. And ever ever ever ever this silent song of wonder, in the traffic in the stars in the faces of the partygoers walking home together or alone, in the grass wet from sprinklers in the fallen peaches on the sidewalk, in this amazing full on poignant teary world laughing dancing madly, just as it is, just as you are. The beauty grabs you and takes you down and smothers you with kisses and rips you apart and you drown

In nothing other than this.

The color the taste the timbre the overtones resound deeply and an ageless song sings itself, paints itself with a clarity that cannot be obscured by language by voice by which paintbrush is used

Butterfly wings dipped in rainbow iridescence sing. Lions roaring or lapping at the edge of the same river the same water the same wetness flowing through us as us. Hearts bleeding tears splattered on the edgeless vastness reflecting what can never be sung yet sings itself through a wind a touch a kiss. Rollicking laughing sobbing in utter stillness and echoed rolling down the endless canyons where time has died. This deep deep current where joy and sorrow merged.

You recoil back to the familiar again and again until you cannot tell which way was back or forward

Words slide off the mirror and it feels like you fall through, yet there is simply no one and no thing on the other side as there are no sides. Flotsam and jetsam continue to swirl on the surface after the shipwreck that you believed to be a vessel sailing to an imaginary paradise sinks as your heart drops. It was an imaginary journey of you and your life and love, with your hands on the tiller, yet there were no hands and not even nothing that they were connected to. You awake as a shoreless ocean, directionless, rudderless as a sea of dreams. Life happening by itself just as it always has done, the sun slides across the seamless sky, words lay down and you slip into the flowing.

There is no one left to be free or not free, wind and light and clouds and life through you as you. You cannot turn away from the magnificence, as it is you. Slipping Softly in as and through your shimmering gossamer light gown of awe.

I tried to pick the sun off my shoulders and became enchanted with my hand, moving, warmth, light, my breath, my heartbeat, seagull song on the windy shore... The waves found me again after I lost herself, wandering among the seashells. Always the yellowy oranges of the sunset loom so beautifully. Knowing you nor anyone you have ever loved has ever existed yet this marvelous passion play will end, the kiss of death your beautiful shadow.

This train wreck on the shores of infinity when time and timelessness fell into and through each other through the imprint of your shadow and there was not even nothing left. Twisting twirling shapes and colors twining through emptiness as words gather in the inky blackness, greeny blues emerge and erupt into the suns brilliance and fall back into themselves melting merging in the sea of dreams. Words paint rainbow splashes that ripple so exquisitely as they sink beneath the waves. Simply amazed bedazzled smitten with life as it is. Gathering on the tip of a crescent moon the warmth of the orangy glow hanging by a sliver of light as it sank into the sea of unknowing. Such unspeakable beauty when meaning and meaninglessness kiss in a soundless echo.

Words that seem to evoke this beautiful unknowing illuminate the sparkling shadows dance. Moon can never be caught in the palm of your hand, endless sky can never be traversed, the brilliance of light can never be truly described. The sun's rays can never be captured in a jar. Like a fleeting memory, yet more familiar than your tongue in your mouth. This is more evasive than the kiss in last night's dream. More amorphous than a memory of a song you never heard yet is always on. Waves sing themselves into existence disappearing simultaneously on a shoreless sea.

Edges seem to appear so we can touch. What seems to define us separates us, yet there is a touchless touching. Starlit sky falling, tears flowing, a glance, passersby with Ice cream, crumpled newspapers swirling on the sidewalk.

Reaching with an idea of emptiness he found his hands full. Crashing through all and everything he found not even nothing. He could no longer find his empty hands as they had dissolved in the flowing.

Filling in the blanks is what the brain does. Creating a seamless stream of this and that even through the blind spot. The imaginary center or self cannot see itself. But an entire story paints the dream that swirls around it. How can you realize that all things and you are made up when all looking is the dream? You cannot look outside the dream as outside and inside is the dream. You find yourself on the edge of the dance floor but you cannot fall off. There is no off or on or you or love outside the dance.

Watching the watching, photographing from the inside of a photograph. Frame upon frame of imaginary reference points lost in a calliope spinning. Trying to escape the Whirly-gig is the gig. Trying to be a non doer dons your new clothes. You are already awareness aware of being aware through this streaming dream that paints itself even with these words that can never capture it as they are it. You are the magic you seek but you cannot have it or hold it. You can never arrive at a place you never left or become who you already are. Indefinable, you exist only as these imaginary lines. There never was a you nor a home to leave. This imaginary time line you have walked, a tight rope between birth and death never held you up, it is an empty cat's cradle in no ones hands. Filigreed ideas scatter and swirl and seem to coalesce into a pattern that forms and erases itself. A whirl pool of magic this dream of love, I weep at the sweetness of melancholy as I dissolve again as wonder. Suspended as awe like the hush of shhhhhhhhhhhhh child it is only a dream! of magnificent supreme passion, of love and sorrow and joy where no one tells the story, no one holds the book that was never written.. Empty pages blossom into wings and soar in infinite sky.
When there is no notion of effort the illusion and feeling of an effort-er dissolves. The end of belief in other better more and next, a life of seamless ease as the dream paints itself, desire the movement of life. Butterfly wings brush stroke my colors, wet in wet, sliding through infinite iridescent tears.

Rainbow reflections on a bottomless shoreless ocean, riding the waves sparkling rippling over and under and through each other. This feeling of aliveness in undeniable. A three dimensional light fabric weaving and unweaving itself without beginning or end, yet always beginning and ending, never actually forming into a kiss as there are no two. An ever blooming ever wilting flower drinking deeply its own beauty. A wave of ever never rippling shadows lit by their own reflections pirouette in their own sweetness, never finding a place to rest on this edgeless sea of dreams. Without time there is no rhythm, no patterns on the sea, just bits of memories of wetness as love slides into love.
Swallowing the sun as the sun swallows you. Stepping out lightly in gossamer shimmering butterfly wing'd threads of reflected starlight, a footless waltz spiraling in echoed brilliance. Wide eyed wonder spinning in its own dizzying reflection, twirling in the canyon,

laughing at the clouds and weeping at your own amazement. Light and wind and and life and love soaring pouring flooding roaring through you as you.

We are shimmering reflections dancing as seamless openness without definition or direction or boundaries, a duet of time and space, a dream time movie echos, singing this very story.

Walking in the rain under a blue umbrella, tire sounds in the wet road, one handed typing on my phone, looking up and saying hello to a passerby, falling in love again, tall skinny sunflowers laying down in the rain, infinitely petaled tears condensing color.

Soft hellos on a wet summer sidewalk, lit by streetlights, blinded by headlights, by this love that is not missed as day time colors pool in leftover puddles. In love as love through love this dance of one of two of many of none. Ultimately sublimely bittersweetly alone, yet there is love.

And it is utterly apparent
Without any effort or non effort
This vibrant scintillating aliveness
Ever present as this very breath
Your very heartbeat
Closer more intimate than your tongue in your mouth
the darkness the hush the pause before the dawn
and brilliant daylight streaming through your window
the longing to hold the sunset
Or make a kiss last forever
Laughing or weeping or gazing at the computer
That lull between the waves
that ache in your heart
feeling afraid of love
and longing for it
the feeling of your bum on the chair
Or your footfalls on the sidewalk
the caress of the wind or a hand on your cheek
Or those hot hot tears late at night
The wondering if there is meaning
or why those tears
Feeling deeply
Or not feeling anything at all
watching a novella on tv

Thoughts of future
Of past
Of loved ones
Or what to have for dinner
Saying I love you
Or longing to say I love you
All of life happening all by itself
Looking and feeling like anything at all
This myriad of infinite kaleidoscopic reflections of color and hue and pitch
Baseless transparent brilliant rainbow'd watercolor dreamscapes flowing silently singing
radiating undertones overtones echoing shimmering dancing swirling flowing soaring
roaring shouting murmuring ripples of a hush a sigh a kiss a story of untellable wonder
A show unlike anything other
There is no other
Uncapturable unpinpointable ever emerging self erasing a passion play painting itself as
it simultaneously dissolves into and through itself
A magician's tale unlike anything
Simply always only like itself
you cannot stop it or hold it or manipulate it or go with it or accept it or reject it or sur-
render to it
you are not separate from it
It has no parts
No separate moments
No outside
No inside
There is no escape
Wanting to escape
Wanting to capture it
Or figure it out
Is it
Simply unutterably wondrous truly truly that anything seems to appear at all
All by itself
Life dances
there is nothing but the dance
And it is you

and they sat in utter ease bathed in the colors of their own beautiful demise

Everyone knows what it's like to hurt so badly
To long for love
To lose love
To fear loving too much
To fear losing love

How strange that I used to feel like tears were happening to a me, like I was the victim of my feelings. Now that hurt!

It was wondrous when joy and sorrow merged into a deep un named beautiful emotion. It was amazing here when anxiety just started to feel like energy. Just life flowing through me as me, Looking and feeling like anything. It's really only the story that life is happening to a you that creates the suffering

It's belief in the stories that hurts so much. Looking for sustenance in a reflection, trying to drink the water in a mirage. Arms spread wide waiting for that hug that will never come. It's like your life has been spent as one set of lips in the dark. Aching for a kiss. Reaching reaching reaching forever reaching and longing for something, what, you do not even know.

Yet you may have all kinds of ideas about it and ideas of love or peace or for fulfillment or oneness or enlightenment, these ideas are what you are.

You may begin to realize that life has never really gone the way you had wanted it to. That flow of thought and feeling just happens as it does. You never had the kind of thoughts he wanted to have. Witty ones or nice ones, just anything seem to appear willy-nilly. And, oh! The feelings sometimes it seemed clearly out of the blue, deep deep feelings. Life didn't seem like anything that you could control at all. All those decades and decades, years and years of fears, and finally, so many uncountable tears. I wept for every reason I wept for no reason and the flood seemed to consume me.

I no longer to tried stretch out my hand to catch the wind to hold onto life to try to change it and manipulate it and I watched my hand dissolve, as light and wind and life poured through me as me. Utterly naked, with nothing wearing this nakedness. I realized he could only see myself through others reflections, otherwise it was just a vast vacancy, and a streaming undercurrent of awe.

Without each other we cannot find ourselves. A thread has no longing to gather a hem without a need of pockets. It is only in the dance that we have any apparent weight. A light without reflection. A song in the dark. Only in the chorus can we feel the resonance the overtones the dissonance that tells our story and paints our imaginary lines. Without a twostep there is no step!

A melody floats on evening breeze swelling and fading a tune that cannot be captured yet it is always your song. Like a shadow that proceeds you and meets you, Just. Here.

We sing for no reason. Stories write themselves and a singer is borne. Such beautiful poignant heart wrenching beauty. Especially those who wish to see that its all a story, not realizing that they are a story.

Nighttime drips onto the page as the story of you is reflected in the evening star. Silhouettes dance into deep blues and a single cloud catches the pinkness turning purply and fades. No longer believing the story it continues just the same, this wild unpredictable unbelievable stark raving madness. You dance to unknown music, no invitation required, no steps to learn, no special clothes to wear. You're utterly naked and unconcerned, yet caring deeply, laughing and crying as the breeze flows through you and stars stream through your eyes.

Time dies yet the waves keep crashing on a shoreless ocean

Belief in separation is the same as belief in cause-and-effect. So if there is thought there must be a thinker. If there's feeling there must be a feeler. all trying and trying to not try simply seem to tighten the noose that no one is caught in. Time and place arise simultaneously with self No one is captured in the cat's cradle that spontaneously weaves and unweaves itself... utterly insubstantial yet feeling real and solid when believed in.

Self is the knots the tangle of beliefs glued together with hope and fear. The knots untie themselves

Or knot.

How I longed to capture the magic

Never knowing I was it. And yet songs flow ...description continues... the dream of separation painting itself. Painting me and you and me. Words seemingly echoing this dream of love in reverberations of sky.

Beliefs are like layers of an onion. sometimes it feels like your skin is getting ripped off when they pop, sometimes it feels like your heart is being ripped out of your chest, but as the layers and layers fall away or become transparent what is in the middle of the onion? After the shift when it's realized that you exist only as this made up story a fairytale, the stories are no longer owned. There's no one left to own them, and you are all stories and no stories simultaneously. Always home and simultaneously homeless. There was never a you nor a home to leave.

Infinite vast array of stars strewn across the fields of night will not bring you warmth or comfort on this imaginary journey. There is no path or trail that need be illumined. No love to be lost or found in your wandering. Yet every tear shed, every insight gained and lost sparkle so beautifully in starlight's shadow glimmering in your beautiful eyes. As you look up and feel you've never seen stars before as you cannot find a home to leave or trail to follow, the utter magnificence of unknowing spreads its wings and your heart bursts and a love without edge or center blooms.

The utter comfort of no longer searching for the infinite intimate embrace you never left saturates the dream, knowing there was no you nor home to leave nor love, yet love dances you into the spinning dream.

It's like you were trying to untangle an endless knot, to re-arrange the stars so they would shine just right and show you a clue a key to a door that was preventing you from seeing the answer, and you realize there never was a knot that needed untying! The circle was never broken there never were any edges to grasp, the center was an imaginary knot of hope and fear that was you. endless tears exploded into everywhere and nowhere, they were never signed with your name. Now the named world shines with your own brilliance and the un-namable soars through you as you.

It is not the goal of this journey to live suspended as nothing ness. It feels so freeing as all the layers are ripped off, but I have been there and it is not ok nor not ok. How beautiful when the fullness of love rushes in, constantly sweeping you off your feet you soar as utter awe, skinless in the warm summer's breeze you are forever bathed in the warmth of this profound all-encompassing silence that sings you, a love song reverberating echoes of yes, this dance this dance this dance, a lovers dance of life kissing and singing itself through your very lips. delicately balanced like a butterfly's wing dipped in rainbows painting the imaginary spaces in-between with infinite un-imaginable colors streaming the dream of you and me and we.

I woke this morning in tears. The beauty the wonder the sublime edgelessness, colors swirling, lines and line less-ness fills me, empties me. This utter weight and enormity of light. Naked and unafraid, smitten with this namelessness that words can never kiss, as I find myself on the edge staring into the vastness, feeling this great emptiness this sublime bittersweet aloneness and this made up dance pirouetting into and through itself and slip sliding a sing song of love.

I am always all the characters, I am everyone I meet I feel their sadness their hopes their dreams and fear and pain and joy and longing and deep deep sorrow. I can see it in their eyes as this magnificent passion play, life full on naked dances itself madly weeping laughing. I am simultaneously suspended as nothingness, and the vulnerable inside out life of a fearless feeler, this beautiful humanness shinning brightly inevitably in this dance of twoness. Without any effort the dance dances itself the song sings itself, empty shoes know every step as it appears without any rehearsal without any plan or purpose or non purpose. The overtones of love resound after the chord has been struck. I am the rippling the shimmering the reverberations the echoes flooding streaming rushing roaring pouring down the Grand Canyon of love. Ahhhhhh this heartbreakingly beautiful life!

How wondrous this uninterrupted indivisible streaming of what we call perception. Ease fully naturally like water flowing, through memories reflection we hear waves. Lapping. We see and feel the vastness of the ocean the weight of the wetness the depths we cannot see. We have tender cheeks that are caressed by the breezes that come from where we know not. We recognize the kiss of sun on our shoulders our feet on the sidewalk our toes in the sand, a memory of a loved one who will never walk with us again and an empty hand waving hello good bye hello. A tear a shadow a dancing a life a love this love this love, this life un-equalled uncaused unfettered, a magic this knowingness that these words sing the dream, the wonder of apparent thingness arising like the sun on uncharted seas revealing its own luster with its own reflection Shimmering Un-alterably.

Light cannot be grasped nor feeling nor life, yet it is felt deeply, these incalculably deep emotions this flow of what we call life but has no name nor limit nor border is not has never been nor can ever be separate from the knowing of it. There is no method to achive this knowingness this intuited feeling tone of unicity

It need not be gathered or attained a new, for it is always on. Inevitably so.

As water flows, you are this flow there is nothing outside of it

The longing to share the wonder the magic that I feel seems to be the core of this illusory self, a deep profound subsonic wave that ties existence together. Poets sing in the darkness whisperers of love that pierce an aching heart.

there is no you to identify with story, as that is your story

Most seekers are really looking for a more elaborate place to hide

Like the I do not exist story

She wept when she realized they were simply mouthing liquid words of love, the longing had become who they were. It painted their echoes in sky's rippling reflection. Colors swirling merging appearing to separate and yet flowing as one all encompassing sigh dancing, love sings like this. The intimacy of sharing this unknowing reverberates our heartbeats throughout timeless time, our tales sweeping through water as wetness swims through my eyes. Wet in wet, softness in softness, light in light sings like this.

Your arm reaches out your heart sings, and it is the universe asking you to dance, and you cannot accept or reject this waltz as it always is, and always has been this very dance that has sung you as you have been singing it. A brush made of starshadows painting a dreamdance with nothing but memories where love never hides. It was never lost nor found as there was never anything other. This dance that never was nor never will be yet exists in the singing of it. She longed for wings to soar and found that love soared always in this dream dance of you and me and we.

In the middle of a pirouette she saw her tears exploding into rainbows reflecting this dance in as of and through all and everything. Without end yet always ending, the kiss falling into the kiss, we are love's memories lost and found and lost again. Words can never catch anything but their own reflection, and we are swirling thought dreams made of words. We are less substantial than cloud shadows racing down the canyon and bathing in the desert winds. Streaming images you seem to see in the steam rising from your tea as the morning sun illuminates the swirling, and yet the words 'I love you' pierce your non existent heart with untold fathomless beauty.

MAY SONGS

What do you call an open heart when there is no one left inside? When no one saw their empty eyes reflecting in the garden glass looking out looking in? No one left their fingerprints on the window pain when no one went out the back door and no one entered leaving no marks on the threshold. No one embraced an empty shadow weeping in the kitchen at the enormity the immensity of a ravishing vastness a burning intimate all consuming brilliance superseding all ideas of emptiness. Brilliant awareness gazing out gazing in and meeting itself in
This
Very
Kiss

I look in your eyes and the sky unfolds. I swoon into you, yet can never touch you. timelessly we dance in silent wonder, as this very ungraspable momentary is neither touched nor captured. As it signs it's name in the sky it vanishes, yet it's vibrancy is not missed. It swallows itself in its atemporal beauty. I am awed by my very transparency. The ultimate beauty of a million poems untold.

Fiery cloud canyons tunnel into blue. sunset's promise of a new day. A wish of love that will soothe your heart and forever ease the fever of longing. The journey to nowhere is perilous. everything is left behind, even love, even nothing. embers are swallowed as you sail out of your dreams and uncharted waters leave the cool hush of darkness to dance with itself.

This jeweled tapestry weaves itself from words and brightly colored bits of glass it picked up looking at picture books. hearing songs of life from ancient mariners it longs to plunge into the sun, and sail endlessly into the horizon without end. Some notice the weaving itself can never be undone by weaving yet more threads into its density, and light begins to shine through the holes left as the weaving unravels. The ends of the thread can never be seen. Wings form and they sail effortlessly past the horizon, where warp and weave are no more, and disappear.
Plunging back in to tell their tale of the sun hanging like magic in the watery blue sky, they can never find a way to tell another of this profound subsonic wave of seamless existence.

You find yourself walking, and you become the sun streaming, the wind blowing as you fall upwards into blue. Your finger dipped in rainbows you are the poem before it's written in sky.

Songs flow through and I watch amazed as they form colors and take wings and fly, but never catch the wind or sunlight yet they create it. They dance in their own right, as are the dance, the heartbeat of existence. It is impossible to kiss what cannot be kissed with words yet I sing, and my imaginary lines write and erase themselves in the air. So scrumptious so tasty, never touching the meaning of this and that, yet swirling through the emptiness gathering moon beams to untie the words of wordlessness.

And this ....what cannot be pointed to as there is nothing outside it to point to it
is always on without time or non time
It is not an it nor a non it
it is the silence the heartbeat the ache the sigh
the crickets in the night
sails catching the evening sun billowing reds across the deep deep purply blues and greens
Wakeless rippling reflecting echoed breezes
You have not forgotten this song it is too close to listen
Too near to see
to taste your own tongue
To taste the taste of taste
The flavor of flavor
The silence of sound
Sings
No singer can be found
Nor listener
Nothing is separate from this
It cannot be captured or held or treasured
This is indeed the treasure you have been longing for
Without edges or non edges
Or place to grasp
No staves or notes that it hangs upon
No ropes of tangled space or light can entwine it
No emptiness can swallow it
As it is emptiness without end

So vast it is beyond imagination
The hum of day and night
Vibrating
Simultaneously
Silent

The idea that there is truth or an ultimate reality that can be known or that there is some-one to know it is simply an idea. That there is a place to rest, that there are any things or places, or any reference points or lines or edges whatsoever.

It can be known in the deepest sense, not conventionally but intuited, felt always, that all separation is made up. This simply cannot be spoken of as every word seems to divide up this seamless edgeless unknowable vast expanse.

You are the dream, not the dreamer. You are a flowing painted dreamscape. Mirrored baseless reflections shimmering on a river, a castle of clouds flowing into images and reab-sorbed into sky. A three dimensional seamless light fabric without edge or center. Pulsating empty aliveness extending infinitely without direction or non-direction everywhere and nowhere. There are no things that can be caught or known and nothing to catch them.

This is it coyote. The only world you can ever know. As conceptual beings we can only see or know concepts. All that happens in enlightenment is there is an awakening to the made up mentally fabricated nature of this pseudo-reality. We use the word dream or dreamlike or a magicians tale or a pseudo-reality or a virtual reality, but really it has no name or non-name.

There is nothing out of place when it's realized that there are no things and no outside or inside, no place or non place. There are no things, yet all things are included, as where else could they possibly be? Looking for the magic is the magic, looking for wholeness is wholeness, trying to escape the dream is the dream.

You are a beautiful painting never done nor undone sliding through the dream. A circle of emptiness with neither inside nor out. Like tears painting echoes across a shimmering unending vastness falling into and through themselves, a hush singing itself, a symphony of nothing echoing your name. Shadows of colored tears skim across purply seas rippling words into an empty cup as you drink deeply. Ricocheting echoes streaming in empty wall-less canyons.

Sweet nothing whispers in the dark alighting like a dragonfly on a shimmering pool to kiss its reflection. Falling through images there is not even nakedness. Underneath your rainbow feathers there is not even nothing.

Yet this undeniable aliveness is felt, and an entire world a universe of unimaginable beauty seems to appear. A flowing yet not moving edgeless ungraspable magic is always on without time or non time.

The utter fathomless beauty of not being able to know the magic is the magic.

Separation is a beautiful tragic dream
Yet it is only through these imaginary cracks that love flows

And he saw it everywhere
In everyone's eyes
His old longing
Where did it go
Perhaps it was the resistance that left
Slipping out the back door when he was in the kitchen
Only the evening breeze
The faint smell of saltiness of distant seas
An image of a moon he had pined for
Lost in the moonlight
The water no longer tried to escape its wetness

Only you paint beauty into the dream. A butterfly kiss a lightening bolt a dance of two and you're goners. Trying to capture the magic is indeed magical. It's the uncaptureabilty the impermanence that is heart achingly beautiful! Colors streaming through the veil of rainbow tears. Rippling memories showering the waving grasses with last nights kiss. We are love's memories, painted echoes of wonderment singing iridescence onto the wetness of tears. No tears without wetness. Trying to remove the blue from sky, to take it into your heart so you will never die...
How wondrous we can recognize this magic that we are!
Tattered echoes dance and swirl and stream through their own resonance into an image swallowing itself leaving ripples of love's memories sliding across the great great endless vault of sky.
There was never a you nor a home to leave. Tracing your own tears as they slide down your tender cheeks. Winds of sorrow and joy evoke the shadow that never was and you watch yourself dancing as moonlight streams through your empty glass.

life is the ultimate intimacy, you are not separate from it
Dissolving into and through your own reflection through anothers eyes.
Ahhhhhhhh... kissed from within

And the force and heat and light of in numerable suns explodes imploding piercing the very core of your being. Erasing all ideas of who you were or who or what you might be. You realize that you are less substantial than even the cloud reflections dancing and sliding across the rippling stream. There was never a you nor a home to leave. As time and timelessness, meaning and meaninglessness, and all ideas of non duality seem absurd. Melted as the suns desire, in this ultimate conflagration, you are light dancing through light as light. Dissolving continuously into sun.

She reached deep inside her naked breaking heart that had sucked all of the light the love, every kiss every tear, from a cloth woven of memories that she had called her life, and tried to hold on to that last bit of love.
Yet love itself died. She thought she would not be able to bare it so she reached her arms wide in order to hug herself, but there was nothing left to hug.
Only an empty circle. Spinning, suspended, motionless. An emptiness so vast it could not contain emptiness. A fullness so rich so unbearably weighty in its brilliant lightness. Life shining without need of cover or corner. All secrets had been revealed to be merely the wind
Singing
A hush
A whisper
A roar
A kiss
From nowhere and everywhere it echoed, ringing throughout a primordial infinite vastness.
Butterflies alighting on a window kissing a mirrored glimpse
of
a
kiss
Simply unbelievable this dance of one of two of none swirling in empty time. A call and answer song rippling across unfathomable un-crossable imaginary spaces echoing a dream time kiss that reverberates in a hollow shell where the ocean sings.
It's a passion play that exists only in reflected memories weeping for no one for everyone. A taste of this bittersweet aloneness twirling scattering drops of moonlight into a web of untraceable bird paths across endless vast infinite blue.

Amazing that through this miracle of imaginary separation, which hurts so much when believed, and is so magnificent when not believed by the very brain that paints it, we can marvel at the unknowability and be amazed at amazement and weep at the beauty of the mystery of love.

It is no longer your eyes your face your smile your heart your tears your love. Or your emptiness streaming on a dark lonely night or your fullness bursting at the first song of dawn. Or the ripping and shredding of the baby blanket falling into deaths arms.

The depths of despair and anguish and overwhelming joy crash into each other as your hands dissolve into the still peace of a silent lake. Hummingbirds hover as whisper winds sail across the surface and tremble your reflection into the moon shadow shimmering and mountains lost in clouds.

I sing of this with the very words that seem to create slices of sky, as crows raucously sing and mountain streams tumble into rivulets of meadow grasses flowing, and rivers roar into a wide delta just before they sink into this beautiful vast unknowing. Unutterably stunning dragon shadows race down the canyon capturing your shadow my shadow our reflections dissolving in mist. Never formed never captured yet obviously apparent your smile like a song arches over the canyon where we twirl and twine in rapturous embrace. Day and night swirl over us through us in us as us. Love a magnificent dream arising only as shadows play in the story book land of time.

Infinite hue and color and sound taste so lovely in an unbroken dream of ever blooming ever wilting multi petaled flowers. Wind rushes down the canyon and cannot be stopped as it echoes in the canyon spilling rushing tripling from pool to pool. Radiant liquid light dances as shimmering ripples slide over and through each other. Life and love and death and hummingbirds and breezes sing flowing dreams where deep feelings and laughter swim among the shadows. Lit from within and without wonder abounds as lineless transparent being.
Under this whirling mirrored dream dress there is not even a shred of shadow.
I cannot find my feet until you ask me to dance. I cannot find a song until you ask me to sing. I cannot trace my lines until you show me reflections of beauty. How bittersweet that we can never touch as there is no you nor me. How marvelous that we seem to appear laughing loving weeping in this dance of one of two of none.

Under the willow tree they sat together in the wind flowing and wondered at the beauty of wonder.

Beyond words beyond the farthest reaches of beyond there is not even a place-less place, and you cannot go there, as there is no you without place or time or another. There are no things or non things yet here we are, singing of the love of loving. Things are names and names are things. Yet the wind cannot be lassoed by the word wind, and the word wet is not wet and the word salty does not taste like your tears. Yet we all know this magic of life as it streams through us as us. Is magic a thing? Yes it is when named. Awakening is the knowing feeling that all thing-ness is made up, a magicians tale, an imaginary universe of this and that and you and me and wonder and beauty, and magic... that is unspeakably magical. We are the magic wand that sweeps across not even nothing and creates many wondrous things.

Evening wove its shadows into the fabric of the light and reverberated loves kiss across the rippling waving branches that seemed to hold up the stars. There was never any reason to count them or your tears as starlight is so beautiful reflected in your eyes.

He looked down at his feet to see where he was
they were slipping
where could he step next if there was no next?

There is a sublime bittersweet aloneness and simultaneously the dance of love in love as love through love, knowing there is no you nor me. Joy and sorrow merge in an unbearably wondrous hue of every color of no color of crashing rainbows singing.

Truly love is an unspeakable wondrousness of knowing feeling deeply that there is no you nor me to kiss, yet feeling the kiss always. A constant union of what was never apart, the pure mind boggling apprehension that there never was a mountain nor anyone to climb it, yet here I am walking with you in ever present wonder.

There is no me nor you nor love
Yet it is love that spins the galaxy of I am into the universe of we are
Shimmering mirrors on her gypsy skirt existing only in each others love lit eyes.

It's like being as cold as sub-zero ice and an inferno of love

Joy and sorrow merged six months before the shift
What is going on
What we are
What is looking
What is seen

Is utterly magnificently unknowable
Neither moving nor non moving
Neither this nor that nor both nor neither

It can be known and felt that there is indeed no separation
No separate things or moments to be separate or joined
Yet only in this imaginary space between us is there
a light and shadow dance.
Defined by our imaginary lines we can kiss and fall and swoon into our wondrous reflection, OUR OWN BEAUTY. Our own ultimate sublime bittersweet aloneness.
A lone Meadow lark singing a song to myself watching the wind dancing through the rippling grasses

And we are the poem as it writes itself in the wind
Footless we dance

As you crash in dream time wonderment into and through your own after-image a silence inseparable from song begins to become utterly obvious and you realize it was always on simply never heard. Your heart spills into the flowing whirlpools that had felt like patterned footsteps written like bird tracks on the river. Like empty fishnet stockings that never told their story, swirling mirrored skirts bedazzled by their own rainbow eyes.
Water floods water and pirouettes without a center or bottom or top in sideless looking.
There is nothing seen no one watching, nor even a shadow of the moon's reflection.
Yet starlight flows through you as you alighting colored kisses in your empty silhouette with love songs as without lips there is no breath nor anyone to tell this magicians tale.
Weeping laughing soaring as wind swept wonder.

Startled by the beautiful stars in her eyes he looked and saw his own reflection

Memories kissed my shadow as unwritten songs danced in the gathering dark. I could not find my lostness... desert winds blew up the canyon. My footprints filled with tears and the edges crumbled into the vastness, ripples reflecting the luminescence of empty dreams.
I stood amazed at my utter nakedness and wept as the full moon sailed through me as I was the moonlight dancing.
At the end of rainbow's pale streaming velvet colors sing the morning sigh across the canyon
falling surging a pause a hush blooming infinite petals dancing reverberating

echoes painted thought dreams in wakeless shadows rippling without movement
nor stillness
transparent iridescence wound a colored thread sewing an unraveling tapestry
A magic that could not be held
Yet felt always
As you are the dawn in infinite delight
You are the dusk
the shadows at midnight
You are the sky showering starlight
and the clouds sailing through the moon
Your footsteps are empty
There was no path in the desert wastelands
Every star you chased fell across the horizon
Every sign you followed
Was written backwards in your own hand
Every path you took
Turned round and round into itself
Until you wept
At the beauty
Of your starlit eyes
Everyone who has danced this dreamscape with me is like butterfly kisses soaring into
my heart song and leaving fingerprints of love.
This unspeakable momentum of love's embrace fills my story with sublime melancholy.
Shimmering dancing echoes I no longer long to follow as it all dances as my hearts
embrace. How could this vast unknown emptiness break my heart so beautifully?
Beyond place and placelessness
Beyond wind and stillness
here and there collapsed into each other
Beyond wheres
Or whens
Or hows
oh my
oh how the starlight dances so magnificently on midnight empty waters
shimmering it's breath of memories reflecting ripples in the tears left in the wake of loves
demise

Rain dries on the sidewalk in elegant swirls and meanderings and tells its story of falling.
Sky erases its reflection with sun. In between the shadows you spy your tears slip sliding

in waves of joy and sorrow extending empty hands into blue. Trails of what never was seem to follow you as you soar along the skyway into what will never be. You feel your vast aliveness whispering moon songs. Magician's clothing of mirrored starlight wonder twirls into a dance that seems to appear just like this.

There is no you to merge with God, nor God to merge with. There is no you nor me that are one. There is no two there is no one, there is no none that can swing and swirl and boogie late into the night. There are no steps to take and no one to lead or follow. Only in the sparkling of an imaginary I do sides of a deep deep Canyon emerge that separate us. Only in this non existent canyon do Shadows dance and illuminate each other.

I feel like a deer stunned by your love light. Like a puppy so delighted to dance in our loving arms. In this dos y dos of contrapuntal madness a passion play unfolds into a blooming light fabric of flowered curtains fluttering in the morning breeze. Rippling pouring rushing roaring tone poems ricocheting against wall less canyons painting colored thought dreams into a facsimile of wordless wonder.
Afterimages of overtones whisper silently calling your name my name into the dance. Echoing our love song into patterns of wind tossed cascading tears flinging droplets of sunshine back into whirlpools that they never left. Our hearts empty buckets that lost their bottoms long ago.
Without a dancing partner I cannot find my footless steps that leave no traces on this vast shoreless sea of dreams.
There is no purpose or meaning in this dance of one of many of none and no one to look or find one. This obviously magnificent fairy tale writes itself and it's castles crumble just as they seem to arise. Your hand my hand fall through each other just as they seem to touch. Your lips my lips dissolve in the kissing.
This is it coyote.
This non existent canyon down which I twirl and sing meaningless songs to myself. Soaring as the wind the wind soars through me. Wingless we fly.
Footless we dance

such infinite array of stars strewn haphazardly across the night sky, never forming tales of love or war until our brains try to formulate an answer to a question that we forgot when the questions about imaginary things goes away we are lost as unspeakable beauty

Morning crochets itself, light into light, space into space. emptiness into emptiness, nothing into everything, everything into nothing, streaming through my fingers, my eyes, my heart, my shadow, flowing and dancing across the flowered carpets, ever blossoming into a love song that never begins or ends yet has never been. Gossamer day dreams of infinite softness ripple and swirl exploding into a call and answer love song without parts with many parts bending and twining into ropes of air that almost capture the sky I fall through as I twirl down the canyon of vibrant aliveness. My heart broke open long ago yet it was never my heart or my love that sings this love song.

These are empty words that scroll across your mind screen and seem to paint a picture of loveliness but it can never be captured as your hands are the painting as it bleeds into itself. It is always an empty heart an ache that explodes, that swoons in the fire of this ever present love song.

Wrapped in starlight's empty gaze, weeping tears no reason, as reason and meaning have hidden itself in a vacant memory of a lost and lonely woman who longed for loves magic to fill her.

My empty footfalls ring on the pavement but I feel like an empty dress singing, like mirrored gypsy skirts swirling reflecting the love light of everyone I sees. Wind soars through the tree tops and the loose ends of my hair and the tattered remnants of my story fly into endless blue.

It is always a love song that sings itself and seems to look like sadness like madness like unbearable joy like deep deep kisses laughing as night swallows day.

Pierced by love songs this love dance of one of two of none continues and it is only this beautiful ache that reminds me that I am. Never here nor there yet here and there. Everywhere and no where silent love songs sing.

The lines are known and felt always to be imaginary. Softness into softness, Light into light. Space into space.

Hearts are dreamt and have never had lines, yet words flung from streaming tears seem to create ribbons of illumined wavicles that sing an all encompassing silence where rivers cross and hearts melt into a variegated love dance of awe. Transfixed by the magic of what we are and whatever seems to appear the dance self hypnotizes itself and love blooms in the interstitial spaces between emptiness and fullness.

Tears an edgless ocean waving as a dreamscape of love's emptiness.

Words are the wings of this and that, that allow life to soar and know it is soaring in love as love through love. The wings of desire singed as all dreams of future past cast themselves as empty shadows across the fiery furnace of love.

Their tempest dissolved in the coolness of these mind-bogglingly beautiful fathomless depths of unknowing where sourceless reflections flow into and through their own shimmering echoes. Dreamed rainbow creatures sing in the deep blue where sky kisses sea and blueness simply a facet of the magical display of love's infinite intimate embrace.

We exist only in this imaginary gap where life kisses light and shadow into a dance of smiles, of tears, of laughter, of heartbreaking beauty. Spinning memories into a diaphanous web, a multifaceted jewel with an imaginary reference point. How wondrous this dream world casting shadows on the cliffs that can never be crossed until the gap closes and an afterimage of love's smile gazes upon your beautiful beautiful tear stained face.

I was the looking for something other than what is going on. I thought that love peace enlightenment was somehow "out there", something I was going to get, to achieve, something special and extra-ordinary.
Well, what is going on is special and extraordinary, fresh and alive and bursting with spontaneous perfection! Even looking for love is a full-on love dance of one of two of many of none. It's not me over here and you over there! There's just all-encompassing love.
"look! look!" I sing! Here is your already perfect love"

Infinite feathers of your winged arabesque dance as wind caresses your exquisite softness. You embrace the wind and silently sing this wind dance as it sings you. Space and light collapse into an unfolding murmuration that swoops and swirls in immeasurable fluidity. Following no design or template or path there are no required or separate steps as you recognize your feet are inseparable from the dance.

You reach out your hand as trees and sky and light are your hand your arm your breath your heartbeat your song every song singing itself as an infinite instance. There is no time, there never was and will never be, simply a mirage that shimmered so enticingly as you longed for a lover to complete you. That ache was you is you as there is no outside to this infinite kiss.

Soaring as wind dreams pirouette into stories of love and love lost your feet never needed to know how to dance, your heart never needed to know how to love. Love a slow dream waltz when inside and outside disappear into the music that fills you and empties you without time or place, in all time in every place, always this seamless love song.

A door shuts and will never open again. Such a beautiful heartache this treasure in our hearts that will never sing our love song again. It is like your breath whooshes out and never returns with the same rhythms. Their tender shining eyes will never sparkle with our love light again.

For truly without each other we do not exist. We exist only from the reflections of others eyes. We exist only in the imaginary space between us.

So when someone we love dies it is very real and the feeling is very real that a part of ourselves has died. Only through their eyes were we ever beautiful. Only through their eyes did we know love.

It's so beautiful and amazing that in our deepest anguish and sorrow we can recognize that we are each other.
A broken heart is the greatest treasure. It's always a broken heart, but it is no longer owned. Love has bled into everywhere and nowhere and yet it knocks on the back door to remind me that I am.

There are sights and sounds and smells and songs that conjure up a tapestry fraying in the wind. Clothed in love's memories as life softly hums a song of one.

It's truly beautiful and amazing that in our deepest anguish and sorrow we can recognize that we are each other. Only through this touchless touch does the river flow. Spinning great webs where whirlpools seem to gather and swirl and reflect our beautiful beautiful humanness.

The dream paints itself with love and laughter and tears and deep deep sorrow and despair and no one leaves the dream. Even when a loved one is gone they continue to paint our hearts, as we are still and always beautiful water color dreamscapes. Tattered dreams of kisses that will never come are woven like jewels into your thread-bare heart.

Shimmering reflections dance as we are bejeweled wonder itself, astounded at our beautiful beautiful reflections as we swoon into each others eyes.

Only in this imaginary space between us is there a slow dance of liquid love pouring into silhouettes of sea dreams.

It is the very tender and delicate wetness of our eyes that allows life to weave our stories into a passion play alighting on a river of deep deep unowned unnamed tears.

We care deeply yet there is no one to care. It's love that reminds us, "Oh yes! Here I am!"
It seems there is mostly simply an enormous all encompassing edgeless emptiness that is so stunningly full of light and life, I am the perfume of awe.

Knowing there was never anyone to kiss except as sparkles dancing on this edgeless sea of dreams, pierces your heart with an unbearable magic.

The twisting and twining of tendrils of empty shadows reaching into pure space and touching nothing other than their own tears.

It's truly the naked impermanence that I feared that has become the beauty that I am.

Utterly unafraid we drink deeply the song of love's desire and explode into spinning galaxies. Whirling swirling kaleidoscopic surround sound pierces you from the inside out and streams penetrating deep kisses of starlight into ripe juicy mouthfuls of wordless words spitting out these seeds of watermelon dreams.
It was always the alien twostep that kissed life into Ged Clampets ce-ment pond where the red fern grew into tall tales of looking for Mr. Goodbar. The words and lines of every story and the swooshing of velvet curtains shimmering in the footlights of every passion play pour through an empty silent sonic boom and weave a bejeweled tapestry of time that flows through your empty shadow.

We exist only as the story, there is not even nothing under the costume.
When it is un-owned, we become all stories flowing, twisting twining into a backwards glance where a most marvelous passion play sings itself.
Just
Like
This

No love letters are needed
No portraits on the wall
No confirmation or stamp
The night sea has an undeniable saltiness

My song has no beginning or end nor words to grasp and put into a box. Like a river slow dancing to the sound of its own echo on the canyon walls, it thunders and breathes a moving silence.

I have no message of clear bright tomorrows or wide open skies or the end of everything or nothing. Mouthing the words of deep deep penetrating unspeakable heartbreak and unutterable joy, I am a clear reflection of your unfathomable emptiness and mirror the obvious love of knowing we are each other, existing only as dream lovers waltzing rippling shine and shadow across the long summer grasses in the evening breeze.

Feeling this unspeakable unknowable vibrant aliveness and knowing there is no language no symbol or sound that can sing this marvelous uncapturable wind blowing rivers tumbling roaring madly from nowhere to everywhere. The song of me sings a heart song of mirrors dancing in a seamless embrace. There was never anyone behind the looking glass, and never anyone peering in trying to kiss her own reflection.

Imagine all you ever wanted right here right now
Without having to do or not do anything or nothing
Tears
Beautiful

If only there were separate moments to glue together, I would concoct a bower of falling stars to hold your love and drink deeply. Knowing there is no substance to light or love or you and me feels like starlight flowing through me as me. You can see your unspeakable beauty in my tears, and I in my lovers eyes.

The seeker cannot see that he IS his ideas and beliefs about enlightenment, and that they are all hearsay. Learned ideas of peace and love and oneness are all conceptual limitations of inter-connectedness.

Words the sages use like emptiness, he believes point to images he has of a glass once full that is now empty. He cannot imagine the sides and bottom and the emptiness falling away. This is unimaginable. Infinite edgeless emptiness does not point to any thing or non thing, and thinglessness is beyond belief, yet it is the case.

People assume that I no longer identify with thought or feeling or the body or the story. It is beyond comprehension that there is no one to identify with thought or feeling and that we exist only AS the story, the magicians tale that sings itself.

Some believe that I have let go or accepted or indeed resigned myself to what is going on no matter what it looks or feels like. It cannot be grasped by the mind of this and that that there is no one separate from what's going on to accept or reject feeling or thought or action, and mind blowing that there are no separate thoughts or feelings or actions or even separate things called thought or feeling or moments or time or anyone to live a life, or anyone to have or give love.

The seeker may begin to feel that sitting around the flickering campfire with his friends singing songs to ward off the dark is not enough. The darkness where the sparks fly and disappear beckons. He wanders off and hears dogs from other camps bark and echo across the vast desert as his eyes begin to be accustomed to moon and starlight. Strange noises are no longer frightening and the end of all known pathways do not stop his feet.

His skin is ripped away in the desert storms and his heart eviscerated as all promises and dreams of tomorrow vanish.

Vaguely he realizes that this is the end of knowing, and yet he cannot turn back as his footsteps have dissolved. The vast immeasurable emptiness is astoundingly ravishingly beautiful far more wondrous than he could have ever imagined or believed.

Out here where there is no here nor there, not even an echo from last night's day dream, he is simply suspended as not even nothing.

In this a-temporal dream he may find his feet slipping back into his old comfortable shoes, so he can dance. Knowing there are no selves nor love does not end the ecstatic love Dance of this and that, as this knowing IS the dance, there is no escape, no outside nor inside to this dance of one of two of none.

Some may become singers in the dark, sirens calling seekers to their own demise.

Some may simply slip back into the flowing. You never hear about those.

Randomly spiraling drifts of daydream, gossamer spiderwebs soaring through the air catch the light in sparkling radiance. Threads forgotten untie the light and burn brightly through ideas of time. Aloft adrift, suspended as nothingness dawn sees itself in the morning flower. Wind kisses itself in the petals shimmering as tears touch the radiance between light and shadow seeing their reflection in the canyon stream.

Echoed halls of wordless wonder wandering meandering ricocheting, soundlessly singing, the day begins swooning into its own song. A dream of lost night.

Swooning into and through itself, caresses from the inside out, the universe swallows me as I fall into my own infinite intimate embrace. Cascades of butterfly kiss my tears.

After the sea crashed into the sun and moon, after the tempest that smashed every dream of what had never been and what will never be, after the ripping and shredding apart of every idea of who I was and what the world was or could or should be... after joy and sorrow merged... I lay on the beach of the shoreless ocean waves lapping at my feet, seaweed tangled in my hair, the warp and weave of tides undone by piercing love light, I began to breath, in and out, and stood, and looked around.

I walked in utter amazement that there never had been any mountains, that there had never been a center of the swirling, and the wind blew through me as I was the wind.

How could I not have noticed this natural perfection, this utter unfettered beauty, this naked unadorned seamless ease shimmering sparkling reflecting echoing streaming rushing roaring soaring flying flowing fleeting down the canyons through the plains across the desert into the shore-less sea.

Vast beyond vast, empty beyond empty, spacious beyond spaciousness, free beyond freedom or bondage, lit from within and without, beyond time and non-time, beyond place and placelessness, unimaginable, unbelievable, yet vibrantly obviously magnificently spontaneously present, life simply doing itself.

Wind is never separate from wind. Yet in imaginary separation wind sings, flowing over tones and undertones vibrating in simultaneous harmonic resonance. As without imaginary spaces there is no melody and no one to hear the wind whisper your name or feel it's gentle caress upon your soft tender cheek.

Light weaves light and space tumbles through space, and love streams though love, weaving and un-weaving an empty dream though which life recognizes itself and sings. Crocheting slip knots of starlight love is never lost or found. It permeates all and everything with a silence an ease an ever arising insight as to the utter perfection of all that seems to appear.

Hush, love cries, you are simply and most beautifully an imaginary character in a dance a dream of love's joy and sorrow spinning endlessly looking for love. All the turning and twisting created an imaginary hole in the center of your heart, an ache for freedom from this dance. But there is no outside to this dance of life kissing you into this passion play, it is only the thought that there is an outside that creates the feeling of a lonely center that fears being flung out with its own centrifugal force into the stars.

Yet the intense heat of trying to hold on to starlight may burn your very heart to stardust as that hole in your heart explodes and implodes simultaneously.

And you wander endless shores, one foot dancing on the sand marveling at the play of light and shadow across endless dunes painting love songs that whirl and swirl into and through each other with unspeakable perfection, and the other foot pulled into the unknowable vastness...
Sea shells rushing rolling in the push and pull of moonlight's gaze....

In the quiet that never left you hear the universe sing a love song. You no longer need to decipher your tears. It's only the weight of lightness
Weeping

and if I could I would write you a love letter with your own tears so you could taste your own unutterable beauty...

Life is wonderfully simple yet it cannot be grasped. It cannot be held or stopped or slowed down, as there is nothing outside of it. Life has no outside edge. There is no other.

What is going on includes this unending description of life made of words and ideas and concepts that were learned. This constant thought stream paints a picture a virtual reality over the vast unknown and makes what is going on seem tangible, graspable, knowable.

It creates an entire universe, like the chatter at a midnight cafe after the concert, saying which were the good parts and which were the bad, which came first, and which came last. Who was sitting and who was kissing whom, and who was in the back room dancing.

This play of imaginary separation where stories slice the music into shards of piercing sound and silence.

What happens when there is no more looking for the author of the story, the composer of the tale?
When the notes of light of sound of touch of taste of joy of sorrow are known to happen effortlessly, and there have never been notes in this unbound melody?

Simply the joy the wonder the ease of seamless being, and love squeezes into the imaginary cracks where terror of not being thrived.

It was in between the storms that she found the pause and began to fall...

and In the dusty hot afternoon of her life she noticed that her fingerprints had never taken in those forgotten photos.

Steams of loosened spider webs swam reflecting the evening sun. Blue dragonflies hovered over left over memories she had forgotten in the wonder of shifting sands. Her tears seemed to clear the air.

She had fallen in love with her emptiness, yet longed for the deep blue sea... Her hands sifted through the dryness and found her tears which she had put away in this timeless placelessness ....

...and she stumbled upon pools of endless reflections ...dreams and memories started to swirl ...she glimpsed her own reflection
She bent down to drink
The saltiness

And found herself
again
emptied
and full

without a doubt that her story wrote itself
it was her own love she found
her own tears
balanced
she lived
between emptiness and fullness
awash in wonder
she was the dance and the dancer

this sublime aloneness is bittersweet
as imaginary selves we felt it a great emptiness, and after the shift knowing there is truly no other, we feel this bittersweet beautiful melancholy deeply.

We are these beautiful stories as they write themselves and simultaneously evaporate like clouds in the noonday sun. Smoke signals writing love songs across the vastness...

There can occur in some brains a fundamental shift in perception where it is seen without a doubt that all these thoughts composed of shared learned words only seem to create separate things and events and a thinker of them. Knowing they are a conceptual entity relieves all that angst of belief in personal autonomy, of all that hope and fear of life of death... of love. It's like time dies when the do er disappears, yet there is no concern that the whats nexts are gone.

no one is spinning the plates, we just enjoy the sparkling as we are it

and these patchwork quilts that are our stories dance in pattern-less patterns and share the light streaming through ...the flowing beauty ...the winters storm and the gathering of spring...
The nests full and the nests empty.

The utter devastatingly beautiful emptiness of light and the richness of all light ripping into shreds all that you thought possible and impossible.
Rich beyond measure and yet nothing at all.

walking up the canyon, cloud shadows race across the rocky cliffs
the hush of the river calling out my name... drowning in edgeless wonder sliding without care...
...wrapped inside out into myself ...the parcel always bursting ....never contained or tied or fettered or lost or found ....nothing missing ....
....every drop of light slips color into the dream where memory is needed to know the names of things... and yet.. no longer needing names or places to rest ...or any things...
.....thoughts of past or future do not exist in this .....or softness.....or hardness ....meaning-less description cannot add to this....or take anything away.....

The tree is not seen as an illusion, it is merely recognized that there are no lines dividing separate things outside of the human brain. The illusion of separation is created by belief in learned shared words. Some brains can sense that the worded world is made up. Yet still spin the dream of things.

This story is the only place you exist. You cannot drop it or let go of it. A character in a novel cannot change the cover or the font, or the plot. It looks and feels like anything at all.
If the story is seen through, if the brain that paints the story no longer believes it, then that is the story. It's all story. There is no outside to the story as outside and inside, like all this and that are made up.

It can become obvious that all thingness, including you, are mental fabrications. And the joy and wonder of simply being takes front stage, knowing that without this theatre there can be no awareness of being aware, there can be no recognition of unicity without the lens of self seemingly creating a play and someone watching it.

People are beliefs and opinions. And if those are threatened, their very existence is threatened. Most people believe that if EVERYONE, or at least more people believed as they do the world would be a better place. As no belief is ever actually believed they go hand in hand with hope and fear. Hope that it's true, like a merciful God, (and fear that it's not), or fear that it's true (like the devil or hell), and hope that it's not.
That's why we tend to hang out with those who share the same beliefs, in religions or clubs, communities, Facebook forums, etc. As if more people believe in what they do, well then, perhaps it's true! Who goes into an empty restaurant when there is a lively one next door? We look for others opinions when we are buying products, but beliefs do not fall into that category, like you can shop for them. As I remember believing in next, even though I never found one.
Self is like a cloak of beliefs glued together with hope and fear. So after the dream of separation is no longer believed, belief in belief ends, belief in disbelief ends, yet the dream continues without hope and fear. Feeling deeply the anguish and frustration of others when they can no longer feel your hope and fear and need of a never arising next. It's like the sign that used to be on McDonalds restaurant, 'one million burgers sold'. Strength in numbers! How many gather in clubs and dark churches singing songs about the light, about some who have seen it, yet fear it?
Truly what would you be without beliefs, or even the belief that there is a thing called truth?

Self is a prison yet the cage can be known and felt to be imaginary and a most beautiful prism where light and life and wonder flow.

Swimming in this edgeless sea is utterly magnificent! I had heard of inter-connected-ness ....but that doesn't even touch this.

....the utter emptiness of light and the fullness and richness of light ripping into shreds all that you thought possible and impossible... hope and fear can no longer be found...
....it is rich beyond measure and yet nothing at all....
It could be called peace or love or bliss ....but it isn't like anything.... ...there is a constant knowing of the sublime 'rightness' of the flowingness ....whatever appears...
....and dancing between nothing and everything.....

.....and clear moonlight spills into the canyon...yet I cannot warm my hands in its gaze.....
stars hang in the silence... and winds ripple the canyon's reflection into paintings of
unfindable beauty ....

All words seem to say something ...they form images that we share....but this is beyond
imagination....it is more real than any concept or idea can touch....

It's like slipping into the warm liquidity of home after a long arduous journey where
you've lost everything along the way....including your skin.

The self is the lens through which we see the world. The objectifying mind of this and that
is seen to be the creation of all things, yet it is also always known that there are no sepa-
rate things or events. So this lamp of knowingness is seen as beautiful in its own right.
Like a net of spontaneously occurring description, never actually dividing the seamless
timeless flowing. Yet this is where love and beauty appear.
How marvelous!

We are the softness of a caress from the inside and outside kissing itself. From everywhere
and nowhere love flows into love and weeps at the utter all encompassing silence, reverber-
ating into echoes like never ending parentheses of hugs. Reaching stretching into your own
infinite intimate embrace life kisses you soundly. You can feel your beautiful aliveness always.

The ecstatic love dance swoons into itself through the prism of your rainbow eyes, rip-
pling colors overflow into and through themselves. Awash with loves timeless beauty.

Seemingly swooshing and swirling and twirling waltzing light and shadow thirst for each
other as night and day drink deeply this draft of love

There's nothing in the middle and there is no outside to this wondrous love dance. It hits
you like a freight train that it has always been this way. There is no more looking for the
other half of a kiss, it feels like the first and last kiss always.

And how could you look long and hard into anothers eyes without weeping at your own
beauty

One foot in the unknowable vastness, the other walking footless in the sand always filling
with tears and crumbling into the skyway

Circling endlessly without beginning or end in a loop de loop möbius, a wind brushed star shadow shimmers through its own reflection. What is pointing out is pointing in, and no hands are looked for as the moon whispers its painting across the ripples it reveals. Your heart like a sinker drops into the fathomless depths as a little plastic toy floats on the waves, bobbing its head saying hello, good bye, hello, and the river continues its meandering, singing of the countless salty tears it has reflected swimming through your beautiful eyes.

Water cannot be grasped with your naked hands and your nakedness cannot be known without your rainbow clothes.

Arpeggio'd plurality ascends and descends rungless sky ladders trippling songs about the end of sound and silence that converge in a pointless point at the end of nothing. Where is the beginning of emptiness when it is not separate from fullness? Where is the love you thought was yours as it crept over the garden wall seeking rainbows blooming?

Where was your song when you had no words nor voice to sing? Where was your heart when it flew away with the sunset? Where are the colors in yesterday's rain-bow? Where is yesterday except in the flowing dreamscape of memories that you are?

When memories slide away so will you.

What I can never kiss with words is a mind blowing earth shattering place less place where no one arrives, as there is no one can travel to no where, and no where is not a place. Seekers are the idea that there is someone traveling on a path yet there has never been anyone seeking and no one ever has been asleep or enlightened.

This is simply beyond all ideas of this and that, all ideas of understanding or not know-ing, all ideas of confusion or non-confusion. All ideas of perfection and non-perfection are burned in this world shattering brilliant clarity. It hits you like a lightning bolt, like a freight train, this devastatingly beautiful recognition of utter and complete emptiness. It rips and tears the fabric of what you thought to be your existence, and like the greatest lover, it pierces you to the very marrow of your being and eviscerates all ideas beliefs and concepts about what enlightenment is.

It is beyond time and non time, without direction or non-direction and yet this vast emp-tiness neither non-moving or moving extends infinitely everywhere and nowhere, encom-passing all things and non things, swallowing even itself, consumed in its great marvelous maw of unbearable beauty.

This huge conflagration of all ideas of truth or God or meaning or purpose ignites your world and burns all ideas that there is anyone to have a world.

This catastrophic change in perspective cannot be articulated, it cannot be thought about, as all words paint the sea of dreams with endless reflections reverberating echoing flowing rippling into and through each other creating this wondrous made up world of you and me and we, and sunsets and moonlight, and deep deep kisses and laughter.

One glimpse of this and symphonies are written, and yet this marvelous unknowable perfection cannot be danced or sung or traced even if all the stars in the universe sang in one unending whoosh.

For the brightness is most often too much to bear as long as it is felt that there is someone watching it. It is too huge to consume as long as it is felt that there is someone separate from it. It consumes you utterly and completely.
All by itself.

the ball had already been thrown
by no one
it painted its picture across the vastness
and fell through the colors of its own reflection
as the empty wake of nothingness collapsed into itself
no one knew it had fallen
and it had no idea how it happened
its all falling
the falling is falling
there are no reference points whatsoever
there is no prize
and no one to claim it
life was ripped away at the seems
Tattered dreams
Streamed like clouds across the moon
seems like a dream
That there were clouds
Obscuring
This light
Beauty seeing its own beauty
Light knowing light

Love recognizing

Ah

Yes

This is love

I sing of moonbeams and I sing of shadows dissolving into each other. I swim as the deep heart current where joy and sorrow merge.

I dance on silent stars

shooting through endless skies.

No amount of twisting will gather light into darkness or darkness into light.

Songs singing themselves ignite the intensity of this amazing seamless ecstatic union of what was never separate.

It is beyond understanding, this ever emerging submerging richness of nothing dancing as everything falling into the dance of nothing swallowing everything.

Dancing at dawn the skeletons rattled their empty charm boxes and jewels fell upon the land. Sparkles of reflected light sang echoing whispers of hidden treasures.

Those listening formed wild dream images of what this precious jewel must look like, and most failed to see the beauty, lost in abstractions and trying to capture them.

Like attempting to catch the wind or looking for a place to land when even the falling is falling. Yet even the attempt is the magic as nothing is excluded from this unitary dancing. Wild dreams of tomorrow create a sense of lack, a hole which can never be filled with more ideas. More concepts only seem to make the imaginary barrier between inside and outside more substantial.

It all happens as it does. The dancing on an illusory dance floor and the music that we can never capture.

...and brushes of emptiness paint imaginary lines with gossamer ideas and color in the nonexistent spaces with rainbows....

Icy winds rip down the canyon and pierce my skin, trees dance madly yet they do not ache for calm. The sun does not long to crest the rocky cliffs and flood this world with color. We are the only beings who ache for something other, and there is none.

When we know utterly that there is nothing other, life simply becomes a magnificent bittersweet impersonal wave of un-named emotion.

No longer caring why tears flow. No longer concerned with what thoughts appear, these beautiful transparent meaningless sounds.

No longer trying to catch the wind, I soar as the wind as it blows through me. It's always been this super all encompassing unknowable pure stainless vastness. A seamless dancing, perfect beyond measure, whatever seems to appear.

Just. Like. This...

there is a location-less place between timeless and time, between hard and soft, between up and down,
beyond conception .
we know this but when we try to speak of it, it slides away ....as this delicious unknowing can never be captured....
morning does not push away the night, nor night await the dawn

she spied her shadow swimming in hindsight
iridescence shimmering in the mourning Dew reflecting
The utter weight of lightness
Weeping

and she was the wind
Filling and emptying its own embrace
Caressing shadows in the night

Spying her beauty in the treetops dancing
Hearing her own Love song in the breath of all
Unfettered symphony of love and love lost cascading down wall less canyons
Echoing penetrating a silent slumber roaring

Sighing a silent peace
Ripples streaming
unwoken without a kiss
sunset glimmered beyond her doorstep
and pulled her into her own light

The dance
Before dark
how beautiful to be the inside of a kiss

Like cloud shadows swirling and pooling at your feet, you are like the breath of midnight in a world without time. You are the untraceable path of a herons wing after it soars across the canyon. You are the memories of a little girl who ached to return to the home she never left, counting her footsteps as she walked home from school and getting lost in the beauty of her feet on the side-walk.

You fall, you drown, as your fingers seem to un-pry themselves from the space you thought you were surrounded by, and everything falls with you. Even the falling falls until there are no more things. There is no desire to grasp the sky as you have been ripped inside out. There is no hand left to grasp.

Just space falling into itself, waves crashing into themselves. vividly apparent reflections of nothing, unheard overtones singing a melody of one. Torn into a gazillion pieces you are thrown across the endless vault of sky and no one is left to put them together. There never were any pieces of sky or stars or starlight separate from edgeless vastness. You were never separate from pure open spaciousness itself.

Mirrored reflections dancing.

Falling into and through each other.

Not one not two not both nor neither, twisting turning shine and shadow shimmering beautifully without rhythm or rhyme.

Such a magnificent song!

Mountain flurry cascade of tears. Forgotten moments blend submerge into what has never been and will never be. The remembering sings of this and that, and loves fury escapes.

Boundless.

Timeless and free.

It took a backstroke

A virgin smile

A wait a minute

For time to dissolve

Poems write my lines as morning floods through me and kisses me into morning. All is naturally perfect, unicity is perfect, twoness is perfect, plurality is perfect. Intuited or conceived, grasped or non grasped, all and everything is all ready perfect and super complete. super saturated like a poppy floating in the sea of grasses catching the evening sun. Rivers of words sometimes caught with fingers or thumbs, twisting turning like ever growing flowering vines blossoming twining around and through empty space never capturing the kiss of day.

Tendrils of light stream through the window and dance in the steam of my tea. My eyes color in color and add the edges of my cup as it dissolves into center-less pure light without source or end. Unspeakable the day, the night, always dawning always setting, swirling yet neither moving nor not moving. This marvelous unknowable endless vastness uncontained beyond freedom nor non freedom.

Always super complete as nothing can be or need be done to recognize this, as all reaching for other creates the illusion. ...of other.

Utterly always sublimely alone, a shadow bird of forgotten memories kissed her cheek. She was the bittersweetness weeping.

Tears for everything.
Tears for nothing. Tears our broken hearts shining, swirling through the canyons, echoing love songs. Music, unrehearsed, plays itself in dream-time company.

Pure shimmering brilliance without root or ground or sky or space, like a rainbow, beautifully transparent clearly seen, yet ungraspable. castles in the sky made of dream stuff crumbling into dream dust.
This splendid flowering blooming wilting singing silence. This shining shimmering play of shine and shadow flowing always ever never. This brilliant spontaneous immediacy doing itself yet neither happening nor non happening, neither moving nor non moving without change nor non change dances itself. Simultaneously arising and falling writing itself as it self releases without time nor non time. Nothing can be said or not said, yet we sing. Just as the birds or the mountain stream or the crickets in the night. Joyously erupting. The song of sky.
We are simply unique beautiful fleeting stories written with the same words. When the story is unowned, we become all stories. We are the stories of ancient times that never were, and times that will never be, as time is a story.

Life which is found to be uncontained unbound unfettered simply flows naturally. Rich and lush, a tattered patchwork quilt weaving and unweaving itself with disappearing ink, with teardrops drenched in rainbows
Butterfly kisses flowing on a river of whir-pooled wonder neither moving nor un-moving.
Ripple less ripples.
Patternless patterns.
Rhythmless rhythms.
Wakeless wakes shimmer a love song.
Singing echoing, yet only seen in a reflection, a backwards glance.
Toppling as they are built castles made of moonbeams,
Erased as they are written,
Unsung as they are sung.
Dissolving as they paint themselves
On a deep roaring ageless river.
The hum of the universe sings.
swirling through the canyons ricocheting echoing call and answer love songs.
music unrehearsed plays itself in dream-time company.
Shimmering iridescence dancing on the wave across a smiling tear. between never and forever, between here and now, between the in between.

Where lips tremble just before the kiss just before the song the breath no longer held no longer let go, life sings itself.
Life breathes.
A heartbeat of shadow and light
This and that. You and me. And love

Transparent rainbow of pure delight
dancing shimmering in its own reflection
Its heartbeat the two-step
The in breath the out
Between lost and found
What is red

When a loved one dies their love light embraces my heart and becomes a most precious part of me
death weaves its infinite beauty into the fabric of who I am

Mirror mirror on the wall... enchanted with your own reflection you seek to find the source, and there is none. It's not that the writing is on the wall
It is it. You are and always have been Bathing in your own natural brilliance.
All description paints the dream.
Amazing how naturally and spontaneously the brain seems to divide what's going on and then attempts to glue infinite subtance-less pieces into an imaginary whole
I love it. When the flowing thought dream is not believed it is a most beautiful under-mutter creating all and everything in this magnificent passion play. It's all in the tender sweetness of our eyes.

What is outside of this and that?
What is in between sides and not the middle
Where is not here nor there
Nor now nor always nor before nor after
What cannot be captured with a song
What has no edges or borders or center or corner
What has not a name
What is beyond imagination or belief
What is not a what?
What cannot grasp itself or hug itself or see itself or kiss itself

Not full nor empty
What has no other
There is no one to choose where to direct attention and no separate places to do so.
There are no things to resolve or glue together or fix.
Life happens utterly spontaneously.
It has no edges or split or division anywhere. It was never broken. Self is the Belief in other better more next, and there is none. We exist only as this dream of separation. There is no escape. Yet it can be realized and felt always that all separation is made up. As an imaginary piece of sky there is nothing you can do or not do to patch together this seamless unbroken unstained vastness. Under and over are the dream as there is no outside of the dream. All this and that like inside and outside are the dream. Truth and non truth are the dream. Anything you can think of is the dream, is made up, all thought, all description paints the dream of separation.
Words can never kiss what is not a what or an it or a non it. Yet they kiss all and everything into existence. A play of this and that, of you and me and love and beauty, a dream of separation, a virtual reality, a pseudo reality a magicians tale.
We are indeed a spell of words
A divine dance with no other
colliding crashing falling
Swooning into itself

He gathered bits of seaweed from last nights storm and slept in salty dreams painting a picture of the distant shore where he knew he would finally see the sun rise. He feels he knows where he is as his shadow slides along the sandy shore, but it disappears as he enters the storm. He takes off his sunglasses as the first drops of rain hit his windshield. Tears so effortlessly catch the wonder of unknowing, mesmerized as the beauty pulls him in.
Chinese lanterns bloom only in the rain, he realized all his efforts to avoid the storm have always been in vain. Silent thunder echoed the future storm as a tsunami of tears washed everything and nothing away. Bare bones dancing on endless sands in between a breath and a shadow to unheard melodies never sung yet felt deeply. He saw that everything he believed himself to be was an empty kiss.
Walking up the twilight sea losing his heart in inky blackness, it was never his. The ember of dawn seemed hidden by the sunset, yet found again in the stars his hand. What's looking in the shade of his shadow as memories flow but they can't understand.
Knowing this unspeakable aliveness and no longer trying to nail it down or capture it or hold it, there is no feeling of separation after the dance-floor falls away. No looking for how to place his feet as he has none, yet they sway and swing. The dance dances itself

the song sings itself. There is no invitation no script the book is unwritten the melody is remembered and we mouth the words to our own starlight dancing in the tree tops glistening with our own tears that we have wept since the beginning of this imaginary dance of you and me and we and time. The unbearable majesty the unfathomable wonder of our beautiful humanness.

His own tears reigned softly in the night and sang of sweet sorrow too beautiful to touch sweeping a windy beach where heart ache wandered aimlessly. Feasting on shadows of dreams half remembered this ravenous desire to stop this incessant roaming. Tip toeing where words can never touch, an essence of loveliness sang, beckoning him further and further into the night of unknowing. A shell placed against his ear reached into his heart and sang of what he knew to be true, but every time he tried to understand it, like a memory of a dream from long ago, it flew into soaring thunder and he could not hear the words or the melody. His very own heartbeat drowned out the echoes where his shadow lay, breathing. His nails red with his own blood grasped his heart and pulled. The very sea boiled in lust for what it could not swallow.

This kiss of enduring lostness. The rush and roar of life singing hello goodbye hello, snarls you slays you grasps you in its arms strangles you drowns you points your nose in its abdomen and yells your name. This is it! It screams like a banshee rolling over you crushing every bit of life of you into a flatness where there are no things. Not even a drop of light or love can be found. Every tear rung out. You are indeed dead. You never existed. It was an elaborate hoax a trick of the tale an enchantment an infinite fabrication of ideas. A scaffold of words built on clouds. The kiss of death by your own lips.
Only the shimmering gloss in the starlight as it fades. Life quenching itself with its own desire through your skin your lips your teeth your kiss your deepest darkest secrets. Unwrapped, unveiled, undone by desire itself and turned ripped inside out till there's nothing left to hide and no where to hide it. Hope and fear like a bullets gasp gone into the night. Air woven by its skin into an idea of love curled by desire for what it knew not yet longed for turned into itself. Desire for more transmogrified itself into desire for what is. Vanquished by the needles sting, love crept softly back after the battle was lost
By no one

The ache is like a dancing heartbeat tango-ing you into town. To see the moon's reflection in your smile that you left there last night, picking over leftovers you realized that nothing is ever repeated, not even that syncopated rhythm that feels like love remembered, not even that poem you're sure you wrote yesterday, not even that forgotten kiss of wonder that was captured in a whirlpool where your song your heart your love lay bleeding and forgotten that swirled into an edgeless love ballet.

Mirrored gypsy shadows spin and swirl, multicolored skirts weaving rainbows in the sky. Simultaneously appearing and dissolving like iridescence on a ripple, a butterfly kiss of unspeakable wonder, like your heart crashing and burning in the abyss of your own love. Drenched in tears, soaring In between the breath and the song, painting this vibrant aliveness sliding through the transparent canvas of your mindstream. Feets lose themselves in the dance, as mist dissolving in morning sun. We cannot capture it, as we are not separate from it, yet we sing. Casting shiny pebbles in unseen springs, hearts echo in deep dark canyons waltzing between the abyss and my heart.

Wind leaves no footprint on the lake yet you can see it dance. Bending and twisting rippling light and shadow flowing through the weight and enormity of brilliant emptiness appearing as time and dimension of sun dancing in and as this fathomless beauty of knowing this unknowing of ultimate sublime vastness.

Rapt into itself the taste of your own love your own blood your very existence soars, exploding on wings of air that were never tied with ropes of sky. There was no one to be free or bound nor prize to catch, just an empty echo weeping. The Taste of taste unraveled itself into this very shining shimmering crest of a wave hovering falling swooning crashing into itself in between what never happened and what will never be. Not found nor lost never actually ever forming into anything other than a beautiful dream of who you were when you softly danced as starlight kissing your reflection in the middle of a sigh. You are the dancing winds and the echo of winds reflection.

At first I used to say it was like I had spent my whole life trying to swim against the current every rock and branch that I hit hurt becoming more and more exhausted until I realized even going against the current was going with it.

After that it felt like I was always, and had always been this flow of life, as there is nothing separate from it as it rushes and roars and trickles and weaves wetness in wetness, painting fantastical currents and ripples and whirlpools, reflecting this unfathomable vastness reflecting your beautiful face your beautiful tears your beautiful mouth your beautiful song that sings you as you sing it.

The moon does not ache for its reflection. How can a touch a delicate kiss a meadow of long waving grasses a rainbow magically appearing in a dark stormy sky, tears flowing at the memory of a kiss, a warm summer breeze a wisp a tendril of spring vine climbing an old gnarled tree, an intake of breath explain or know or touch itself? How can your tender heart grasp it's own love? Does the night time cloud covered sky long for the moon to play its light and the moon to reveal the truth of night? Only a human can wonder at the magic of love and existence and wonder itself. Only your beautiful eyes can paint color and form and joy and sorrow and beauty and love. In the dark the desert trumpet blooms unobstructedly. It's fragrance fills the wind swept air with butterfly kisses. Only in the telling of the tale is there beauty.

This be-jeweled saber pierces your heart and leave no prisoners. Ripped apart torn asunder drowned in your own utter emptiness. It is your own hand your own dagger your own love that lies bleeding, and every attempt to catch yourself only precipitates more tears. That you cannot stop. That you cannot hold. That you cannot allow or reject. They overtake you. They swallow you. They subsume you. They are you. Your own all encompassing love. I was adrift on a tiny island that was flooded washed away by my own love, drowned into unknowing vastness. Appearing again in the tides of my heartbeat my breath my humanness unfurled but filled no tattered sails, the prayer flags of hope dashed on the rocks of sublime sorrow, the deep deep knowing that the sun is always setting and there never was another breath another kiss another dance.

In the placeless place where shadows overlap the deliciousness of every taste and no taste, patternless patterns melt into each other. What was always on the tip of your tongue, dimly remembered like a lamp lit in a faraway dream, like a melody that was never written or sung, haunting you with it's wordless overtones. Light blooms without resistance and the shimmering lights itself. Many petaled fields of wonder unfurl velvet tongues of un-knowingness written in your heart. Lost beneath the blood of gaping wounds pierced with the shards of separation, the rain washes your salty tears into the ocean without a shore as you slip into the vast liquidity of home which you have never left. Looking around after a lifetime of hope and fear you realize you have never left your infinite intimate embrace.

I dance and laugh and sing of this trembling tenuous precious aliveness. Riding sailing surfing tumbling falling our utter gut wrenching amazing rip your heart out overflowing humanness. Every tip toe dances in air, every heartbeat resounds through the canyon. My breath is the winds that dance flowing through the pines singing these songs of love. Falling into nothing, words form, bursting through the flowered curtains shaping emptiness into a poem and fly away, nothing was ever captured. There are no things.

Drifting sideways through feathered cups of reflected light, your handholds dissolved into a fingerless touch. Your beautiful petals could never capture the morning that bloomed in your heart. It was not sorrow or joy but deep deep despair that Ruptured the sutures that bound you and unraveled the dream of memory of time and place and your dancing footfalls echoing in mirrored halls of wonder. Dragon clouds soar through you, winds caress your rippling shadow as the treasure of this very breath sings you. Your tender lips never kissed anything as soft as your own lips that had hungered for this taste of freedom that collided with all ideas of freedom and boundaries.

Love was the song you longed to sing as it sang you so wistfully in your bittersweet loneliness. Looking for a partner or a hand to hold you always found your own hand your own lips your own song mouthing the words to a primordial heartache that you finally saw was the incomprehensible jewel that had no center or chain to wear it. It was always displayed upon your tender breast. Under this nakedness there is nothing to hide in this dream dance of love. No messages were sent and nothing was received but the call and answer sing song sings you, a transparency of light falling through light this winged beauty of your sublime aloneness. Life tastes its own sensuousness through your very lips.

She wept for every reason and for no reason. For the enormity and transience of this rich and lush life, for the little girl who was so lonely and longed for love, for the magic of love and love lost, for the glance from the woman in the bus that pierced her heart, for this wondrous heart ache of life greeting itself through her eyes, and for the bittersweet beauty of tears and of sorrow itself.

We are always a part of each other as we exist only in this dance. Only through our reflections in each others I's can we see ourselves, and know love. Yet we never can actually touch, as we need our imaginary lines to reach... We need our selves these words that define us, our tender skins the imaginary boundary between inside and out.

Watching your arm your hand your heart reach out for another knowing we can never touch, hello good bye hello. We exist only in the touching, this touchless touch of reverberating echoes a thump thump thump of the heart beat of love dancing, this dance of one of two of many of none. Knowing there is no you nor me nor we nor love, life feels like a waterfall of love streaming in me through me as me.

Hot winds rushed up the canyon from the deep desert floor and brought the scent of dust and ashes where many had died, eons of blood spilled into the sand. It blew your skin off in tattered strips as the sand dug into your flesh and you heard your heart beat echoing on the canyon walls. In your despair you tried to catch each tiny piece of glass before it hit, argued with them, yelled at the storm trying to make a deal. Yet the pain became so great, you stopped and watched even as your heart was ripped out and your bones were gnawed by nighttime creatures.

When all that you had believed to be yourself is found to be empty, every drop of hope squeezed out like a tumbleweed flying across the barren desert, tears rise and fall like the sun grabbing your heart and pulling it into the sky. Dawn sweeps over the canyon walls and it is constantly astonishing. Such beauty of every sunrise pales, the magnificence of every counted moment had been missed. In the measuring with what had never happened and hope for what will never be, in the figuring in the determining in the comparing and the judging the brilliant silent singing was ignored. A lifetime of tears watered the dust and ashes and a shadow bird rose, effortlessly soaring.

Yet the heart never closes, it is perpetually blooming and falling in love. Breaking into waterfalls of loveliness, the heart never heals from the gash of imaginary separation, and who would want to shut out the light of love? uniquely human, this tender vulnerability this aliveness that cannot be caught. This centerless spinning jewel that you are shines so magnificently so beautifully as our deeply unprotected hearts.
True unalterable unfathomable beauty is in the sharing, the touching, the singing, the magnificent emerging of you and me and we in this imaginary space this Grand Canyon of love.

Where was the sorrow that waltzed in my footsteps? Who walked across the threshold of no tomorrow? Whose shadow was illumined by crystalline tears left on the backseat of forgotten lullabies? Crumpled empty chip bags drifting down the beach catch the mourning in their exquisite wind ballet that arises after the storm. This dance of sublime melancholy took my hand my heart and spun me into whirlpools of reflected faces that mirrored my eyes and my emptiness. 'Hello' said the river of sorrow of joy of waves surging collapsing rushing to the sea. 'This is your last and only dance and has always been yet never was. It was never your hand that held back the sea, it was never your tears that ran in rivulets down your tender cheeks. Yet there has never been anyone else, and will never be. Never another moment, just this sigh swooning into itself, falling through the falling. Your one and only kiss, the first and last, no ones hand to grasp not even your own. You are simultaneously less substantial than the cloud reflections on the sea, and yet you extend infinitely, intimately. Yet there is the dream of love of heartache, the only place you will ever know." And knowing this, I sing, and hear your beautiful beautiful song echoing in the canyon.

Your heart doesn't actually explode, but it feels like that

All you ever wanted all you ever wished for unseen unheard unformed melodies in the dark hidden, lurking under undiscovered corners behind rainbows
Waiting
You turn around and face yourself and there is nothing, only the memory of love.
You are the swirling memories of all the love that simultaneously wrecked you and created you and flooded through you and washed you away into moonlit pools singing a song you once sung but cannot remember exploding your heart into infinite pieces that

gather again like mirrored shards of sunlight weaving stitching themselves into a dream of you. Of your own heart your own love ravishing you burning you like a wave crushing you and becoming you singing this beautiful passion play. You are demolished knowing there was never anyone to die or return, yet here you are, always the first and last kiss. You cannot find yourself without love. We exist only in the touching knowing we can never touch. Only in this kiss can we find our imaginary edges.

Wanting to be free of story of self is like wanting the world to stop
Wanting the oceans to call your name in the night
Waiting for a prince to kiss you
Love is an idea just like you
You are a story
This is it coyote
Life whatever it looks or feels like
There is no escape from the story you are it
When the story is unowned you become all stories
Like ricocheting parenthesis echoing the primordial hum of we are

The crunch of the gravel beneath my feet
Where was my foot
As it slipped over the rainbow
We all know this deep un-namable current of profound sorrow and unbound joy
No one need remind you of your undeniable aliveness that looks and feels like anything at all
Whose hot tears slide down these cheeks?
Nothing but a lovers breath
Between the lips and the kiss
Wrapped in yesterday's newspapers her tears wrote poems of loves beautiful sadness in their meandering.
Night swallows your love as you weep for those who wish to swallow the moon. The moon consumed you long ago and you found moonlight streaming through you as you. There is no dancing naked in the moonlight without another to join in the dance. This effortless dancing to music that was never written or sung, it has no words yet is felt deeply. It requires no invitation or rehearsal, it is unceasing, yet has no time. A pas de deux of wingless wind soars effortlessly down the canyon of love and death.
How did it feel when the wind blew through you, when your hands loosed themselves from the tiller and all you could see was no where to go? Morning sings you into the universe and sings itself to sleep.

My feet crunching on the gravelly path ......looooooong late summer sun highlights every pebble, my shadow spills over the canyon and I see myself waltzing with the trees.

We exist only on that razors edge, that tightrope walk between birth and death. And as there are no separate things or moments there are no steps to take and no one to take them. Yet on the way there is love and the bittersweet beauty of impermanence.

We can only touch in this touches touch, dance in the Grand Canyon of love, in the imaginary space inbetween us. We are ultimately sublimely alone. There is no me nor you nor love. Yet knowing this is not the end of love... We find ourselves only through our reflections in each other's eyes. We do not exist without others, yet there are none. Just this brief always emerging always dissolving momentary dreamscape where everyone you have ever loved will die and be forgotten, and as your lovers slip away so does a part of you, as you can never see your beautiful dancing echoed back to you through love again.

Self is like a patchwork quilt. There is constant effort to keep the seams together. When the efforting ceases all by itself, Cascading jewels shimmer unloosed at every intersection unwoven, waltzing on rainbow reflections. Falling up spiraling without location, I reached out my hands and the universe grabbed me and flung me into unnamed galaxies. Reflecting beautifully, perfection unmasked. Directionless spinning spiraling into unnamed unowned beauty.

Dancing in front of the fire sends shadows into the clouds. Sparks fly like hair streaming into the stars, indivisible light dances. When theres no where to go the dance is stunning. Wingless love soars effortlessly across the canyon and swirls in the imaginary gap between you and me. Emptiness pouring into itself, sparks flying, Undeniably astounding. they fell into and through each other and spiraled into starlight.

ah! And I know how you ache for love
......as I once did .....
How I wrote love letters in the sand ....and the wind caught them and blew the grains like knives deeper into my wound....
....and I wrote my missives of love on the river and my tears washed them away...,,
.....and I scratched poems into the dirt but the grooves filled with blood and were illegible.....
.....and I wrote notes in the sky but they fell apart in the wind....
.........and I sang my love songs loud and clear ......and they always came back to me....
unanswered ...
And I realized it was my own love that I sought ......
And I fell into myself like disappearing ink ......

As you are
We are
nothing
But a lovers breath

and the wanderer passing by the village heard them singing in the dark
about the light
some of them had seen
and how they longed to find it again
and he asked if he could sit with them awhile
and as he listened he began to weep
the light you long for is all around you
in you as you of you and through you
it is only your ideas of what you are and what the light is
and your longing to capture it
that create this imaginary barrier between inside and outside

Perhaps you feel you're going somewhere, on a path, and you notice that you're calmer and life seems to be going smoother. You've planted seeds, watered them diligently and a tendril of green appears, a tree seems like it's growing…
One morning you look out and it's been crushed completely! You run out desperately and try to determine what's gone wrong! You are shocked to realize that you have been trying to grow a tree in air. As your tears water the ground, you realize it was all a sham. You had nothing to do with this, ever.
It was never about you.
The vast empty night is utterly completely dark. The light has been sucked out, the air, swallowed. Life, captured and put in a bag. Put on the back burner, warming itself for later…
Waiting waiting waiting waiting…
A hush an in breath a single tear, withheld…
The expectation consumes you
Hope, for the Big Bang
Fear, that there will only ever really be
This
And all your dreams will never come true
And all your fears will never be calmed
And all your tears will never be done
Falling

It's what you hoped and feared in the silence before dawn, as you watch your feet move through the waving long summer grasses drenched with starlight's tears. Like a song you sang. Once, but have never heard, yet you long for it and fear it. As you might be ripped apart by infinite sorrow and unutterable beauty and overwhelming joy and shredded into galaxies of tears and drown, washed away by the tides of your own love.

Once known without a doubt that this indeed is it. Once touched, this perfection cannot be unknown, or un kissed as you have become the kiss itself. You have been drunk by life as you drink it, the sky swallowed you as you twirled in awe at the beauty the beauty the beauty, never captured, inseparable from you. Lost as symphony's shadow, the dream spinning itself, never looking for another song another dance, another next, every nuance every wisp of melody every barely remembered breath resembling words that tell the tale of no one. How extraordinarily perfect,

There is utter rest

All life sparkles undoubtedly

Beyond belief beyond expectation beyond understanding beyond wonder itself

And he rose to greet the dawn

And remembered oh yes

This is how it smells

I had forgotten

My footsteps were in my way

How many ups will fly me to the moon and how many downs are in the great rambling story of our lives

Where were the yellows when you were hiding in your darkest night sunk into the well of darkness

She thought if only she could capture the stars they would fill her darkest shadows

The singer danced in the dark and heard his fingers ripping her heart to shreds

She could not find him

Only her song

Echoing moonlight

No longer looking to right the boat it sailed without arms

And always the oranges and reds of sunset filled the sails

Love blossoms where sky kisses sea

And why and where never sprang from her lips

Only songs that could never kiss the piercing of her love for this as it magically appears

Unfettered untrammeled uncaused unbidden

She reached out her hands and was swallowed by sky

She stretched out her toes and stars pulled her into the bottomless edgeless sea where her tears echoed salty dreams dancing across the stars rippling reflections.

This is it coyote she sang in the darkness
I don't know why you would want a lonely prairie song
But it sings your name sweetly in the night
The rushing of grasses in the moonlight
A cricket calls your name
Your loveliness
Unseen
only starlight echoes your heartsong
It is the fullness of emptiness that enlivens the night
Breaking Dawn
Swirling through you as you the wind losses itself in your own love
Your own ache
For nothing other
Than your song
It's all you ever wanted
It is all you have ever heard
these petals seem soft but when they disintegrate on the sidewalk all your dreams are gone
Shattered
Startlingly
….into tiny bits of color flowing away in your tears of loss and destruction, flowing without cause. You self implode, Your heart unleashed flies everywhere
And nowhere
Flowers dance in the shadows born of the wind's inescapable kiss, and there is no running away from silence or towards cacophony. My heart beat so loudly it crashed into my nighttime dream. The pure terror of utter nothing squeezed every ounce of fear out of me, and that I was made of fear did not escape me. It became an unsigned note in this unwritten symphony that left no traces. Just a tear streaked face and eyes no longer trying to hold the afterglow.
Soaring effortlessly without need of dreams or hopes or fears or need to capture the moon, or write your past on a potato peel and bury it under the magnolia tree at midnight. Moon shines without cause, reflecting sunlight in half circles written on your lovers face as you realize with a shock that there was is never will be any separation, any other. Your love letters were always written to

You

Sometimes a sweet melancholia sweeps down and kisses your cheek, a shadow bird remembered. Transparent crystalline edgeless wonder sketched lightly on your face, pierced deeply into the very core of your being, skewers your heart and holds it aloft and says here I am.

Have you not noticed your unutterable beauty?

Whose naked heart glows and sings

Whose tears flow through me

Whose love am I not?

Where is sadness what is joy what are blue and green and how can you tell where one begins and one ends

When does the day turn into night

What happens to your heart when it bursts

Where were you when life began where does your shadow hide in the dark

It was your own sweet lovers breath, hot upon your neck, that kissed your tender naked-ness and ripped apart all ideas of love to shreds. It reached deep deep deep into your very essence, exposed every secret corner where you used to hide, and eviscerated your outlines, your in-lines and the very substance of substance. Love erased all ideas of emp-tiness and fullness and crashed every dream of a beautiful tomorrow filled with endless rainbows, until your hand that had forever come up empty as you tried to capture this life and any bit of meaning suddenly unfurled into seamless sky.

Memories of love

Memories of dreams

Memories of memories swirl into watercolor tears and whirl pools of joy and sorrow caress your most intimate nakedness as songs pour through the dream painting your footsteps in sky. Your very being feels like a flood of love. This exquisite sensuous feeling of seam-less beingness, of life and light and love soaring through you as you feels like a timeless dance of patternless patterns rippling into and through and over and under each other, never separate, never joined, a continual union of what was never apart. There is no need of next, no one to lead and no one to follow, yet we can only find ourselves and love in the dance. This desire this heartache that finds us is this penetrating immediate brilliance, this piercingly unfathomably intimate kiss.

The urgency left when time lost its footsteps and you found yourself waltzing with an empty shadow whose silhouette resembled someone you once knew. You found your own kiss on your tender cheek and wept a thousand sorrows as a joyous melancholy emerged in the wake of love's demise. A heartache unlike any other reminds your feet where to step, and your heart that was never caged nor yours, falls continuously in love as love through love.

Such beautiful magic in knowing this magic you longed for is not separate from you, that it is you. This soaring wingless wind ballet.

Slender weeds can weave themselves into a daisy chain of hope and fear. A yellow kiss on your chin marks you as a dreamer for something other than a waltz in the moonlight. To ache to grab the moon and swallow the incandescence and translate its soft rays into rainbow dreams of starlight dancing in drifts of flowing softness that will cushion you and feed you endlessly with drops of love. You will settle for nothing less than perfection. And when all hope is gone

It is like that.

A filigree curtain that you thought was you was merely a river of reflected light. What might have been stirs into what might be and dissolves. How can life kiss itself? Moonlight eases its arc of brilliance into your night time dream. Can you catch it? Can you capture the jewel of life?

You reach out your hand your fingers as tendrils of emptiness untie all ideas of freedom and anyone to be free. The brilliance of what can never be known is like a beautiful falling that can never be captured or stopped up or held in your tender heart, a love for what you never were and for all this.

Whose heart whose love whose pain whose tears whose unutterable sorrow who's unbound joy

Who could claim a rainbow or a storm? Trying to kiss your reflection you fall into the river of your own sweetness.

Without love we cannot find ourselves

Or lose ourselves

Love spins

And we fall into and through each other in the flowing.

Her hands moved methodically through the morning feeling for the tears she shed in last nights storm. Without any effort without any doing or non doing, she was consumed by her own fire of love of desire of unutterable joy and bottomless sorrow. She lost herself in the lostness, and found herself riding wings of love. There was neither up nor down nor inside nor out as her own love song sang her. Beginning with a hum and a tremor and a light in the vastness that echoed in the canyons, love formed into a lightening bolt that struck the very core of her being, bringing her back into these footless shoes that danced like this.

A timeless song that could not be caught nor captured soared through her as her

Dancing madly as only mad women can

There's a point when a shadow... dancing across the pavement... meets the leaf... falling and disappears

you are nothing other than a hint of a memory of a song you will never hear

My teacher was a shadow felt yet unseen until the war was over
A hum of all rightness not heard but felt deeply in the last nights before even love died
All those summer nights
Frogs and crickets singing starlight love songs
Laying in the long grasses cool and damp
Weeping
Sobbing
empty of even emptiness
the wake of love's demise
Ripped open fearless nothing left undone
Ruptured in the veins the arteries the heart blown apart by life and love itself
Raw inside out naked
nothing under the new costume of nakedness
Nothing to hide and no where to hide it
Not even nothing is left
It all blew away
There is no looking for what never was
Only the echo of weeping
The echo of weeping
weeps

How amazing that words concepts ideas cannot capture what's going on, yet they are all we have.
The worded world is all we can know, as we are conceptual beings. Words are like Tinker toys pretending to be life
Words symbols a wink of knowing
Deeply piercing us
Like stitching together tears
Into a waterfall of love

We are the illusory center of a shoreless ocean
An imaginary crystalline ship
...rudderless

on a sea of dreams
The prow of a phantom ship
Singing dreams into being
We are nothing other and nothing more or less than what is arising in the uncatchable
unstoppable uncaused unfindable inseparable momentary
I am a conceptual beings trying to sing of edgelessness

You were simply an idea that there was something to get ......
And you discover that your hands are off the steering wheel and there never was one
We are the shimmering reflections
In seamless openness
without definition or direction
without any boundaries
Of time or space
a dream time movie
singing echoed reflections
a story
of sublime wonder
there is no this nor that nor both nor neither.........
there are no reference points what so ever
no place to rest
no understanding to get
and no one to land or rest
you are the dream of other
and many feel deep down that there is nothing solid or stable or fixed and it is scary........
wobbly......... dizzying........
so they try to pinpoint them selves.......
always trying to find where they are on this imaginary time line
it's like walking a tightrope
and the noose is around your neck
and they might always be taking polls or surveys.....
what kind of person am I
or look into psychology
or philosophy
or religion or spirituality
or astrology............
and yet the moon cannot dance in its own moonlight
and the sun cannot bask in its own warmth and light

and there is nothing separate from what is going on that can catch it or hold it or figure it out
or understand it
there is no place to rest
and no one who can find it
self is the longing to rest
self is an imaginary reference point around which the dream swirls........ made of an ever emerging ever slipping away kaleidoscopic hodgepodge of thought emotion sensation preference belief seemingly all referencing a feeler thinker doer chooser...........

Isn't it amazing that we as a product of the thought stream can watch it paint a symphony of colors arpeggio and fall
....blooming in infinite incomparable forms merging flowing rippling shimmering into and through castles of ever moving clouds and thought dreams and pictures and sounds of pasts and futures and stories of brilliant immediacy shooting through edgeless space and stopping pausing hanging by threads of weaving bejeweled wonder illuminating the inky darkness seeming to settle and Rocket again into dancing shadows lit from within shot through with myriad unfindable specks and sparkles of hints of weightiness of the enormity of utter lightness
and oh my
........feelings that run and sparkle and pierce the day
.............and a you that is not separate from the forces blooming and falling and that this pulsating aliveness you feel you know so intimately so tenderly so wondrously shooting through you is you
And empty winds blew through the morning and echoed songs into the vastness of love and love lost and shadows dancing in the night
Neither here nor there nor lost nor found
Waves crash on the edge of a shoreless ocean and without any hope of harbor her heart sank
And the stillness of evening rose in the ripple less wake of Dawn
Colors shapes timbre and hue drop from unfathomable depths and sing into form and fade simultaneously
The scaffolding the myriad planes of an ever shifting dance floor fall away and there is no more place to hang your hat .....no corner no center no edge can be found
and starlight weeps at its own magnificence as it sweeps through your skinless mind
Falling through the mirror everything and nothing must go
But a reflection of who you were
a shadow a phantom dances

Lit by shimmering starlight a pas de deux sings us into being
And he longed to bathe in starlight
But his skin was in the way
He could not rip it off as it was him
And he longed to sing like starlight
But his mouth was in the way
He could not remove it
As he was the words
And suddenly without warning starlight swallowed him
Neither here nor there
Neither lost nor found
Homeless mind

For those who think they want this, it is terrifying to get close to the edge of everything
and nothing sensing that everything must go, most recede into the familiar
Curled up again into a wall of fear of unknowing
Gripping onto methods and practices that have never worked
...the loss of a path would be the loss of themselves

You begin to hear a silent language, indecipherable, yet it sings your heart song like a
dimly remembered lullaby that you sang long ago. You cannot stop from crying as the
beauty pulls you in and begins to rip you apart so painfully so beautifully.
After the guts and heart and blood and bones have been shredded
And burnt
ashes blown away
You are simply an empty shadow
Whirling streaming shimmering light rippling echoing without edges or sides
Like a constant ease of suspended awe...
Until you meet another and can find some imaginary lines to fall through .....
Edgeless centerless love in knowing we are each other
Your heart must drop
And love die
To know that it was made up like you
To fully swoon again
We are echoed glances of flowing tone poems ricocheting in wall less mirrored canyons
Amazed at our own amazement
Delighting in our own delight

Light life winds songs flow through us as us
we are the dance itself
This is all there is

When the angst and fear that accompanies the belief in separation in the belief in personal volition falls away
There is no more self judgment or self correction....
No more is every perception judged as helpful or harmful to the illusory self
So the main activity that was protecting and defending the imaginary self is gone
Whoosh!
There is left a hyper awareing of awareing
Like life felt experienced more directly and intimately without the wall of hope and fear clouding obscuring the obvious perfection of life as it is....
An unutterable joy and awe of simply being
Self remains but has lost its relevance
We still have beliefs and opinions
We simply know that they are imaginary walls they become transparent and are not believed
There is no longer the urge to fix or change oneself or others or the world
All apparent 'thingness' arises mutually
Say the word tree and suddenly there is everything that is 'not tree'
Sky and ground and you and me
As conceptual entities we can only 'see' or know other things
The brain recognizes unicity it is always on
So when the lines are seen to be imaginary by the brain
The illusory separate persona loses its opacity
And unicity is always felt always known deeply
This is the peace that passeth understanding
The sides slipped away
The bottom dropped out
the emptiness poured out
I opened my hand
And found
Not even an empty hand
The world became immeasurably sweet
Dissolved as it were into nothingness
Your heart is pierced with loves heart magic and is no longer yours

Empty dreams explodes into everywhere and no where
You look around and the world has become covered with your tears
And everywhere is a reflection of your love

Awakening cannot be practiced or arrived at through effort as all doing or non doing simply and obviously perpetuate the illusion of a doer and belief in separation.
You cannot hypnotize yourself into it or try to return again and again to a 'state' of peace as it is not a state at all but an underlying ceaseless profound sense of seamless ease, of sublime quiescence and utter knowing and feeling of unicity is always on when the belief in separation falls away
There is a huge physical and psychological release
And that is not slipped into by the person like entering a warm bath it us rather like a ripping apart a violent shredding of all you held true about yourself and the world and all ideas of time and dimension and causality all ideas of meaning and non meaning and truth itself are slayed in this conflagration
It is not a pleasant process it hurts like hell
It is not like growing wings and soaring over an abyss it us like crashing falling down an endless cliff of rocks with jagged edges razor clouds and fire burning every last shred of anything you held to be true
Not like an angels kiss but like a stint in a Dante painting of hell
You cannot arrive at it as unicity is always the case and all feeling of being on a path is always seeming to create division
any attempt Any doing creates the illusion of separation
It cannot be arrived at through introspection or inquiry as it is not an intellectual knowing at all
The razor of thought can Never get this as edgelessness cannot be grasped
There is simply no grasp-er
Nothing outside of what's going on to hold it or understand it
Awakening is not about achieving a state of bliss
It is not about going anywhere or attaining something anew
As unicity is already the case any effort or non effort to achieve it creates the illusion of two
It is not about feeling better as the full range of human emotions is still on
we are fully alive beautifully human
It is not about becoming a better person or improving oneself or the world
It serves no purpose or non purpose

It is truly an empty prize for no one yet I would not give it up for all the riches in the world or long life or world peace or all those other things i thought I wanted.

Glimpsing your ultimate aloneness is ravishingly devastatingly beautiful, yet a beautiful sensuously sweet melancholia prevails. Words fall apart as they form on my lips on this page that erases itself into simply a kiss with no other. Knowing there is no you nor me nor love it is felt deeply when our imaginary lines meet and dissolve in this touchless touch. Such a beautiful aliveness awareness aware of being aware, life tasting touching seeing feeling it's own aliveness through your delicate tongue fingers lips and eyes. You are the prism the lens that paints color and form and love and beauty into the universe. A brushstroke of iridescent tears reflects life and loves majesty and mystery. The wet of wetness, the taste of taste, the wonder and unspeakable joy of unknowability and impermanence through your beautiful beautiful I's.

Without lines it's obvious that love is immeasurable

The future is an idea
Just like you
C'mon bring me your self and put it on the table
Gimme a cup of future to go
Pieces of a non existent puzzle looking for an endless kiss
Wandering the desert dream your tongue dry and throat parched lured ever on wards by an idea that there is a way out
What if there were no goal
What if this WERE indeed it?
This IS the storm
There are no guarantees
It may or may not pass
It's the utter honesty and intimacy that pierces you
Deeper in places that you never knew existed
It is NOT an intellectual understanding
It is a personal Armageddon
The passion play writes itself, it always has
unrehearsed unbidden uncaused
With disappearing ink of endless tears
There is no better or worse

Before or after
This is it coyote
The song writes itself
Sometimes it breaks your heart sometimes it soothes you
Or washes you away
And you are nothing other than a hint of a memory of a song you will never hear

Self is a wall of fear of unknowing that is quickly repaired when threatened when concepts may challenge the ideas that you are, or a glimpse of the unknown is intuited. There is a grasping for more and more beliefs ideas concepts to try to fill the great void that many sense lays beyond the river of words.

There is simultaneously a great longing and a huge fear that there really are no reference points whatsoever, that what is going on is fluid and un-graspable and that there could be a conflagration of the known world and a drowning in your own fear and longing. Oh! how so many are terrified of all that love they long feel, as they might lose it.

What broke her heart?
Where did the knife come from?
How did she get on this gangplank? She knelt down to fix the loose ends of her hair, and became transfixed by the yellows and blues and deep deep watery greens. She fell into and through her own reflection, her own tears were like knives biting off her air flow. She lost sight of before or after or better or worse drowning in her own sobbing the sound of her heartbeat her last breath, this death dance with her own shadow. Finding no way out, there was a halt. No key was looked for, no corner was left to hide in, there was nothing left to hide, not even her nakedness. She was simply these reflections of tears that echoed her own beauty, her own humanness. All that she had longed for was already here, yet it could not be counted or spoken of or put into a box.

Shadows dance in ancient patterns across the dreamscape as moon peeks from behind the curtains and laughs, waltzing with her tears. Gypsies twirling mirrored skirts catch a glimpse of what was never hidden or lost as she remembered the cool breezes, the warm hearth, the universe flowing in her as her, through her.

It cannot be named this preciousness this knowing of the fleeting nature the beautiful impermanence of what we call life. Like a rippling echo dancing through a deep abyss catching a glance of its own beauty in a curtain of sun streaming down kissing a song that was never heard before, it was just a song I seemed to miss when I was looking for the melody. A shooting star dissolving into the night, my story writes itself with tears on a moving river of sky. A patternless rhythmic dance of space flowing through space.

These are not our thoughts our words, it is a musical landscape beyond measure. We are the notes in an indefinable unrehearsed symphony, we cannot isolate our part our song our heart our love. We cannot see our selves without our reflections in each others beautiful beautiful eyes. We are the lover the love and the beloved, existing only in this dream dance of love.

Tears slide catching late afternoon sun. I see memories of rainbows uncaught, love blossoming, falling, like sunshowers erasing themselves in the mist.

JUNE SONGS

What do we see when we greet ourselves through liquid eyes?
ahhhhhhh, darkness reveals its stillness in morning bird song echoing through the tall trees where the moon disappeared last night. I hear the murmuring of hearts singing oceans of tears drowning in the desert of love lost.
Mystery collapses into itself in this breath of awe that streams through the day dream and leaves a silent hush singing. All this intense feeling of unbearable joy and deep deep sorrow and despair and great floods of wonderment have merged into the unspeakable beauty of unsigned tears painting my footfalls echoing in sky. Reverberating in endless parenthesis like one hand many hands all the hands that have ever reached for the magic they believed that they had lost. It cannot be found, nor left lying on deserted beaches where love went bathing in its own tears and you lost your footprints in the surge of tides.

Turning in circles seemed to etch a path that would lead to the center of wholeness but you found there are no edges that need be crossed, and no prize at the end of the moonbeams that gather in the pooled reflections where you lost your shadow on that late midsummers eve. Naked and unafraid you cast your last dreams upon the sea to watch your silhouette dissolve into itself and you found your self bleeding on the empty beaches, seaweed tangled in your hair. You found you had never left the love you longed for, that the dream of love simply echoed across the vastness to pull you into and through yourself.
There was never a you nor a home to leave yet you find your feets dancing on the shores of nothing. They have always known where to step in this dance of life that sings your heart into a rippling shape of perfect wonder.

This roar this rush of brilliant silence singing your song, everyone's song, this song that is everywhere and nowhere thrums thrums thrums. So nakedly obvious that it can't be seen or held yet you feel it deeply always. No need to remember it or forget your forgetting as it sang you as you sang it long ago in this timeless time that you have never left and never appeared. A beautiful heartache a wondrous broken heart weeping, melting in its own tears, it has no melody and there are no words but every word is outlined in love.
There is no outside or inside to this dance as all sides have merged in a duet of one. A chorus of stars kissed their shadow and wept at their own shining brilliance that echoed your name as you pirouetted into the winds caressing your softness into a dance of light

in light. Life such a beautiful heart ache extending reaching everyone's hearts, no ones hearts, empty hearts crying out for love. All you find is your infinite intimate heart dancing solo on a crescent moon. The darkness creeping into your very last breath. Like this.

Just as the wind blows effortlessly and just as the suns rays radiate effortlessly, warming and illuminating all things equally. Effortlessly life happens, and is effortlessly recognized. The flower of love blooms, when the borders between you and me are seen through.

Words seem to cast a net on an edgeless measureless seamless directionless placeless infinite unknowable unknown and capture separate things and events and you. They are a closed loop and it may feel like you are caught in it, like a noose they capture and form you and separate you from all other illusory things and events. The painting of this magnificent dream of separation, this streaming thought dream is always spontaneously singing itself, even these very words seem to describe what cannot be caught with words. This spinning of the cats cradle seems to weave a web hanging on a breeze, and we feel the breeze of freedom yet there is no escape as we are the dream. Freedom and non freedom more imaginary threads in the jeweled fabric. Trying to find the beginning of the thread, or the beginning of a thought or feeling or moment, like trying to capture ideas of truth or meaning is impossible as a tangle of thread cannot untie itself.
Thoughts twist and swirl and weave tattered memories and dreams of the morrow into a patchwork quilt of ideas that appears to change and rearrange and slip and slide around an imaginary center of the cyclone that is you. Lightening hits and hurts as it marks the spot when the dream is believed. Out of the net the web the tangled dream we do not exist. All words can only be defined by other words and never ever touch or kiss or capture whats going on. How many books can you read about flowers? Poems and biology and chemistry, until you realize flowers can never actually be known?

The fire is on, it is your own love and desire, as wind fans the flames and a siren's song fills your heart, catches your sails and tatters and rips apart your dreams of next. It's no longer your journey your words your song your tears your heart your life. All promises are off as all ideas of what is going on and who you are crash and you are ravished by your own emptiness. It is simply stunning to find nothing, and stunning to return, and see again through baby eyes, edges dissolve in misty eyed wonder as you slip into your own love. This shoreless ocean touches itself with songs that echo across the surface and reverberate into the bottomless depths. It's sublimely okay that oceans will never kiss, salty tears are the same, yet longing flows as you are it. This sublime ache of joy and sorrow and love. Continuously you drink yourself as love subsumes you and this bottomless treasure of life and death spill into the dream as overflowing awe. You never existed yet the story of you ends. This symphony plays itself, unrehearsed, no one writes or rehearses or knows the score.

Many petaled whispers rise and dance among the hovering cliffs, they silence the crow's evening call and pierced by vast infinite nothingness your heart drops. A despairing cry leaps from your heart and falls into laughter and weeps at this unfathomable beauty. The canyon waltzes in the breeze and you are lost in the rhythm-less winds that sail through you as you. You find that the broken-ness of the sky was only a mirage, simply infinite beautiful mirrored reflections of you. Walking alone singing to yourself drenched subsumed permeated as awe, an untouchable peace resides in the knowing of the majesty of the this marvelous impermanence you once so feared. It always feels like the same timeless time, always familiar and always new, the first and last kiss. Where time and timelessness crash into a song. a silent duet that has no pattern or rhyme, yet it this magic is always known deeply. Brilliant clarity permeates this passion play this love song of one of two of none. Tales untold echo soundless reflections that reverberate into resounding tales of light and dark who's echos skim across and through but never touch and yet are not separate from the ripple less shoreless ocean of simple uncaused joy and awe of everything-ness as nothingness.
There were never obstructions no obfuscations to this magic that you longed for. Between time and timelessness a sigh falls through itself. You are suspended as awe.
Amazed at your own amazement
Delighting in your own delight
Adrift aloft lit from within and without skimming across the edgeless sea of dreams.

What would you be without your ideas about enlightenment?
All ideas of this and that of truth beauty love meaning and non meaning are all subsumed consumed permeated dissolved in light beyond light. Space beyond space. Infinite beyond infinite

Knowing we can never touch, existing as a touchless touch. Our sublime emptiness and our magnificent fullness, death dances adorned with love's sparkle. kissed from the inside out and outside in with this unquenchable thirst of the joy of desire. Without it there is no humanness no love no life.
Sublime melancholia of a sage

This all pervading all encompassing unknowable unknown super saturated utterly spontaneous spacious beyond measure emptiness that is not a thing or non thing seemingly exploding and simultaneously imploding into as and through all that seems to appear! All description pants the dream like this.

It can be innately intuited, deeply known without a doubt that there is nothing to know and no one to know it. That it is the very brain that paints the dream that seems to not believe it. Here there is always a disbelief even in disbelief.

Nothing and everything, the worded world and the knowing that the worded world is made up, awareness and perception, emptiness and fullness not two nor one not none. The words seem to create a knowing as most mistake description for understanding, yet the words when not believed are the sparkle, the dance of this and that, the heartbeat of existence.

To truly irrevocably recognize the utter emptiness of all things and the holder of them is amazing! We were not brave, no one chose this, it does not happen to the person. I had never heard there were no things! It was over a year and a half until I met another who also knew.

Slippery sliding down the rainbow and knowing there are no separate colors or edges, yet delighting in and as them all, as they slide in you through you as you.

Knowing that there is no you nor me nor we, feeling deeply that we are each other and that we can never actually touch or know each other is unspeakably wondrous, yet there arises a sublime melancholia that paints a butterfly kiss on your lips, a beautiful brush of death that enhances color and light and the feeling of vibrant aliveness. We are always swooning falling into and through each other in this heartachingly beautiful dream.

We are simply love songs, of one of two of many of all, of none. Of dust dreams shimmering, hovering, soaring like cloud shadows over endless empty sands. Some stories are hollow shadows walking bareback in circles following endless signs, longing to drink, dying of thirst. Others sing of this thirst for everything for nothing, and the beauty of empty footfalls. Shimmering emptiness overflowing dancing in an elaborate mirage, a sparkling echo resounding in this unfathomable vastness that seems to form yet never does, into a love dance that looks and feels just like this. We find we are all walkers all dancers all lovers like the great desert winds rushing up the canyon to warm the mountain peaks, swirling caressing your beautiful face in the brilliance of the noon day sun.

The light may seem so beautiful that you long to run naked in its golden rays, swim in its warmth, and dance in the winds that swirl around you. Yet the nearer you get to your love, the hotter it becomes, and you burn in love's fire. Crystallized desire reflects rainbows that cut even deeper your hopeless heart. Yet when not even nothing is left, this great emptiness vacant even of emptiness, the winds of love stir your ashes and a phantom bird emerges, soaring effortlessly, wings circling the sun, swallowing the sky as the sky swallows you.

A song of nothing pulled our heartstrings and played a symphony of one. A touch a tear rips your heart into infinite pieces and pulls you moves floods the very core of your being in places you did not know existed. Blood flowing until there was nothing left, tears sobbing until they became who I was. Rain spattered path. River of tears shimmering in moonlight. Drying of the sidewalk in intoxicating patterns. Aleutian Islands. Continents touching and falling away.

We are the inside and the outside of the kiss the embrace the soft caress. As empty shadows dance and weave and unweave the dream in contrapuntal timeless time. A never done nor undone primordial fabric dyed by the sun and moon glow in the desert, the warp and weft the heartbeat of existence. Footless wingless butterfly kisses without weight sing of softness falling into and through softness. Our songs sing us as we sing galaxies into existence. Spiraling ever outward into space less space light flowing into and through light. Brilliant stillness sings this song of one of two of many of all. Stories unbound revolve into a dance of love we call life, marvelous and superb.

Delighting in all and everything. Knowing there are no things. I point out things to my friends but could never explain the utter amazement at this life no matter how it seems to appear.

Without words we are not. A flow of words grasping imaginary shadows and swirling into them as they weave themselves into a diaphanous light gown. Feeling deeply can never be said yet these smoke signals of loves essence can pierce the darkest night. An echo a reflection an overtone of a chord that has never been struck yet pierces us deeply. Lightening in the inky blackness illuminates the story of you in sky. Dancing only in its own reflection soaring through the bottomless edgeless see. It winds and unwinds with other light dreams into a shadow dance of love.

Perceptions of colored iridescence moving are remembered into a dance of butterfly. The story of you writes itself and self releases. A passion play kissed into being by its own reflection. It echoes in the canyon and we discover ourselves falling into and through each other through our beautiful beautiful eyes. Singing a song of unwritten love, life kisses itself with your lips your eyes your own trembling aliveness. An inside out dream weaving and unweaving itself, singing of its own demise, lost in its own unfathomably wondrous infinitely faceted bejeweled reflection.

Does the seed long to be a plant a leaf a flower a tree a fruit f a l l l n g?

Ripening in the summer sun, it is devoured and its heart thrown under the raspberry bushes in the cool moonlight. Longing, desire is the moment of life sung through our rosy lips waiting for a kiss. After dawn exposes the empty center, desire still swirls. It has fallen through your heart and merged into the big wow and there is no looking to other to fill an empty grasp. Shadow arabesques on a lonesome sidewalk dance transfixed by the rainbow afterglow.

They sat as empty wonder and sang echoes into the vastness. No one heard and everyone wept. Symphonies of love painted dreams in smoke signals.

Cloud cover cracks. a window of blueness leaks in and vastness seen, and longed for. You want to jump. Trees burnt by lightning glisten in their wet blackness as your tears that were hidden by the rain are nakedly spectacular, your utter vulnerability shines. You discover you've been grasping desperately to handfuls of air, dreams of an imaginary future.

All that you know slips away as all ideas of solidity are seen to be false, including ideas of truth. All that you've taken for granted is consumed in this fire. All the assumptions of what you were. What you are cannot be known, no one knows what life is, what a relief to no longer ask. Crystalline raindrops slide down the window like a priceless necklace reflecting colors from within and without simultaneously.

Ahhhhhhhhhh ....infinite color and hue and timbre and overtones and undertones of echoed reflections weaving and unweaving bits of tattered memories into a love story, a gossamer mirage of an endless broken heart reverberating ancient songs that have no beginning nor ending yet are always beginning and ending in a silent kiss roaring through the rainbows soft caress on your beautiful beautiful tender lips. A primordial kiss of life falling in love with life itself.

You are the heart song of the universe singing itself through your breath your song your lips your mouth your tongue your heart your very own vibrant aliveness swooning through itself in as and through your infinite intimate embrace. There never was a you nor a home to leave, in all reaching for other you find your own tears streaming, in all looking back and forward and inward and outward you find your own magical reflection singing I love you.

Silent land of dream-time wonder sings of cloud shadows racing towards the inevitable storm. My garment of starlit tears shimmers as death weeps at its own beauty.

Streams of clouds merge and dance and slide across the sky, some wisps form dragons with icy fire's gaze.

The shadow dragon does not miss the sun that creates him. He swims along the canyon eating my shadow in his coolness. I disappear as and into this seamless pirouette of the wind ballet.

There is an audible hush when time dies. Light saw itself in a sideways glance shimmering without shadow. Wakeless tears caught a rainbow. Weeping.

As we are nothing more or less than an afterthought, a sigh, a wisp of a daydream. Dancing shadows in the dark. Crocheted with wings of light.

No where cannot be found. All space collapses and there is simply shimmering. When there is no one feeling feelings and no one thinking thoughts, a still wind embraces the song of you.

There really is no you to be blown away anymore. Just the silent wind. Singing.

Lazy raindrops splash on the windshield
And are blown into cat prints running through sky

Most teachers tell you what to do or not do simply perpetuating the belief in a do-er.

The stillness of which I sing is always on, the recognition of seamlessness happens or not, yet either feeling it or not feeling it is it, as nothing is excluded. If this infinite seam-lessness is all encompassing, without edge or center, can you take something out of it? Where would it go?
Can you add something? Where would it come from?

So this that cannot be named as it is not an it nor a non it, and you are not separate from it as there are no separate things or non things is super saturated and complete always. Therefor it cannot be perfect nor imperfect. There are no separate things or moments that need to be put together or that have ever been apart. Without time or timelessness there is no future for awakening nor past when there was not, nor even a now that can be held, as there is no you separate from this brilliant seamless flow that can step outside of it and grasp it or change or manipulate or accept or reject or surrender to it.

There truly are no things nor non things yet everything is included. Existing everywhere and nowhere you are not separate from the flow of perception and its simultaneous inseparable recognition.

We are shadows dancing unseen by time or place illuminated by reflections of love light. Ever blossoming ever wilting ever falling ever weeping ever soaring ever roaring ever never caught. We are the tempest at night. Dragon clouds sail across the moon.

We are the blush of dawn we are the drop of dew we are the oceans song we are tears timeless ancient and new. Forever and never weep silently in the imaginary space between the breath and the song. The universe breathes and dances us, sings us, paints us. Our stories write themselves. I am all the stories that ever were and will ever will be, never separate or merging. Coalescing echoes rippling over under and through each other weaving and un-ravelling a dream never done nor undone.

An unwritten unrehearsed symphony unbound unfettered scatters empty pages empty staves empty footsteps empty shadows empty winds singing our song softly silently like cats paws on the garden path.

Tears in the dead of night weeping for everything weeping for nothing.

Radiant spontaneous knowingness, open pure crystalline clarity, center-less edgeless unfettered ungraspable supremely spacious, un contained, uncaused without any inherent qualities or characteristics naturally subsumes all things yet it is not separate from them. Simply seamless all encompassing indivisible unicity, a most marvelous dance of one of two of none. Brilliant beyond measure, always on, this perfection, utterly intimate as there is no other. Truly indescribable yet felt deeply, as it is what you are. Knowing and feeling this there is boundless awe.

All that we ever longed to escape from becomes the most wondrous wondrous life more than we could ever have imagined no matter what it looks and feels like. The fleetingness this rawness this tenderness is the beauty, is your beauty.

This transparent center-less jewel spins showering rainbows of infinite variety color timbre hue overtones reflections shimmering sliding rippling into and through each other of this and that. Your heart beat your breath your song singing itself.

Tears brushed with rainbow dreams reflect the universe in your heart.

All remnants of belief in separation are smashed to smithereens as all feeling of inside and outside pours itself into endless sky. Burnt in the heat of sun's desire, love ignites the ashes into a sparkling shadow dance illuminated in this canyon of streaming winds where we kiss.

Pierced, eviscerated, it felt like you died, but it is known without a doubt that you never existed. You look down and you see your feet, starlight dancing, but no one is moving them. Not even the stars look for a place to shine.

There was never anyone to be broken. Never anyone to lead or follow. Never anyone to wander in circles seeking a way out of sadness.

Yellow finches hang on the sunflowers you planted in the spring, and the very magnificence of color and flight and softness and the tender delicate wetness of your eyes is unbearably beautiful.

Life cannot be grasped. Reaching to grasp the flowing is the flowing... trying to escape the flowing is the flowing...
the silhouette of the mountains cannot hold the moon-rise. The river cannot hold the moons reflection

A friend asks me to judge whether a news story is true or false. I am dumbfounded! How could I say that every story, be it the Cat And The Fiddle, or Star Trek, the Magical Mystery Tour or the story of Nancy seems absolutely made up?
Time is like rushing meaningless shadows. Someone cries, "Off with her head!", and I wonder why everyone is scurrying about.

Yet simultaneously suspended as seamless timeless nothingness there is the heartbeat of this and that. Every color and shape and taste and sound and feeling hyper real and surreal.

Every secret corner of my being has been flung out into interstellar space, alighted on the stars, burnt and blasted into infinite sparkling smithereens, and dances swooning merging folding unfolding blossoming blooming infinitely empty pure brilliant light rushing roaring collapsing and exploding constantly into and through itself in ecstatic union... the kiss of the universe kissing itself.

Butterflies seem to carve a path in sky and color the spaces in between with love. Spinning ricocheting iridescence weaves itself into a flowing edgeless heart with reflections of tears as colors of reflected light blend into an indescribable unspeakable hue of love's heart magic. It was all we feared and yet all that we longed for, this terrifying overwhelming beautiful fleeting ungraspable impermanence.
There was no need to paint the flowers, or your tears.

That wistful melancholy I had felt since I was small is who I am. We are our beautiful humanness surfing oceans of tears. The kiss of death weaves beauty's reflection into your love light. It's only the space in between us that is imaginary, yet that is where we kiss.

The dream paints itself with this and that and infinite color and sound and joy and love and deep deep sorrow and despair and awe. When it's no longer believed even love is known to be made up, yet this is not the end of love, as seeing it as a dream is the dream. How beautiful you are my dear dream lovers.

How many wondrous stories have painted themselves into my heart? How many heart songs are simply woven memories unwinding themselves into the fabric of who I am? I exist only in the touching, knowing that there can never be really touching. It's so beautiful knowing that we exist only in a touchless touch, a cloud shadow racing down the canyon, always ending always beginning, never ending never beginning, the stories of you of me of we intertwine until the edglesss glance reveals that there were never separate people to kiss.

Love rains softly through me and sings. Without singing of this there is simply no singer, not even nothing, just a magnificent unknowable unknown gazing in amazement and bewilderment at an amazing unknown unknowable vast supreme spaciousness.

A touch a kiss a song seem to paint a reflection of an echo of a flowing dreamscape, a sigh, a rippling iridescent arabesque of me. Sky in sky, not lost, not found, kisses itself in the whisper of wind. Every word writes a book but there is nothing inside. All there is this seamless radiant edgeless brilliance. Singing. Just like this.

This beautiful sublime ache to kiss what cannot be kissed fills me and empties me. This longing to share what it feels like to bask in the warmth of my own infinite intimate embrace and pour my heart song as liquid love into every secret pore of your being paints watercolor tears into my crumbling footfalls and weeps liquid sky into my empty shadow.

Where were your footprints on the diamond path? Where were the echoes of your song? Where were the traces of yesterday that would lead to a promise of tomorrow...
How can you grasp the sunlight and pour it into your being and find this love that you have felt before, but seems to evade your grasp as you reach for it?
You stumbled down the path through summer breezes and lilting melodies and turn your head as night falls.
You can no longer find your way.
night moths in the moonlight... a mist of golden showers... a song you can not remember a love you cannot forget wrenches your heart it into a gazillion pieces and wrings out every tear from the universe. In that flood you drown in his own saltiness.

the edgeless sea, the seeing, that it was your own love
And from far away and from the inside of sidelessness echoing
Reverberating
coming from here and there and nowhere
like a tinny radio in an old convertible on a summer evening just as darkness begins to
kiss your sight away
Your hand a shadow
when you try to grasp the sparkling
Until tears flood your empty footsteps
Igniting the earth and sky
In a conflagration
That burn all ideas of pathways
Or anyone to walk anywhere
And the ashes blue into the desert dream
And turned into diamonds everywhere
Long long light begins to form a shadow of your footsteps upon the sidewalk
You can hear the tires on the road
It curves and swerves everything comes and goes surging fading and coming around
again
And you no longer care to make out the words of the song because it is everyone's song
it is your song
it is your lovers song
it is every lovers song
It is new and it is familiar it is inherently deeply always known
Always felt
Always sung
Always on
It is the heartbeat of existence
The hum of the universe
Sighing silently singing
Overtones of wonder begin to fill your heart
Till bursting
Overflowing
It is the recognition the constant recognition of this
on my
of this
on my

of this
oh my
This vibrant aliveness seamlessly dancing
punctuating the darkness with this and that
Like stars in the night strewn across the heavens
Thrown from no hand
Revealing every hand
Every face
Every heart
Every song
That rests in the songless night
Waiting to be sung
Waiting to be heard
This Song of magic unlike any other
Is you

Night time swims in revealing sky kissed lights strewn across the darkness. Treasures unbound in patternless patterns stepping lightly
punctuating unending vastness on the staves of electric lines. A song is born for those who read them. Unsung songs for those who hear them.
Long long lights from cars far down the road cast my shadow on the poppies and catch their red before they pass by leaving a hush of a journey that never was.
The waves were empty
A heart was full
But was never yours
It was only a story
Unwritten
Overtones reverberating in the sound box of the night

Circling endlessly around an empty center, searching for the end of my own footsteps. incising the imaginary line between inside and out deeper and deeper, perpetuating the illusion of a solid center. Every round hurts more and more, tightening the noose, longing for emptiness, and wholeness, longing to let go, and be held...
I remember when I learned the word infinity, I loved the concept for something so big that even the adults just left it.
How I hungered for the big wow, looking for more of that magic, when the mind of this and that would be left hanging. Longing to follow the tracks to infinity.

I read of this concept called oneness, and it just seemed right. This had to be the way it was. Using the only tools I had, thought and imagination, I tried to grasp this. As I had this great knowing, this deep down sureness that if I could recognize the sameness of inside and outside, this would somehow soothe the edges and erase the endless trying. I knew this was the all rightness I was looking for. Yet every thought divided what was going on, more thoughts divided it even more and soon I was lost in a complex diagram that had no end, spiraling and spiraling out of Control. Never did it come to a conclusion never could I find a place to rest.

The shadows lengthened, the night deepened. I could no longer see. I was terrified that the darkness would overcome me, and it did. I could not collect the pieces of color that ran down my reflection as my frozen heart melted and gave up its edges. It is most beautiful like a beautiful release of everything and of nothing. I found everything I had always wanted, always here, and yet it is nothing at all. The imaginary center of the cyclone broke free and was everywhere and nowhere. Without me doing a thing the trying released itself, and all the lines disappeared on their own.

This was inconceivable, it was beyond belief. It is far more and far less than I thought or imagined it would or could be, and I wept and wept and wept.

Infinite ripples sliding over and through each other rocking the imaginary solidity of something someplace someone sometime. All edges collapsing cliffs sinking into the sea as dizziness loses itself when there is no line between here and there, thee and me.

Rippling lightly flowing over and through itself dancing light and shadow reflecting the marvels the colors the iridescence to what no finger can point to. To what no lips can kiss.

Where all ideas concepts and beliefs about who you are and what the world is dissolve in this river of tears.

Empty feathered wings fly silently on unseen waves. Roaring unheard through canyons where time was lost and never found. Between remembering and forgetting you found not even nothing, yet it filled the empty space with untold joy.

You dissolve into your own emptiness and un-named unbound tears merge with the ocean from which they sprang. The un-uttered wow, remembered as tears watered your own grave. No longer looking to define or capture emotion or life, it swirls into itself and has no place to stay.

No one leaves un-teared. They flow and create an imaginary path that reflects the wonder of the universe.

Canyons roar with the echo of desire. It beats your heart and swallows your dreams. The last gulp for air chokes as you slide into yourself not lost within the vastness nor found. Simply gleaming treasures, sparkling centerless gems revealed reflections of rejections an empty prize for no one.

It was a clap of thunder between everything and nothing that lit up this fire in you. The scent of lightning stirred you made you believe and know deep down that there was more to this.

Where was the darkness when the sun rose? You searched for your shadow with a flashlight. You looked under every word you looked under every leaf. You looked under every footprint of every star in the sky. You tried to look between the shadows that danced on hot afternoons for a cool breath for a welcome wind.

Your tears collected in empty footprints rippling sighs across the vastness as your reflection hinted at the echo of a song barely seen in the distance. You found a love sonnet that you knew came from you and all you saw in everyone's eyes was your own reflection, yet you wanted that love that magic you saw.

Under that song there was no singer. You fell through your own love and you feel through your own reflection. You fell through your own sadness and you fell through your own joy. You fell through your own emptiness and suddenly all there was was simply this. There was never anything more or less.
Your tears cried 1000 shadows.

The edges of this centerless multifaceted jewel that you are have been blurred and you recognize your unadorned beauty everywhere. It seems you spend your waking hours falling swooning through rainbow tears, and simply a wordless wonder that cannot be kissed away.

A stunned silence when the electricity goes off in the night. He could hear the crickets and all kinds of sounds when the refrigerator stopped humming. He thought he heard the moon-rise over the edge of the darkened Canyon.
If we were to meet in person we would simply fall into each other slip into and through each other. You need to have a little imaginary space in order to look into each others I's.

We stir the cream into the coffee and fall into the clouds.

Swinging from the stars, ropes of air, hearts on fire, castles burning. Love unowned sweeps away imaginary distance. Like the first rays of dawn streaming into the canyon. My face is etched with smiles, tears form rivulets and colored dreams fall into sky.

A song unlike any other sings forming ribbons of untold tales spinning turvey topsey dreamscapes castles tumbling into silent singing mountain streams flowing into deep roaring rivers into bottomless oceans where there is no harbor or safe place to rest. Only the shimmering surface reflecting moonbeams of star shadows echoing the laughter and love of all the smiles and tears of everyone who has ever been and everyone who will ever be.

Thought draws in imaginary lines and seems to throws a net over the vastness, so we can find ourselves.

It paints in infinite colors, a bottomless treasure chest reveals itself in the swirling. Light and color and sound and movement appear, and we seem to be on a timeline, yet the center of the cyclone as well.

We feel we are doing the painting, but life paints itself, there is no author, no puppet master, or puppet.

Words seem to divide the unitary flowingness, but there is no actual separation. Just waves ebbing flowing into and through ripples of meaningless perfection merging and emerging into sparking rainbows falling softly down reflecting themselves timelessly.

Broken wide open the heart sings. Songs unseen undo filigree threads as tendrils of emptiness untie softly parcels of meaning. Memories lose their grip in the flowing. Space pours into space and reflects the light in lovers I's.

When I look around at all these beautiful tender hearted people is that they feel alarmed and out of control when emotions are in full swing. Everything they've heard and every-thing they've read

has played upon their fears of feeling too deeply. They have been told that if they want this love of God or life everlasting, they must act or feel or think in a certain way.

So what they long to prolong is the very thing they are afraid of, feeling so deeply the essence of our humanness. In the configuring of trying to keep these emotions alive this knowing of you alive

you have to get rid of these things that you love the most. In the fear of not being we look for anything we can to keep being, and that usually entails denying the reason we want to be at all.

Without emotions we are not.

Oh how our shattered dreams are us!

The function of self is to look for solidity, because the assumption of self is accompanied by fear that it does not exist and hope that it does. So on the journey of self-discovery we look for reasons for rhymes for a purpose for anything that will tie this feeling of all these separate things that seem to be flying apart together!

Searching through self-help books, psychology philosophy spirituality and religion. Anything that seems to offer any hope or promise of unifying it of healing this hole in your heart.

Self is the pretense of knowing, the fear of not knowing, and the belief that something can be done to know or to capture life. Deep down there is an intuited knowing that is largely ignored that what is going on is not separate from you and there fore there is no controller or chooser of thought feeling or action. If this fear becomes too large to ignore it may consume you in the gaping maw of your own love.

"Oh my! Now I know the answer! Everything is energy!". Well, what is energy?

"Oh my! Now I know everything that happens is supposed to happen!". How would you know if you can never go back and see if things could have gone a different way?

All there is is description whether it be scientific spiritual philosophical psychological. What is going on simply cannot be captured. It's ideas all the way down. Nothing to rest on. No one to rest. Like the stories told of love and war about pinpricks in the night sky, real is just another idea. The hope and belief that it can may or may not fall away.

It may dawn that we have never had control, and there has never been anyone doing anything. Life in its fullness and richness has always done itself. There is utter ease rising writhing rushing

living between this this rush this fullness this flowing of emotion and not even nothing.

Knowing that you know, being amazed that you're amazed, delighting in your own delight, wondering at your own wonder. All magnificently only human!

All her life it was like being one half of a kiss searching for the other set of lips, and reaching reaching reaching, and finally finding that it was always the first and last kiss. She was the love the lover and the beloved. Life dancing swirling emerging falling through itself in an atemporal rhythmless rhythm flying soaring through prisms of untold beauty of rainbows delighting in their own wondrousness. Light and color sweeping through shadow and shine as leaves trembling in the wind.

Wall-less canyons echo the silence of the universe singing a dream of reflections shimmering in shadowed light. An uncontained symphony of overtones and after images of sideways backwards glances into where you have never been falling through illuminated manuscripts of where you will never be. A hush of memories sliding through a sigh of nowhere, and no place to convene, like kisses in the dark.

There were never any sides to nowhere, there was never a song in the wind until her heart beat madly in tune with her breath did the song emerge. Silently roaring the blood surging through her body she heard the universe sing her name. This it is she whispered, this is the only song. It sings me as I sing it. My home is everywhere and no where. There has never been anyone to land as the falling is falling through the falling. Such a beautiful bittersweet melancholia sings a song of indescribable beauty dancing as joy and sorrow merge with love in an undercurrent of sublime aloneness.

Light folds into light and unfolds through filigreed reverberations that echo starlight's song. Space shimmers and streams through space singing in and through the darkness. Sound ricochets through shadows lit from within and without. A primordial dance where time falls into non time and leaves ripples of lovliness endlessly pirouetting a wind ballet echoing in the heart of emptiness.

A shimmering edgeless symphony full beyond measure or time or meaning or non meaning, this dance of one without sides.

Beautiful gossamer threads of belief untied wrap around a centerless gem spinning, like tears awaiting a dream.

The picture paints itself, the dance dances itself and nothing has ever been out of place.

Not one tear, not one echo, not one note, not one song. This is a seamless recognition that there are no separate tears or echoes or notes or songs. Yet without imaginary spaces in between there is no perfection nor beauty nor music nor wonder nor love. Always super complete as nothing can be added and nothing can be taken away from what is going on. There is simply no one can step outside of all this to do so. There is no outside nor inside.

All description paints the dream as the singing creates the imaginary singer and listener.
It sings itself
just
like
this
watching the dream sing itself
is the dream

....and how I longed for the love of another ...until there was no other ...and the white horses glow as the moon rises in the canyon....

and he looked around... and the colors and forms swirled through him... as him... one dance ....edgeless......he could no longer tell where he ended and the wind began.... merged into and through the day falling into night.... an undeniable amorphous essence he could no longer and no longer cared to catch.... the brilliance that flooded through him..... as him.....

yet there was scintillating on the surface of the wind...... an appearance of a rising sun..... over a line drawn by thought... yellowy orange tears sparkled on a timeless wave of dreamstuff.......

the constant concern of the end of his wave had dissolved into the edgeless ocean... all there was was this trembling quivering tip of what could never be caught or named...

it felt like a constant swoon... falling always into his own embrace his own kiss his own love

Across the great divide my heart sings
Echoes calling each other
And you can only hear your name
From the mountain tops from the depths of the bottomless ocean
It resounds echoes pierces you deeply it is always your heart song
Saying hello
welcome home
.....I love you

There is no holder nor things held. Self is the imaginary line between inside and outside. Self is the grasping, the clenching, the feeling of a line between inside and out.

What is going on cannot be caught or captured with words concepts and ideas. Sometimes poetry can evoke the ambiguous nature of fluid slippery unknowable flowing that has no movement. Like broken shards of empty mirrors scattered across the vastness reflecting that what you have always known but seem to have forgotten, revealing this seamlessness of what is, this sublime Edgelessness from which you are not separate.

Every word seems to create more and more things that are you or are not you. Even nothing seems like a thing. The unknowable endless edgeless vast expanse becomes painted with heartbreakingly wondrous vistas of stories of joy and sorrow, love and love lost. All scribbling of these words believed is like more and more concrete pouring over the sun. Until your brain realizes that you and all thingness, this passion play that writes and erases itself, is made up, is its own mental fabrication.

You lay down in the rich grasses your hair entangled in moons ray. After the battle you can no longer find your shoes but it no longer matters. Rippling softly colored reflections of loves last dance plays on your mind screen yet you have forgotten all their names. A song that you can barely remember echoes without meter as you fall into the sweetness.

There is no one to be lost or found yet you keep your feet as your old shoes have become diamonds of starlight dancing. Here is your old house, but the walls and ceiling have become transparent. Here are your old clothes they have become a gossamer light gown of wonder.

You are the dance, this streaming light show, galaxies imploding exploding rushing roaring Star light sparkling iridescent three dimensional rainbow painting butterfly kisses intimately felt. Here is your own Beautiful humanness.

Walking down the empty road long head lights find you in the darkness. Shadows linger and shorten and disappear in taillights glow. Without the differentiation of light and dark, shine and shadow, there are no things, there is no movement without the imposed measurement of time. There is no music without measured intervals and there is no love without imaginary others. Without this brief brief moment of imaginary twoness there is simply no awe no wonder no everything
no nothing.

You can feel your heartbeat the blood roaring under your skin. You can hear the canyon rive'rs song the same as you hear your own song. It is all singing you.

You can feel and hear your own breath sighing speaking ready to kiss as you hear the wind in your ears and feel it on your skin. Windsong is Windsong. They are the same. Hearing it feeling it touching it seeing it is it. Is you. There is no separation.

Obviously vibrantly apparent, the symphony of perception is simultaneously recognized as your brain paints a picture of inside and out. Yet it is all the same song. You are never separate or apart from the symphony of perception of life showing itself to itself. Tasting touching seeing hearing feeling it's on aliveness through you. You are this beautiful windsong. Listening to yourself.

Images form and sing. The dream paints itself as sound and light and shade and color swirl magically appearing as they simultaneously self release. Reflections of reflections. Echoes of echoes, we are mirrored dreamscapes dancing in our own magic.

I see a kaleidoscopic flowing of seamless beauty. A cascading slipstream neither forwards nor back silently flows arpeggiod dreamscapes through my mindstream singing brilliant unequaled immeasurable unspeakable songs.

Painting an a-temporal time scape, where form and line seem to appear. Yet the softness of no edges, of nothing cutting or sharp. There is always a deep sigh underneath the apparent flowing. The knives the swords the razor of this and that always felt and known to be an imaginary magical illusion.

There is both the knowing that there are no mountains and no one to climb them, and yet gazing into the vastness where suns slide across the vault between imaginary edges of canyons spilling flowing as castles crumbling life flowing a brief brief window of life touching life. Feeling it's own aloveness through you.

I am a song I am a tone poem singing itself. Steps in the dark. Notes on a stave. Intervals are Imaginary spaces between this and that. A contrapuntal backbeat. A heartbeat dances me sings me and you. A love song in the distance begins barely heard. Yet grows and grows, bursting, full on aliveness. A dance of shadow and light, of deep kisses. And laughter.

The rain falls through blue skies shimmering diamonds at your feet. You look for a rainbow but you cannot find it. It is in your heart, it is you, just as you think you are.

When he longed for something his heart felt empty, and when he felt he had it, his heart felt full. Yet his heart was never absent it was always there either empty or full, never separate from the feeling, never separate from the song, never separate from the feeling of lacking or fullness. There was never any separation, he had never been separate and apart from what was going on. It was simply a most painful misconception.

The idea that thoughts are good or bad is simply thought.
Can you find the beginning or end to a thought or feeling or moment?
Are there really separate thoughts feelings or moments?
Is there someone separate from thought feeling and this edgeless ever emerging self releasing momentary?

Watching the dream unfold into an unwoven weaving of spiraling reflections of faces of stories of technicolor vividness without time or meter painting an edgeless vast spaciousness like a delicate fingertip touching a flowing becoming the flow.

These very blossoming rippling words exploding into a watercolor dreamscape where we live and love and sing together. A chorus of one written with the same words yet uniquely precious.

Like a magical incantation an open sesame of wonder. A hologram of pure delight pierces my heart deeply as the dream of us unwinds itself tripling down the sidewalk of sideways glances over shadowed vales and sun dappled forest floors loves heart magic sings.

So sublimely beautiful this bittersweetness of an almost kiss hovering in the canyon winds swooning into and through itself. Singing the song of you and me, this silence murmuring in your own voice your own whisper your edgeless own heart, "I love you."

Without edges we cannot kiss or dance, yet knowing our lines are imaginary is sublime. We merge in the current of un-named un-owned emotion, and it seems to pull us along, this softness of softness weeping at its own beauty. Our tears reflecting and forming the magical flow of all that seems to appear.

It is our beautiful humanness soaring, wingless. A sigh beyond measure, a hush without breath, breathing. A naked sky so vast the blueness merges with deepest darkest space and sings rippling empty after images dissolving into rainbow trails leaving no sign or wake. An unsung song of tears raining falling into rivulets of wonder merging into the deep roaring river beyond time or shadow. Merging slipping softly through soft itself into the vast unknowable unknown, this mystery touching itself through you. These words are description they are not meaningful nor meaningless. They create sun and clouds, and moons and moonbeams, and starlight dancing in your lover's eyes. Love vibrates in the imaginary spaces in between and we slide in as tears pour color running streaming with out intent blending in the urges and surges of rippling dreams.

Through this broken open heart butterflies kiss and love flows. The shimmering irides-cence is always whatever seems to appear. We are our stories as they write themselves. You are the pretty pattern, you are the colors weaving themselves into this beautiful dream.

The tapestry waves itself with gossamer threads of this and that at every intersection an unimaginably brilliant Jewel. A tear shot through with rainbows simultaneously weaving and un-ravelling itself like light pouring into light.

This sublime supreme spaciousness is un contained. This utter silence is never over-whelmed. Bursting acceding descending starlit notes reflect your heartsong as it emerges unscathed within the rhythm of the universe. It is never out of step it is footless dancing. It is unrehearsed yet recollected, no end is needed in a beginning less melody as it rips you to shreds without reason or rhyme and leaves a most intimate embrace, a kiss from within and without.

Verdant beyond measure, lush without end this vivid fullness bursting blossoming from inside and out. A caress like no other. A wild heart sings.

This surreal blurred vibrantly articulated movie. In focus out of focus. No one behind the projector.

There is simply no source or true self or pure consciousness or timeless awareness. There would have to be two things to have something unchanging whilst the rest changes, and there are no things.

And oh! That hole in your heart has to explode! A dream time dance of whodunit. Where was it, where is it, where will it be, where will I be, what will happen, when nothing happens? Who writes the song?
How could it be that the song sings itself? The questions drop away, they were your clothes. Like leaves off a plant that is no longer seeking the light. Only a barrenness an unowned nakedness remains. Then the nakedness slips away. Simply an uncaused unceasing silent brilliance singing. Humming this song.

Oh I believed all the songs of the enraptured bedazzlement. Transfixed. Transmogrified. Pierced by love. Of the end of my achy breaky heart. It was the idea of love, it was the idea of fulfillment, it was the idea of complete and total rest that were discovered to be empty ideas, like me.

Yet dissolved completely only to return just for that kiss of nothing of nowhere. Just a smile and hello to a passerby swoons me.

And stars shown through her nakedness, yet every tear was exquisite in it's indefinite distinction.

You are the cricket song storming through the night. You are the tires singing on the tarmac. You are the low engine roaring streaming by you and fading into the darkness. Light behind you and shadows dancing you on the sidewalk. Low red lights as they pass, two eyes fading into the distance. The scent of cooling summer breeze flying down the canyon from mountains passing clouds. The hint of river roaring, the man on the cell phone talking. His quick step passing your slow wandering.

Meandering evening sliding through you as you. Bright and beautiful dark and clear, light and shadow singing you as you sing the night. This cowboy song on the radio flowing through car windows, of love lost and love found, through tears and yesteryears.

Such beauty such richness! Fullness bursting the seems! The scenery writes itself, without beginning or end. Painting your part in sky that is perfectly played by no one, disappearing as soon as the voices are heard.

On an empty bench you spied your shadow. The one who was waiting for all this. Only to find the waiting was it.

Everywhere you look is magic. It is you and you are it. Inside and outside have merged, collapsed into each other. Yet you need your feet to dance. Although all and everything is known to be made up, dream-like and vibrantly real, marvelous beyond measure, the love ballet pirouettes and appears to be two hearts, two songs spinning together apart together. Only in the vibration of this and that can love sing.

The beauty is obviously apparent, a tender flower blooming and fading. Even plastic flowers fade. Life ever emerging ever fading happening utterly spontaneously, looking and feeling like anything at all. Only in the touching do we exist. Only in the imaginary space between each other can we know love.

A magical breath a soundless kiss singing. Clear unbound transparent edgeless pages streaming canyons rivers oceans the wetness of wet.

Un-written, they write themselves and never quite emerge. Whispers of emptiness dipped in rainbows falling through whirlpools of sighs. Shimmering ripples of wet on wet. Softness falls through softness as the hush falls into the hush. Space reflecting space, light mirrors light, falling free formless touching kissing a a story of me of you of we sings.

Life unadorned. All of your senses unbound. Vibrant aloveness. Every secret pore of your being has been turned inside out. All the things we feared so much, fleetingness, impermanence, the not knowing, the utter devastating emptiness of emptiness, the utter ravishingly beauty of nothing. The placelessness, uncapturablity, the un figure out-aboutableness. The beauty of beauty the taste of taste the sheer enormity and weight of light, of vast endless sky, of shoreless oceans, no safe harbor and no one looking. So beautiful, so fleeting. Simply always one kiss, the first and last. Exquisite in all perfect in one supreme in none.

Ascending descending starlit notes reflect your heart-song as it emerges, the rhythm of the universe sings you as you sing it. You are never out of step as you are the dancing, of joy and sorrow and untold ages never scripted unrehearsed never sung nor unsung. The dance-card is empty and the floor falls away. No no end is needed in a beginning less melody as it rips you to shreds without reason or rhyme. All the lines collapse into themselves. It's like falling through your own shadow, and you are soaring skinless in a warm summers breeze.

its an empty black and white world that switches to full-color. This full on unadorned raw life, like you've been trudging along with iron square tires on a bumpy hell track and suddenly it hit the smooth road in a beautiful sports car top down on the coastal road.

Self is seemingly created just as all life happens, all by itself. Self cannot be destroyed or disappear or die as it is simply made up, like purple unicorns flying through my onion soup. There is no supreme intelligence or energy separate from the universe animating it. Life does itself. As belief in separation fades it seems that the I am falls into the we are. It truly feels like there is nothing here. A supreme vacancy shimmering without in or out or as or through the centerless center. Self does not go away after the dream is no longer believed, it remains the imaginary center of a swirling imaginary vortex around which the rest of the dream spins. Empty of even emptiness. There is nothing there or here, not even nothingness.

Simply through shadow and light seeming to dance in a magnificent passion play, the story of you, awareness can be aware that it is aware. Oneness swallows twoness swallows oneness, and all ness-ness known and felt to be made up. All ideas of truth or false or meaning and non meaning lose their place in this sublime quiescence. As this perfect crystalline unbroken sphere of knowingness, uninterrupted by time space dimension always empty, ever overflowing. As infinite unbounded greens slide into amorphous blues sinking deeper and deeper, shadows sliding away as starlight illuminates sparking reunions of what was never apart.

There is a common misconception that a sage is no longer a human. The sense of a me does not disappear, yet it is simultaneously known and felt that the dream of you of me of we of separation is indeed made up. it is as if this hyper awareness of being aware without time or place, yet not possible without the dream of time and place, permeates and subsumes the dream.

dandelion seeds aloft
catch a flowing kiss
gossamer moon glow weaves ancient stories into a cat's cradle that held your song of love and love lost unravels
feathered lines left by the tides do not claim the beach
waves rolling in cannot be caught
after crashing they are gone forever

and the sun glistens on the sparkling sand as the water percolates diamonds into your mindstream

words, like tiny bits of broken mirrors seem to cut up the sky into separate shards of blue, ripping you apart from the seamless flowing.
and words can fly you to the edge and leave you hanging, and elicit the vastness of which I sing.

This is so clear, so simple, yet it cannot be kissed with word or thought.
like trying to capture the amazing clarity of water
creating ripples
that reflect your reaching hand
your beautiful mind
it is far too vast and unknowable
to be sung of
as are you
this unspeakably wondrous uncatchable jewel is known only by its sparkling. everywhere slips through no where and even nothing falls away.
sunlight sparkles on the slip stream and colors touch. it moves you swirls you it leaves you breathless in constant awe. music trips and falls down the mountain stream through rivulets of dancing colors
Desire is the dream unfolding. The quivering tenuous trembling tip of a tsunami appearing to hover as it crashes flowing ever emerging into what can never be known or touched or captured. rushing tumbling soaring flowing, streaming without edge or purpose, undeniably present, unthinkably marvelous.
Beauty strikes you pierces you deeply and rips apart your walls of fear that prevented loves flow
let loose from the illusion of separation its all sweet spot
all the flow
and never a mis-step or fault
we are winds and grasses streaming
shine and shadow dancing. running free in utter delight .....wind whipped tears glimmering with sunset colors
desire is so beautiful
and a broken heart is more beautiful still
that's how love flows unimpeded by fear
only with imaginary twoness is there dancing .....and desire......
knowing it is illusion does not end desire or passion

it simply is not personal
life sees itself and says
may I have this dance
and answers itself
with a resounding
YES!!!!!
the passion to sing of this forms my lines
the banks of the deep roaring river pouring into an edgeless sea
Sparks fly, we are desire. Yet it can be impersonal yet passionate at the same time. It is truly an inside out life
Feeling everything fully, yet it has no center. Edgeless love, soars through you as you are the soaring.
tender tendrils of emptiness untie knots of sky
Life kisses itself as in of and through you. Seamless dancing without a dance floor as music reverberates echoes of loveliness off the canyon walls. This unfindable melody of one.
Love wrote its name in the shadows and was lost in its desire to see itself
The indescribable beauty of beauty knowing that it is beautiful. Jewels everywhere, sparkling of reflections, like looking through a tear as it falls through itself. Ever blooming ever wilting, ever emerging ever falling.

it was the longing to know that defined her
to wrap herself in bejeweled clothes, in dancing starlight
she longed to discover lengths of story
a warp and weave to cover her nakedness
where she might hide
forever
from the aching stars
but the moonlight unraveled the day time dreams
and light was left un captured
under the flowing swirling dream skirts
there was not even nakedness
love was not lost
nor found
it was the fabric of the universe
telling all stories
as hers faded and illumined in the light of knowing she was, this was, simply all beautiful story.

Golden sunlight shifts and fades, swirling shadows consume the riches that dance across the carpet, delicately anointing your heart with a kiss remembered. Looking to see the lips that have emboldened their traces upon your tender face you see only yourself. Glimmering heat waves carouse innermost depths tormented by their own arising. Does the bud ache to flower?

The universe makes love to you and you discover it's your own intimate embrace. When it's truly known there is no other the infinite pieces of your body are strewn across the universe like stars piercing the ultimate darkness of the inky blackness, delighting in illuminating the obvious love dance.

The parcel of love is unwrapped and flows uncontained filling every secret corner where fear and hope used to reside. Everything and nothing revealed at once. Swallowing itself the knowing is you. It un-writes the songs of memory and paints a pirouette on the breeze as cyclones emerge from the depths and race your heart beating in time with no reason. Swirling all and everything into a rhythmless dancing in the clear blue vastness.

The echo came from everywhere and nowhere. Reverberating ricocheting shimmering down the wall-less canyon mirrored songs blooming blossoming swooning withering, dappled love songs swaying in the breezes without time nor place nor rhythm or sign. We are the imaginary walls. Without our lines we have no story. Without our hearts we cannot swoon. Without imaginary edges the echoes cannot vibrate into my heart your heart our heartsong we longed for is us.

Chalk less designs draw and erase themselves. Fishnet stockings walk in the dark. Patterned emptiness sings.

Without the brain constantly describing what is going on with shared learned words there is no story, there is no you. We are memories singing themselves into a symphony, like a wisp of an echo, like a forgotten rainbow. Without touching of imaginary sides, without feet there is no dance, without lips to kiss or sing. There is no softness nor hardness, there is no vibration. The tendrils find no purchase, the vine does not grow, there is no wind to blow. Love does not paint colors into the lushness of your heart. Your story writes itself. An empty echo in a lost Canyon
sings

We are the inside and outside of no sides. Knowing meaning is imaginary is wondrous. Watching with unadulterated awe as the dream unfolds. All story, knowing it is story, oh my. It is nevertheless overwhelmingly wondrous!

My beating heart these beating wings touching feeling intensely. These soaring winds flowing through me as me, edgeless sky flows though itself

Dancing as this and that is a mirage of unspeakable beauty. We are not separate from the dance as there are no separate parts. No invitation or requirements or special circumstances, no steps are necessary for the dance to be seen and known and felt as a dream.

Dusty nights sleep in the bath of cricket song. Laying long and luxurious, Stretching stretching and never finding an end nor beginning to the longing for the longing of this richness of an un-owned life.

Neither here nor there nor in between
Dancing as no one as everyone as everything as nothing.

Where does starlight end?
Where does it begin?
In your eyes it reflects your unutterable magnificence.

I walk at night, the uninterrupted symphony of perception streaming through me as me. Sight sound touch bodily sensation thought emotion, and the simultaneous inseparable recognition of it. This thing we call life has no edges, there is no separation anywhere it does itself, simply without any effort or non-effort.

This is described as cricket song as cradling my phone in my hands streetlights pooling on the black tarmac my feet softly padding along the sidewalk my shadow preceding me or falling behind. My breath my heartbeat, the sound of my gravelly voice in the telephone watching the screen as the letters form my thumb sliding across the glass. The smell of campfires people cooking from the campground, laughter, faces lit with firelight. The tires soon preceding the engines... I could spend a lifetime attempting to describe one infinitesimal moment. I could write books and books, yet they are all words. I can never ever ever ever ever convey you into me so that you can be here experiencing this. Words are paltry pointers to what is going on. They cannot capture it, they cannot even touch it. There are no separate things that can be lassoed with words, yet words are all we have, we are words, this fleeting description. We are the dream of separation.

Truly truly truly you cannot step aside from what is going on in order to capture it or stop at or slow it down or add to it or subtract from it or accept it or reject it or surrender to it. There is simply no outside to what is going on, and so there is no inside. It's not a thing nor a non-thing. It is vast infinite spaciousness that can never be known. The magnificence of the unknowability is mind-boggling. It is stupefying. It is exceedingly beautiful!

The wondrousness that the knower cannot be found or known. How marvelous to know and feel that they are not separate, how sublime!

To feel deeply deeply deeply that there is no separation that there are no edges that there is no time that there is no other that there is no outside that there is no inside that there are no things nor non-things is indescribably delicious.

This is the peace, this is the sublime quiescence, the seamless ease I had been looking for my entire life. It was always on, simply not noticed. Now it permeates subsumes the dream, for awakening is the dream as well.

There is no doubt nor any place for it to arise. There is nothing to hide and nowhere to hide it. There is simply no concern to what others may think or believe about this profound shift in perception.

Awakening feels like being ripped apart and shredded stabbed with knives turned inside out ravishing you devouring every single place every single corner. The tiniest little pockets where you thought you could hide are eviscerated until there is nothing left to hide. When the tiger, my own love, was eating me alive, I simply knew it was just right. There was no fight. It can be terrifying as you are falling and everything is slipping away, yet you are astounded that it is happening with no one doing it. It is like you open your clenched fist and not even nothing is there. There was never anything to get, and soon you realize that there was never anyone to get it.

All the frames fall off the pictures, the parcels of your life become undone, strings untied, wounds ripped open, blood flowing, rivers merging. All is lost as it was never found. There is no place to rest and no one to rest. Your flailing arms give no purchase in the flowing as they are the flowingness itself, dissolved utterly with no speck of sand to be found as you crash into yourself the beach is submerged. Yet in the deepest blackest night a spark of light rages and burns you to your very core and you discover the light that was always on. Nothing is ever captured or contained or stable or fixed or summoned or pushed away or caused or uncaused. This is beyond imagination or description. You lose everything and gain nothing and it is the most marvelous nothing at all. Marvelously utterly everything you've ever wished for is this untying. You are stunned, it is more real than real, and yet it is nothing at all.

All of life flows through you as you. Everywhere and nowhere, and yet it is felt deeply passionately but impersonally. After the shift you can't go back you cannot put the blinders back on. There is no back. There is only magnificently marvelously this momentarily fleeting brilliance arising and self erasing simultaneously. A rainbow of unutterable beauty forming and falling away, a cloud shadow erasing your footsteps. Ever blooming ever wilting. Untouchable. Un-kissable. Unknowable.

We are only and sublimely smaller than a spark yet far greater than a conflagration, more ephemeral then the wisp of a thought and louder than a lion's roar, softer than a butterfly kiss and an atom bomb, a silent sonic boom. The wetness of a tear, the wet of wet, the taste of taste. A memory you can barely remember, and more obvious than an arrow piercing your heart. A run away freight train has hit a mountain.

It is truly felt and known deeply that there is nothing outside of the dream that you are, and there is no more longing to escape it. There is no more need to hang on and no one who wants to hang on or who can even try to hang on. Time dies with the belief in a do er, as all ideas of effort and achievement of a goal or of something to reach or something to attain evaporate. Your eyes are wide open and every pore of your being is vibrantly alive. Ripped wide open no place left to hide, this raw skinlessness with not even nakedness underneath the clothes of awe. Dancing between the lips and the kiss, the breath and the song, always ever becoming and nothing left to become.

Simply amazed at your amazement blown away by the utter deliciousness of not knowing. The utter unfigureoutability. This impermanence, neither moving nor non moving is immeasurably wondrous.

All our attempts to describe emptiness are stories written in air, this baseless shimmering brilliance can never be kissed from within or without. Mirrors can never reflect themselves and the sun needs no method to shine.

As my shadow meets itself at my feet it appears I am on a path, yet there is no direction to nowhere. No story that doesn't fall apart as it's written. No notes that can be pulled from space, as the song sings itself it ripples in its own vibrations.
Empty shadows dance across the thousand pillared hall, swiftly moving shine and shade reveal no lines at all squiggling across the screen. Stories emerge and dissolve in their telling. Life is written from echoes barely heard and roll softly downstream in its own seamless flowing.

tendrils of nothingness untie your secret dreams touched by no other than your own velvet touch as you are unwritten unraveled undone and your heart is cleaved by your own love.

I swoon into you into me into we into and through myself. The simplicity of unending wide open spaciousness sings us as we sing it, of hearts pierced forever with love's magic.

Goin' dooooooown the faceless highway, climbing up the river of tears. How many paths did I follow trying to feel my way through the endless cloud covered night. Longing to touch the great unknown, my heart shattered into shards that pierced all the hopes and fears and dreams that I was. I was ground into powdered tears that showered glittering stardust through a mirror brightly as I crashed into and through my own brokenness. Infinite pieces of nothing flew forever and never touched the end of the sky.

The essence of life cannot be stopped or grasped with words. Trying to lasso a rainbow or hold sunlight in your hand, run your tender fingers through a kitten's fur in a picture or kiss a lovers reflection in your eyes. Yet words fly through your window sometimes, and as they break the pain and your heart wide open, you realize you are the dragons fiery breath as it burns you and the golden treasure you longed for.

It was your own arrow you shot, long ago, before you slipped into your suit of armor made of all those ideas of what life should be like, like a straight jacket, as you hid in secret places where love could not touch. Your heart falls apart and the wind blows it away. All the seems that held you together fold into themselves and erupt, and a river of tears flows through you and washes away the lines.

The storm clouds part and the vastness is seen. Light floods your being as you throw away your umbrella. It never could stop the rain or prevent you from drowning in your tears. Mist clings to the rocky mountain tops and swirls through space blurring the edges of where you thought you were as there is no concern for where you believed you must go. It's like a welcome home, I love you, sliding into your own warmth that you had never left, the all encompassing embrace of this utter intimacy of yourself.

Your face is etched with smiles they are rivers for tears. You cannot think of anything that needs adornment, fallen in between the cracks, enchanted with unlined edgelessness.

No one can color between nonexistent lines with crayons of fixed hue, morning is a magical brush sweeping across the canyon. Sky dresses itself in an ever changing miracle and this sweet song of love paints your beautiful reflection in my eyes.

Songs flow through me and paint my reflection in sky, yet sky is never captured, nor this utter unafraid nakedness which clothes no one or thing. Tattered remnants of memories fly across the vast ness and sing of what has no actual substance, simply cloud reflections swirling and rippling into and through their own echoed reflections painting this dream of sighs.

Whose words whose tears whose rainbows soar through this un owned broken heart? Echoes of echoed reflections dancing and sliding on the rippling winds pirouette into a ballet of love and sorrow and joy and tears that reflect rainbow dreams in each others eyes.

Petting the cat, steam from my tea rising in sun clad spirals, bamboo chimes singing in the breeze cast by the swamp cooler. Only humans can wonder at wonder, be in love with love, know that beauty is beautiful, and weep at the magnificence of this unspeakable magnificence and sing unendingly of what is not a what. This unbearable beauty of life simply spontaneously appearing looking and feeling like anything at all.

Swooning in love as love through love, love the ecstatic dance of one of two of many of none. As the farthest reaches of this deep unfathomable unknown sea explode into infinite spaciousness and collide into and through the known world of dimension and time, we emerge, our feathers wet with the surf of sky, breathless on the beach where everything and nothing remain in the still silent love song humming the primordial words to this song that sings itself. Utterly obvious this brilliant aliveness pulsating as the rhythm of your breath and heartbeat, the back beat of existence itself, this and that in an unending dance that has no beginning nor ending yet never was and never will be.

There is a beautimous longing for what will never happen
It feels like a gentle breeze blowing through me...

I no longer see people as the instigators or chooses of thought feeling or action, and never really feeling that there are separate thoughts feelings or actions is truly beautiful! Naked awareness staring out through a veil of tears

JULY SONGS

You may find that the love you longed for and yet feared has turned around and kissed you full on the mouth. Reached down into the deep dark secret corners of your being that you did not know existed and pierced you and burnt you and consumed you. All that you thought you knew of yourself and your world unravel into tattered clouds raining endless tears washing through your delicate wetness. You may spin for awhile looking for a familiar face, a loving embrace, but you cannot find anything or anyone who will stop this ravishing pain, no idea or hope or dream will fill this astounding utter blankness.

The searching for handholds may stop and you will recognize everyone as your familiar face, and all and everything is your infinite intimate embrace. There are no reference points and no place to land as everywhere is home, yet no one lives there. Such a marvelous unknowing when there is no one to know or not know, no one to be confused or non confused, no one to be free or bound, no one to awaken or stay fast asleep. Gazing out is gazing in when there is no need to grasp life as it swims through you as you. Such unspeakable beauty in simply life as it seems to appear. This seamless ease this sublime awe this marvelous bittersweet aloneness of no one to kiss.

Memories of memories drift in swiftly moving tides of joy and sorrow where rain never lingered to catch your name. You searched and searched for the meaning of the light that sparkled so deeply on the shallow reeds, dipping and sliding across your sadness with no concern for a morrow that never held a forgotten kiss. Where was the moonlight that seemed to hold your beauty in its touchless reflection? Where was the love of last summer's dream? Where was the laughter of an innocence remembered as it waltzed in the back room and wept without end?

Where was your hand as you reached for the shadows where love hid its memories and danced? When was tomorrow and where were the promises that whisper your name in starlight's glance? Was it all for naught this longing of longing and what would you be without your dreams? How could you wander in endless circles without a center to this flowing dream?

And without any warning the night parted as morning mourned the death of darkness. Trippling light and shadow across the vastness, dancing the waltz of endless beginnings sliding into and through the ending of time and timelessness revealing a naked wonder at a beautiful empty hand reaching. Reaching for everything reaching for nothing the waltz of mans desire planted a kiss on your shadow and beckoned you back into the dance.

This is it, this touch this worried brow these tears cried for no one for everyone that ever danced in love as love through this lovers dance of joy and sorrow and the kiss of midnight.

How could you not weep at the beauty of your tender heart? If you have no more tears I have plenty

For I know your beauty

Your song of love

Your sorrow at the recognition of no tomorrow

And I dance with you on the footsteps of time and we will rest on the edge of nothing and everything and weep and laugh and marvel at this brief magnificent human life.

Whose heart was it that sang of a love so fierce, so compelling, so intensely intimate that it broke open your fortress of fear and scattered infinite sparkling reflecting your beautiful tears in this starlight dream? Who danced in this silence that sang your heart song into a waltz that only seemed to flow in a river of tears? Without direction or cause there was no movement yet the pull of your watercolor shadow sucked you into and through yourself. As you found your feets bedecked with moonlight, there were no words to sing of this amazement yet they were heard in every sigh.

Painted dreamscapes alight with three dimensional seamless brilliance, a fabric of jeweled wonder is never woven or undone, yet flows through your mindstream as it dances your adornment in starlights gaze. Knowing there is nothing underneath your nakedness is the most amazing dream of all.

It was your own love that shredded the old clothes and ripped out your heart until you were no more significant than the wind caressing your tenderness that allows you to say, yes, this is it and has always been, without time or dimension yet including all, the dream as it seems to appear is all I have ever wanted, yet it is nothing at all.

Love soars through the dream painting notes on staves of wonderment, melodies continue to arise that sing of this obvious explosion of life! Yet words can only murmur overtones that blend into a primordial hum that has no hue or shadow without the back beat of time dancing down main street.

Who are you to follow your own footsteps glissading down this broken trail, where tears left imprints of your rippling shadow as light found its way into the locked vault of your heart and threw away all ideas of a key to tomorrow?

No one led in this footless dance and no one found a place to rest or hide in this sublime collision of everything and nothing. Remaining as a flowing scar across your tenderness you blossom as the night unwraps the delicacy of day with tendrils of emptiness as the fullness sings you sings me and we meet in a timeless kiss where deep laughter and tears have always resided in time without time this dance of one of two of many of none.

You have never missed a moment of your life as there was never a you to have one and there has never been a moment to miss or catch. This has always been the song that sages sing of so sweetly, it has never needed conditions or parameters. You were the measurement that found lack, and that was the sweetness of your beautiful lips. Finding that there is no one to find and no one to lack is also the unbearable beauty of being, simply and irrevocably always life whatever it seems to look or feel like.

Spontaneously so

Just like this

Life sings itself

Where never and forever crash into each other these daylight dreams waltz in rhythmless slumber. Life whispers uncountable melodies where the last note seems to be always missing and creates a feeling of lack, of just missing the right key that would resolve the questionless questions that pirouette into a spinning tale of you and next.

Looking for wings to enfold you and stretch across the starry skies with lullabies to hold you in the grasp of love's embrace kept them folded into your next breath your next heartbeat your next step that never occurred. What if this was truly it and no prince or princess or eternal now would save you from a kiss-less kiss?

Searching for that other half kept you feeling strangled yet you had no choice but to swoon in love's swan song creating ripples that mesmerized your fear of dying into vague fairy tales that now

You cannot ignore.

What if this sparkling life just as it seems to appear really is all there is? Will you fly into a gazillion pieces if you stop trying to relax? Deaths shadow always at your bow still the sun slides across your tears as you water the ocean of love. Showers of moon light beckon your nakedness to dance, and you find the ship you thought you were sailing has always sailed itself in the sea of dreams where even love lost its shadow in the murmurings of all your dreams. Aglow with wonder knowing there is no one under your mirrored glance of awe, still the dance of rippling tides seems to keep your heartbeat thumping in the rhythm of the night.

Life, a constant swoon of wind into wind, space into space, light into light, me into everyone I greet. I could never fall in love as I used to. How could sky fall in love with sky?

There is no pre-conceptual world, nor truth nor infinite awareness nor pure consciousness nor god that is the source of all this. No key that you need to uncover or find or become in order to discover the wholeness you seek. All of this just as it seems to appear is indeed this oneness this wholeness this unitary edgeless flowing of which the sages sing. All and everything is included as there are no edges or outside to what's going on.

There never was a you nor a home to leave. Seemingly shattered by concepts there arises a longing for other yet there never has been nor never will be anything other or next. Nothing has ever occurred or will ever arise except what seems to arise in the ever blooming ever wilting all encompassing seamless uncatchable symphony of life.

It is all your infinite intimate embrace. You have never left.

Plastic bags scoot and dance down the empty sidewalks after the partygoers have gone home. I am caught in puddles swimming in street lights. Thrilling awe slides through itself and I drown in my rippled reflection. Songs arise between the pause of my heartbeat where the edges of the mountains and the vastness of edgeless seas kiss the sky and I fall up into my own love.

The clouds lift off the mountain and flowing feathered light petals bloom and dissolve in the brilliant summer sun. Just as clouds rain crystalline tears reflecting your innermost dreams, they dissolve in this pure brilliance of unknowing. It was a war of beliefs and fear of unknowing that smashed to smithereens all belief in next. Whose heart will never stop crying? Sailing away on an ocean of tears my heart flew away on the crest of tomorrow, love was never mine.

The very act of looking for meaning creates a purpose, and a separate you looking for one.

The lines write themselves on the untouched vastness, and the story of you needs continual upkeep. The colors fade unless filled in with thoughts of past and future blooming into a story of you

Here, Now

Crumbling under the weight of this fantasy of hope and fear

Crushing the light out of life

Waiting for it to begin

You know the future is an idea

Hopes and dreams regrets occurring in the unfindable all encompassing now

Everything you've tried to grasp

Every idea of knowing has collapsed

You know there is nothing there that will save you

All ideas of life are not life

Yet are included

The unfindablity the ungraspability indicate there is no grasper
And what is left when even your heart flies out the window and is no longer yours

It is impossible to describe unicity, some call it nothingness or emptiness or oneness. Named, these are all concepts. Thinglessness cannot be grasped by the mind of this and that, but it can be felt deeply, always. But never is it a belief or understanding as it is beyond imagination or conception.
How could there be no things?
Picture a tallllllllllllll glass of water
pour the water in the river
take away the sides and bottom
pour away the emptiness. . .
what is not moving nor non moving
what has no outside nor inside
nor sides at all
what has no place nor non place
what has no center or split or division or edge
what has no time nor non time
what is not a what
nor an it nor a non it
what you long for you cannot grasp
as it has no edges nor center
no split or division anywhere
or no where
you are the idea the concept that there are separate things
and you long for one of them
called peace or enlightenment
you are the grasping that creates the illusion of a grasper and something to grasp
have you ever found a now or a next
trying to capture something that is not a thing nor a non thing
your hands are empty
your heart is empty
your longing will never be filled
your cup will never be filled
though you thirst so deeply
you are the thirst
the longing to be filled
to catch the magic

of what you do not know
and the longing for an empty idea
a wish for what will never come
never happens
no one ever gets this
there is no one separate from what is going on
space cannot capture space
light cannot capture light

Willowing leaves of sun swept grasses rippling songs of ancient melodies are the waving of infinite seas caressing your eyes your hands your heart, weaving this ever enchanted dream of fathomless beauty that you are.

Reaching out to gather the light you realize you cannot kiss your own lips. Life dances itself and you find you have never left your infinite intimate embrace. There was no one to lead and no one to follow in this waltz of meandering thought dreams. No one left home as there was no here nor there, nor anyone left knocking at the kitchen door. It was Simply an ache to swallow the moons reflection as it glided over edgeless waters that seemed to lead you astray and forget the magic that when labeled is still never captured. Life bedecked bejeweled by the song that sings you as you sing it with this thought stream you find running through your skull.

Traipsing skipping pieces of blue on blue, the rippling is uncaused, reflecting the endless fount of sea kissing sky where imaginary lines appear. It was a fruitless goal to reach the end of tomorrow. Cascading through you the magic is unearned and cannot be brought about by any method, as it is you, always on, always unfettered, constantly blooming and wilting simultaneously endless petals of super complete perfection reveal your own spectacular luminescence.

Brilliant beyond measure, light pours into light and there is no safe harbor or secret place to hide, for it is everything and nothing this unfathomable treasure that I see sparkling in your eyes. It is love knowing love is absent, beautiful beyond compare knowing beauty has left, wondering at the magnificence of wonder itself it leaves, smiling, gasping in amazement at its own reflection in your beautiful beautiful eyes.

When the fullness rushed in I thought
Oh my
Here I am
Vibrantly alive
But dead
And all that I had tried to shed was back

Self is desire
I wept for months
Beautiful beautiful hot tears laying in the long summer grasses
starlight pouring through me as me
My friend singing with me sometimes quoting poetry
Whitman
Leaves of grass
Just the enormity of what had happened
The unreality of this
The reality of this
This amazing dream of awakening!
Although I never looked for confirmation or another who knew this no thingness it was a
relief to meet another. Singing of this keeps my imaginary silhouette pirouetting in sky.
How beautiful! Desire the movement of life!
The longing to sing of this, Knowing it cannot be kissed with words and that there is no
one with whom to share paints my rippling reflection into heart songs.

He wanted to be Someone
Who didn't have a self
Not realizing that all someones ARE selves
There is not even nothing under the costume
You don't have a self
Ya can't take it off
Like a winter cap in spring

And what is that pain you have felt so deeply for long as you can remember?
Where does it go when you try to avoid it or forget it. Does it ever go away?
How much of your life have you tried to pretend it isn't there trying to get rid of it. Yet you
never could forget that gnawing sensation that things just aren't right. That life shouldn't
have to hurt so much! Oh! The reaching out and grasping for something solid as you feel
like everything is slipping away except that pain.
For surely if you could find a place to rest, or surely if you could get rid of that longing for
something permanent, somehow the knots would turn into bows and unfurl into wings
as they untied you and you could fall into sky! If there were a place from which to launch,
Light would unfold its wings and you would find yourself soaring without end!
It might suddenly or overtime dawn that the trying to let loose the noose creates the feel-
ing of constriction. Trying to erase your lines draws them. Trying to smooth the ripples
in the water creates them. All ideas of trying. All ideas of better or more or next or other

fall apart. There never were any knots to untie. No laces to undo. No wings to unfold. No barriers to cross, and no one to undo untie or try or not try. No where to land and no one to land
Your heart is empty
.....yet overflowing

At first you're swimming, then you watch amazed as your fingers feel like they're swishing through the water, in the wetness, then the wetness is no longer outside or inside, it is all, you are, a seamless liquidity. Your arms dissolve, you feel your feet are no longer kicking against the waves as the waves move with them in an edgeless flow, no longer knowing where the movement originates, or if anything's moving or not moving at all. Your head melts into the depths where the temperature is your own. It feels like drowning, as all ideas that defined you and your world dissolve. Yet you discover you can breathe underwater.
The iridescent colors reflecting on the surface and the bottom flow through you as you have become transparent. Imaginary lines between land and sea and sky dissolve in a kiss. Brilliant radiant light streams from everywhere and nowhere. It is magnificently all right, and you know it's always been this way.

I was afraid of all anger, mine and others. Yet I was terrified of just about everything! We do not become selfless doormats after the shift. We feel it all deeply when there is no one inside an edgeless heart but an echo. I block people all the time on Facebook, but I'm not angry. I just don't have time for spiritual bullshit or sexual come-ons.
We are our brains preferences and beliefs. I prefer not to have my loved ones feel bad depressed or angry, I feel their intense pain like a knife. I do love everyone in the sense that I know we are each other. But if someone starts to cut my leg off I will try to stop it or run away. The self looks out for itself. I exist only as this self. Yet I cannot find it.

The morning kissed her with her own wow. She watched the beautiful streaming dream unfold and collapse into and through itself. Castles of wind of space of light, sky shimmering in space, arching echoing vaulted magnificence merging in the placeless place between here and there, up and down, between nothing and everything, between here and there. A magical appearance a reflection a hologram a magician's tale filled with wonder and enchantment, amazed at her own amazement. Enchanted with this magic that she was. Delighting in her own delight

Life streamed through her as her. Golden rippling sunshine dancing sparkling as her heart, no longer hers, had exploded like stars strewn across the vastness. Shimmering iridescence everywhere, untouchable unshakable beauty, an indescribable splendidness of all and everything.

Pattern-less vibrant aliveness bursting imploding exploding concentric circles spiraling, shimmering, rhythm-less pulsations of shine and shadow emanate between within and without, a centerless unknowable jewel lit from inside and outside without sides, reflecting everything and nothing. There are no corners or edges, there is no place to land, there is no special state to achieve and no one to arrive, the falling falls though itself. There is no place to hide and nothing left to hide. There is nothing to find or lose. Not even nothing or emptiness.

Trying to capture one tear the flood released itself and she was drowned in her own magnificence. She stretched out her hands and the sky swallowed her. The path collapsed and the earth consumed her. She melted into the dreamscape. Laughing twirling weeping sobbing at the magnificence of all and everything and not even nothing.

Infinite variety hue timbre tone overtones vibrating together, infinite inseparable facets of an edgeless fluid gem shimmering singing humming sighing a chorus of one of many of none.

It is the very indescribability which is so magnificent. Yet all attempts to capture pure vast spaciousness write the dream of you of me of we. The naming of what can never be kissed spins all encompassing shooting starlight that pierces you burns you till the ashes blow away. You find you are the wind and the wind slides through you, and you are light and life and you are love and life and love fly and soar through you.

She looked out and she wanted to tell everyone how wondrous this was, and there was no one there. Yet in the singing there seems to arise a singer a song and a listener as life sings itself. Just like this.

What is separate from the rippling reflections shimmering in the lake reflecting the story of you? How could your song be sung without words? What is neither changing nor non-changing?
What is not a what?

What is going on is indescribable because there's nothing separate from it or that can step outside of it and capture it or hold it or slow it down or add to it or subtract from it or accept it or reject it or surrender to it. Is it really your mind, or are you a product of the mind stream, a flowing thought dream? Are there any things or non-things without words?

What I sing of cannot be captured with words yet it feels like it is always on the tip of your tongue.

It is felt deeply but is way beyond any ideas of this or that. It's like a song that you have sung a gazillion years ago and you are trying to remember the words but there are none. As you are not separate from it, trying to capture it is it. Looking for it is it, trying to deny it is it. The dream weaves itself and there is nothing that is not the dream for outside the dream there is not even nothing as there is no outside nor inside. All this and that is the dream. What is going on is neither an it nor a non- it. Simply so. Life does itself.

Have you ever been able to capture the shadow of the moonbeam? Have you ever been able to hold love? No matter how lightly you aspire to tread there are footsteps. No matter how softly you sing there is a song.

When you thrust your arms out trying to grasp the sky, is not your arms the sky? Is not the sky your arms? Where is the line between the grasp-er and the grasped? Where did the ideas bloom that there is all of the stuff which is you and all of this stuff which is not you?

The perception of other happens just as naturally as the perception of self. The perception of light of trees dancing in the canyon arises just as naturally and spontaneously as the perception of bodily sensation or feeling.

The imaginary safety net may slip away, falling through the cracks where time and non-time, forever and never kissed and erased themselves.

It's like your entire life you've been throwing a net over the river trying to capture the wetness and you are so thirsty you're dying of thirst and suddenly you slide down the mossy bank into the wetness, and you realize the net was never meant to capture life or love. It cannot be captured as you are not to separate from it. It cannot be owned as there are no edges to grasp. It was never your life or your love.
The illusion of control slips away as you rejoice in the searing of the dross. The costume shredded,
your heart melts, and love bleeds into the dream.

Yet at every intersection of imaginary lines there is unspeakable jewelry shimmering and you see your reflection in every drop. Priceless centerless jewels everywhere and nowhere singing a song of infinite timber and hue..... overtones sliding through undertones, an afterimage slides through its own shadow.

The deepest richest darkness and brightest penetrating brilliance dance and dance and dance and dance...

Like this

Like a moth burnt in the flame of desire of love reemerging in all encompassing light, untwisted unfurled unpinned unloosed a tangle a twirl a knot unfolding loosening and turning into the sensitive trembling ever emerging ever dissolving momentary. The newness always blows you away, into streams of flying feathery rainbows and lifts you as the dance floor falls away and you fearlessly sing utterly naked of this supreme splendid unknowable wonder.

Amazing that under the story there is nothing here

Or there

When there is no hope or fear or need of next, I fall in love with whomever I'm with. Love is made up. What we really longed for is the knowing feeling of no separation, which is love but not what we thought love was before. This is beyond any ideas of this and that is a feeling that is truly indescribable. Yet, well, All feeling is indescribable.

It's like you're walking barefoot and you realize that your feet are dissolving. You are soaring but you have no wings. You have disappeared and yet there is dancing. There is no need and yet there is love.

This is a most passionate embrace of two knowing it is one, as love sings itself into the dance, playing like dolphins swimming in the breezes. The passion play painting itself as pure delight delighting in itself. We are a moving rainbow dream. We appear and melt into each other again, falling through the falling. A swoon swoons into itself, and a ripple touched by rainbow reflection shimmers and flows through itself into a memory of a dream of what we thought we were. A bittersweetness descends. First a butterfly kiss and then a stab in the heart.

Knowing there are not two to love, yet love continues is not joy nor sorrow. This is deep passionate heart Magic.

The belief that there is a space between you and a moment
You and a feeling

.......Or thought
You and a kiss
....is immeasurably painful

And trying to erase it cuts even deeper

Moonbeams dipped in rainbows paint a memory of you across the sky. Drenched in tears the colors run through you and rise again as magnificent plumage. With wingless wings there is naked soaring, surfing rolling down banks of clouds as utter delight itself. Such a beautiful illusion, all this, magically appearing all by itself, all color sound light touch, feeling, music. Love.

Living the dream, simultaneously knowing it is a dream, a passion play that writes and erases itself with seamless ease. All that we know and all that we thought we were, and all ideas and dreams of what life and love are like or should be like fall into the canyon of wonder. Melting dissolving in edgelessness your walls fortresses of fear, your heart crumbles falling into the shoreless see. There is no more straining at imaginary ropes to keep the clouds in the sky.

Love songs weave themselves into a beautiful web that catches every tear, reflects every Moon-song. Rainbow dreams are where we live and play, and love so tragic and passion-ate burns deep this temporary tiny brief window where life can see itself, catch a glimpse of its own magic through this unique precious window of you.

Her hand stopped combing the air looking for lost or stolen jewels
And starlight swooned into itself as she found not even nothing, simply words painting castles of space.

marvelous and tragic
the ends of a rainbow shall never touch
only in the dream
in the circle of shimmering mist revealing the direction of wind

I thought I had wept every drop.
We are nothing more nothing less than this indefinable unknowable unknown, coloring painting itself like a tie dye flowing through a river of tears. Twisting twirling whirling spin-ning weaving un-weaving flowing under and over and into and through itself. Wet into wet, light into light, space into space.

Vibrant aliveness dancing as you in this river of skulls, river of joy of love, river slides and kisses its own wetness of indefinable beauty in the sunset of sea.

Rhythm-less waves crashing, sea-foam clouds reflecting in seadream'd vastness. Vast endless dynamic sky canyons bursting into bloom, fiery heights spilling blood and tears into your heart through our hearts singing madly of joy and sorrow of love and love lost. A dream unlike any other begins to form and dissolves as your footsteps enter the dance. This sublime aloneness, so beautiful so bittersweet this magnificent ache is what we are.

Soaring skinless in a warm summer's breeze, a naked ease of transparent being, a touch-less touch a soundless symphony roaring piercing light sings a flood of sun stars, as the birds hush in the noon day heat. Distant river roaring echoing the canyons stillness singing.

Simply your soft footfalls on the barren path your shadow falling before you. In the hidden under a sagebrush a cricket begins to capture the dark, a moon Lilly begins to un-whirl. All of life streaming through you as you equally and evenly as wind dances in the tree tops, you are the wind and the leaves and the shine and shadow sparkling. The taste of taste a seamless ease.

Looking out is looking in, all day I fall in love. This naked aloneness swoons through the imaginary spaces and weeps at its own beauty reflected in everyone's unique and wondrous I's. This ache of love of joy of sorrow touching itself, reuniting what has never been separate. This is a constant, oh yes, oh yes, oh yes.

The eyes of the universe looking through the prism of self that seems to break up the streaming colorless brilliance into infinite variety of shimmering treasure. Every one every sigh every tear every laugh every cry, every heart weeping laughing singing every ah ha of beauty recognized is beauty is love is me is you is we.

Without you there is no sun and sky there is no blue. There is no one to sing and no one to hear the song of the universe. Everywhere I look I see my own unutterable wondrousness. Everyone I see reflects my own sparkling centerless treasure chest. This bejeweled wonder reflects your beauty as without you I am not. There would be no delicate tender touch without the delicate wetness of your eyes, the universe touches itself through us. Utterly indescribably beauteous.

We are the river we need our banks to flow, knowing there is no where to go but to the edgeless sea, to the saltiness where tears no longer collide. We are desire itself, life moving through in and as us as through us there is a very brief glimpse of the river knowing it flows, feeling the wetness streaming through us as us. This miracle of knowing sorrow, joy, deep aloneness. Such love when our imaginary banks overflow, merging waters that make it bearable, wondrous beyond measure.

Shimmering tears are such unutterable beauty. This rawness this richness of life so many are trying to escape, love joy sorrow are really all the same ache. All such a wonderful confirmation of your beautiful aliveness.

Without the tender wetness of our eyes there would be no sight, or the delicate rawness of skin there is no touch, or the breath there is no song. Only tender leaves play in the wind and sparkle in the moonlight, just so.

We are the universe touching itself. If life were not so delicate, it would not be life.

Trying to capture life kills it, trying to figure it out is like capturing a butterfly and pinning it to a board and trying to watch its beautiful iridescence whilst it flies. When I was little my mom would brush my face pretending to put make up on me. The very lips that kiss, sing.

Singing, describing this emptiness is like love flowing through me as me with me of me in me inseparable from me as the singing paints my lines and erases them. Full and bursting forth as infinite unstoppable uncatchable radiance, beautiful in its impermanence, magnificent in its ineffable nature that can never be pinned down as there is no pin-down-er. It can never be touched as there is no toucher, never be kissed as there is no kisser, never be grasped as there is no grasper. It never understood as there are no separate things and no separate understander. It is this very not knowing is what is so stunningly beautiful. Simply a swooning constantly as into what's next, and a deep unshakable insight of the utter ok-ness of this as this in this. In this gale force wind if my hat were shaped differently I'd fly away.

What would I say if she asked? How could I reach in her heart and kiss away her fear? How could I show her that this ungraspable life just as it appears, just as she appears, is sublime beyond measure That all reaching for more or other or better, all trying to escape what is going on, is the cause of her misery?

She longs to realize that this is a dream so she could have a bit of relief from the pain of feeling separate. Yet how can I show her that she is dreamed, and not the dreamer?

How can I tell her how utterly marvelous she is, so that she would believe me? How beautiful if I would see that light of recognition. Oh yes, oh yes, oh yes, and that long pent up river of tears she so longs for, but is terrified of, as if all that sadness all that love she has been hiding in the innermost depths of her being were unleashed, her heart her love her life would no longer be hers. The love she aches for would be the end of her.

Searching frantically for truth, to untangle the mess he felt himself to be in, SOMEONE'S GOTTA HAVE THE ANSWER! Death really can't be real......

Trying desperately to believe in oneness, and that this really is a dream....
Left alone in a pile of E-books looking for god

Dreams of what life is like, dreams of what life should be like, dreams of what we are,
dreams of what we should be or could be...dreams upon dreams upon dreams...
Dreams of rainbows stacked to finally kiss the light, or that kiss you've always wanted that
touch that welcome hand, that love..
Kisses you every morning and stays with you until you fall asleep.
it was always your lips
it was always your song
it was always your emptiness
it was always your love

it is all you ever ever ever wanted
more than you could ever wish for
more than you could've ever imagined
more than you could have ever dreamed
far beyond anything you could have believed or pictured

no one is at the center of the cyclone
there is simply nothing there
you slide away and disappear into and through yourself
....yet remain vibrantly alive and fully passionately human

it is that desire that longing to let go to fall into nothingness that keeps the illusion of a
you holding on or can let go
how can a mirage let go of the water?

...and all his wishes emptied into baskets made of sand... falling through his empty hand....
he lost all sense of time in his remembering... and he fell through his own shadow
His own kiss
....and as he sang of nothing he
wove fine tapestries of shimmering echoes
....reflecting castles that could not be lost or found
....yet radiated glimmering with un-owned wonder that never left

Stretch out your hand into the sky and notice the stream of perception is indivisible.
Sight sound touch taste bodily sensation, an indivisible symphony. It is only in the

description that sky and arms and hands seem to arise. Yet all of it, the stream of perception and the simultaneous recognition of it as well as the described dream weaving and un-weaving itself happens all by itself without any effort or non effort. All flowing without edges without lines, ineffable un-capturable seamlessly fluid with out moving or not moving.

Trying to capture or hold the flowing dynamic watercolor dream scape is the flowing. There is no escape. Trying to escape weaves itself into the flowing.

The river paints itself. Rushing roaring silently streaming, a sigh a hush a song unlike any other. Stories writing and erasing themselves, never done nor undone, reflections falling ripping over under into and through themselves.

You are the whisper the song of love that calls you swirls you around in its empty glass and swallows you. Only the fragrance remains.

There is only the tip of the wave, no before or after, and the sea is unknowable.

I reach my hand into the vastness, swirling colors stream from my fingers, infinite hues arise from my breath, symphonies are painted with my eyes. Through the lens of I am all things sing their song in supreme harmony as I bathe my face in the flowing and watch the ripples echo, singing silently through the words, tumbling falling as everything and nothing. All meaning and memory have lost their hold as the holder never was, and yet there is dancing.

A single footstep has nothing to say. Life, vibrant raw unrehearsed painting and erasing itself. This amazing streaming water colored dream world constructed by thought. A streaming dream of infinite variety, the pure light of clarity erases the shadows of apparent duality, yet the dream continues much as before.

As wonder winds leave empty leaf prints in the sky, blue without end never touched this never moving always moving supreme brilliance silently singing this great aloneness this sublime aloveness greeting the touchless touch of morning of day of night of evening songs streaming falling roaring caressing all pervading limitless winds soaring nakedly skinless throughout and in through themselves. This unutterable ease, this unspeakable vastness, softness falling though softness, a sigh falling though a sigh, a hush falling though a hush, light into light...

There is a feeling that you are learning something that you're gaining ground that you are getting somewhere and you believe that you can know this that it can be known and that you can do something to get this.

Learning words can take you so far but at some point you may look down and see that you have gotten nowhere. The ever elusive gem of all that you long for is just as far away as it always was. You have tied all of those ropes of words of learning into an idea of understanding and you have tried to lasso the moon, but actually those ropes of learning ropes of air have tied you more firmly to the ground... and all you ever wanted was to fly...

If you hear your heart song there is no denying it and you will do anything anything anything to bathe in these beautiful waters of home the nectar of love
Yes ....it is the waters of home that you have never left that you seek
Seemingly muddying the waters
It is you precious beautiful girl
There is no other
There is no next
Mega tears smiling
It has always been you
You have been in love with your own love and emptiness

ALL description whether it's science or philosophy or religion or psychology is the dream...
It paints itself.

He looked and looked for what was in between the between. Every time he cut off the end of the stick there was another end, and it was sharp and it hurt. He tried to bend the ends together to join them and the breaking. Everything he did or not, there was a stick with two ends. Somehow for no reason
the ends fell through the ends, and when he saw they were imaginary he saw he was imaginary.
and he picked up that stick and walked along,
sometimes Jabbin' people
singin

he looked his entire life for the gem
the treasure the key that would unlock the door to the knowing what was going on

and every key melted in his hand
every clue along the way was ripped apart in the wind of unknowing

and his imaginary cloud of knowing blew away

even his footsteps blew away
there was no path there was no past there was no future
there was no where to go

and no one who wanted to go

Tear stained cheeks smiling in the porch light, remembering when the future held prom-
ise and terror. The past was like a deep gash slowly filling with water, the ever elusive
present a tightly clenched fist that sometimes relaxed enough to hold your hand. This
ever arising self releasing pure wonder at this expansive space with no handholds.
Sun weaves itself into wings of light
Bathing in the warmth of its own beauty and sees itself in its own shimmering reflection.
Trees dancing in the morning wind rushing flowing down through the canyon to cool the
desert sands.
soft breath of my lover.

You turn around to see your footprints but they have been washed away by your tears,
gathering in the soft wetness iridescent butterfly wings catch the evening song.

Words are like fingers pointing to the moon ....but there are no fingers
And no moon ....
Yet words can race like arrows
And pierce your heart...
what could I possibly say to strike an arrow deep into your heart my heart our heart. these
words are meaningless, like smoke signals, like empty looking glass reflections. Yet signi-
fying nothing they can pierce you. Utterly. They swirled around me like waves of unseen
joy and sorrow, pointing to the overwhelming splendor of just this as it is, never different,
never the same, and gather momentum like a rocket ship, an arrow, a haunting melody.

It's right here! it's here it's here!
....and there is no here ...
You start to smell the smoke of your life as you conceived it burning. You feel it slipping,
and you grasp for more handholds, discovering yet more smoke and mirrors. It burns
your nose your head is spinning, your hands loosen, your fingers relax and the fire fueled
by desire finishes it's job.
Winds blow down the canyon and blow away your ashes, river cools the desire for other,
for knowing, the longing to grasp the magic ends and you know you are it. You wander,
deliciously adrift as wordless wonder sings.

It felt like I was spit out of the loving arms of a warm seamless sea and walked a ravaged burnt landscape for eons. Every pool of water reflected my face but I could not drink, although ravished with thirst, as its alkaline bitterness only made me more thirsty.

I was following a voice that permeated my dreams, that promised me what I knew not, but seemed to lead me to a place of even greater sorrow. The promise of sweetness kept me walking, until the sorrow merged with joy. It was as if I had spent my whole life trying to rearrange the clouds in the sky and sometimes I thought, "oh my it's working!" Yet always they would reform or dissipate or merge in uncharted unplanned magnificent patterns. One day without any effort the blueness swallowed me and I found myself soaring naked, raining saltiness upon my ancient footsteps. Constantly sobbing my tears filled my empty footfalls and formed new pools that cut a river through the desolation, and led me to the shoreless sea. Wetness into wetness, love into love, merging sliding in without resistance back into the warm liquidity of home that I had never left.

There was never anything to get, it is more like an undoing of imaginary knots. It's like a brilliant edgeless silent stillness that moves and swings and dances and sings.
Winds paint the air with memories forgotten, brushstrokes fly softy on wings of untold dreams, and the picture is so stunning I am lost as the dance. This unfathomably beautiful dance of magic twists stories out of empty skies as they fly away on seamless wakes that cannot be followed. Clouds slide effortlessly across the canyon skies tracing un-findable moments that leaked from the day and dripped down into my heart and through my veins coloring my reflection in the sky. The universe sings my song with wordless words, striking chords of emptiness into this symphony of perception.
My lips longed for the kiss of what cannot be kissed. My fingertips yearned to touch what cannot be touched. My song echoes through the empty canyon, and I fall into the wind as the wind streams through me as me. We exist only as a call and answer song.
Light reflects so beautifully as a seamless wave in of and through our beautiful beautiful eyes. Only through your eyes can I see my wondrous unspeakable beauty. Such delicate tender wetness of our eyes shine reflecting the face of love.

He walked out in the pouring rain. Hot tears streaming for no reason for every reason, all his reaching revealing nothing, all his reasoning, no answers to all his questions. Nothing fit into the keyhole of his mind. There was nowhere left to go. There was nothing left to get.

He could no longer remember why he wept

Flying through the dream of next, there is not even nothing on the other side. There is no this side, there is no other side. There are no sides, nor non sides.

You cannot remove the filter of hope and fear, you are it. Trying smears the window, and is the dream painting itself. Trying to remove the cobwebs that have caught last year's leaves and spring seeds flying and ashes from a fire beyond the mountains, sun shimmers in this net. As winds blow it dances and sings the story of you. You have never found a next and yet you have been chasing it your entire life.

Your hands are empty, yet your imaginary pockets are full of dreams of tomorrow. You know there is nothing there that will finally quench your thirst.
There is no one to drink deeply. Life drinks itself through you.

Through the cracks in the fence long afternoon light streams across the garden. Winds breathe the dust to write messages in its sparkling. Golden ciphers flow through liquid air and are caught in spider webs, seemingly loosing their lost-ness, but nothing can catch the sun and give it concrete boots. It's all a runaway train with no driver and no one on board, yet we sit and watch the sunset consume us in its fire.

Thinking cannot untie the knots it makes, as the knots (beliefs) are thoughts. It's like stepping into a river to dry off. Intellectual speculation is endless, spiraling, circling, creating imaginary lines in what cannot be divided or split. What's going on has no edges or corners. there is nothing that can separate from it and capture it or change it. It is not an it nor a non it.
Yet the dream world of separate things and events is also what's going on, there is still no separation.
You cannot let go, or release, or prepare to release. There is no preparation no where to put all this emptiness. No one can prepare for nothing and not even that. All effort or non effort simply tightens the imaginary knots .....incises the imaginary lines deeper, and tightens the noose. There is simply nothing an imaginary character can or cannot do to see that it is an illusion. Thought cannot undo itself or see through itself. There are no special circumstances for this shift in perception. Just as all of life it is utterly un-caused.
There are no special thoughts or emotions to have, no special way to act nor direct your attention and no chooser of these things. There are simply no separate things to choose from.
Total complete and utter letting go happens but no one lets go

The river of life needs its banks to flow. To have movement it needs an imaginary reference point.
Sun shimmers on the rippling wetness and a kiss is born. An echo, a reflection, a hologram, the sparkling sees its own light dancing and loses itself again in the flow.

Songs echo in around and through the emptiness and never catch the wonder of rainbow .....but they make them and the colors and curves and pots of gold......

writing your story across the vastness ....The precious uniqueness of you opens the door to many wonderful things, including wonder. Thought create all things imaginary .....you and me and sunsets and beauty .....We are the precious window that brings color and light into the vastness .....and dancing

.....and love

And the morning winds rush down the canyon yearning to greet the desert sands

Cool it's brow

Ripple it's mirages

The loose ends of my hair and my skirt dance in the movement as the treetops echo desire

Like a great roaring river longs for the ocean begging to dissolve into itself.

Life moves dances and swings. It is all of a peace without edge or center.

Yet without an imaginary center of the cyclone there is no wind

I dip my brush in rainbows and slide into my colored garment ....it runs down my body as I slip again into and through myself, into the warmth where I can no longer find colors....

And you can't remember if you actually heard it

that echo of a train in the distance

coming from everywhere coming from nowhere

Calling you

Calling you

Home

As soon as we meet we are long lost lovers

Missing each other

she could not imagine being in the grip of hope and fear, but she remembered the pain

Like being pierced by shards of blue from a shattered sky...

And she watched while everyone tried to glue the sky back together

And her heart ached as she felt the pain of their bloody fingers and aching heart...

The longing to feel whole

....The longing for their own love

The longing for their own embrace

Which no one has ever left

Self is a diaphanous light gown swirling in unnamed tears that flow through your open centerless heart. Like a song like a rainbow, like an echo of a dream you used to just miss as you woke up every morning and re arranged your garment of fear.

We are all simply fleeting unsung melodies singing themselves. Made of off beats and rhythms, tuneless memories whistled in the dark caverns of echoed dreams. A flowing thought stream raging flying soaring tumbling rushing roaring as the tip of an unfound un lost wave between the betweens of this and that, where the source of the echo can never be captured, as there is none.

We exist only as a story, a dream. We are the running commentary, the under mutter, a beautiful song singing itself.

Songs between forever and never, and yet including both, but neither both, nor neither. Between inside and outside, exploding and imploding simultaneously, without time nor non time, yet including all illusion of this and that. This is vibrant unfettered naked raw inside out living as there is no more looking though a filter of hope and fear.

Truly truly there is no outside to this story that you are, that I am. Where we dance. There is no inside. It is all inclusive. There are certainly not things nor non-things. Yet this includes all thingness and non-thingness.

When everything is gold it has no value. When everything is chocolate including your tongue there is no taste. It simply requires imaginary separation for awareness to recognize that it is aware.

How marvelous to watch your hand pick up a pebble and throw it across the water. Skimming lightly rainbows reflecting everywhere the mountains sky the dark the light your face your smile a tear. You are indeed a soft breeze of the evening just at nightfall. Kissing me kissing you singing us.

All words are like a noose strangling a piece of sky. Seemingly creating the beginning and an end to a piece of string. A beginning and an end to a moment or thought or feeling. Seemingly creating a swirling of self referential thoughts. An imaginary reference point around which the dream swirls.

He looked and he looked and he looked and he daydreamed and he night dreamed, and never ever ever could he find an edge or an end to what was going on. He stretched out his hand and he watched his fingertips touch an idea of the end of sky, and the sky pulled him in pulled him out. Pulled him through himself. It was obviously certainly undeniably indubitably the universe singing him, kissing itself through his lips his song. Exploding imploding effortlessly this Rainbow dreamscape. Singing itself.
Just like this

This is a silence singing, humming a vibration of you and me and we. This hush of supreme spaciousness falling though its own silence. Calling out for the sky to untie its blueness, your tears of reflected echoes crush you as you fall up and through your own vastness. 'Just this', she whispered, 'yet it includes that..'

...a life free from the desire for freedom and the fear of death...

Wind slides through these words and disseminates the seeds of nothing into your empty breast. Weaving infinite light tapestries without threads it's silkiness circles and embraces the dream with the warmth of a thousand suns bursting into galaxies breathing a single note of all encompassing sound.

The song of sorrow, the song of joy, the song of wonder infused with wonder itself. Many songs all songs one song reveal a brilliant super saturated hue of infinite pure space. Words that cannot be thought about twist your lines into themselves and untie the tight knot that you thought you were. Your feet are enthralled to dance this dance of life as it dances you.

Just a shadow of a glance can shake all ideas about who you think you are.

A smile and you're gone.

There is no you nor me to be separate or joined...

Crystalline jewels of momentless moments strung together creating an imaginary timeline from here to there. Made of reflections of memories, imaginary points in time Starlight drops into itself and the necklace becomes a Garland of skulls of your own face of your own love of your own teeth gripped on your neck, your own love ripping your own heart. When nothing is left, chewed to the bone, there is nothing but imaginary pearlized heart drops of moon shadow reflecting the inky blackness

There simply is no inside and no outside. There is not a little kernel of an isolated individual you and an alien world outside. Not even a true self or pure awareness or consciousness. And all ideas about this or that or the dream. Believing in the dream is the dream. Not believing in the dream is the dream.

There is no outside to the dream. There is no inside.

The dream is all this and that, here and there, inside and outside. In and out up and down, all duality is conceptual. Whereas unicity is only intuited, so it cannot be captured or spoken about it cannot be described. It is beyond all this and that and both and neither, and yet includes all this and that and both and neither. It is not an it nor a non- it. What is not a what?

And in the evening as the hummingbirds are dancing and swirling down the canyon, and the shimmering voices of passersby tell their tales, there is always the hush that you are, the stillness of seamlessness that this is

Recoiling

Submerging

Flowing

Extending

Deepening

Shallow wing......

This utter vast clear spaciousness that we are pulled us into and through ourselves, unfolding infolding weaving unweaving endless cats cradles rocking falling spilling flying into explosions imploding utter wonderment. Sighing singing breathing us dancing us in atemporal rhythmless rhythms. Strewn like stars across the night sky draped in love light spiraling effervescent luminescence rippling into and through itself.

It cannot be spoken of and yet we are the speaking of it

And that

Simply

Makes me weep

Ripped into existence.

What can be said about what has no words?

What can be said about what cannot be said?

The illusion spins into and through itself, spiraling into and through pirouettes painting splashes on the wall of this and that.

Through the rear view mirror she watched the sun set an endless sea. There was a night-hawk, and froggies calling, and the hush of an in breath of lovers walking hand-in-hand.

Oh! This river as it empties into itself!

Like when your mother put your lunch into your lunch bag and folded the ends just so.

So that you would know that it was she who made your lunch.

So that you would know that it was she who loved you.

And you have spent your whole life waiting for that special touch, and you finally found it.

It was your touch those were your tears those were your hands lovingly folding the nectar of love into bite-size proportions.

Utterly totally and completely bereft of any ideas or non-ideas about how life or love or now or then or next are supposed to be, knowing that this is indeed it is sublime.

It is always the caress of love that you feel so deeply, those goosebumps on your skin as the wind as the breath of a sigh says I love you. There is no more concern or non concern

about where is the inside or the outside of this touch of this kiss, of this caress, of the great aloneness
Singing you.
Where is your heart weeping?
Where is it not?
When is it?
When is it not?
Is it not this flowing cascading tumbling roaring sighing screaming rippling life ripped into existence?
The moment it seems to appear it disappears.

...you are this unspeakably wondrous infinite love song constantly writing itself... soaring as vast thundering splendor through the vastness in glorious magnificence... disappearing as soon as it is heard like lightening flashes in the deepest darkness... unbound unfettered enchantment fills your being... ever lost, ever found, ever love falling into and through itself...

All 'thingness' arises in the undermutter or thought stream that many call mind and believe it to be a thing. The brain which emits thoughts which are composed of shared learned words seems to create a universe composed of this and that, a pseudo reality a virtual reality. The brain seems to either believe in this worded world or not. It has nothing to do with the imaginary character it creates.
I sing the universe as the universe sings me...

There are no separate things to have lines between them. It is the thought stream which seems to create seams. As is this line, as I am writing it, it writes me. Notice how the dream of this and that paints itself. A watercolor passion play dissolving in the river as soon as it seems to appear, looking and feeling like anything at all.

There are many who will tell you that you are already enlightened and all you have to do is sit quietly or come to their satsangs to realize this. Many sing about changing the world with a new age of awakening. There are many who sing about expanding your consciousness or finding ever lasting peace or bliss or enlightenment and will give you some technique to change or improve yourself. If you find a teacher or guru that soothes you and seems to put you to sleep, into a very relaxed and comfortable place, you have not found a true sage. Enlightenment does not happen to the imaginary character, you, and is not about feeling safe, or better or becoming a better happier helpful person. Awakening is not about changing the world or yourself or others. It is knowing that there was never anyone to awaken or feel better, and there is a consummate knowing that nothing, not you or the world, was ever broken.

She was neither moving nor non moving as she circled and spun, spiraling expanding and contracting as her breath left dust devils of fairy tale Castled dreamscapes in your minds I as she danced across the sun. Glittered eyelids could not hold the tears of future sunsets that know one could ever know. Where did your shadow and evening go as they spun into the night?
How did day find you weeping star Shadows, eyelids that covered up the moon trails beckoning you into the night time dream, lost again the invitation of light?
Where was the ticket that turned to dust when it was realized that no key was needed as the door was merely a memory an assumption between what had never been and what would never be?
It wasn't until you felt the rhythm of the night deeply and truly did you find your feet dancing, did you find your lips kissing the dark, your arms reaching for the light, your breath the sigh of the universe aching for release.
How did it happen that you realized your dance card was empty as the dance floor fell away, along with your lover? The passion play revealed to be a beautiful precious dream. Every kiss you had stolen was only a glimpse of your true unknowable magnificence. In shadowless pools where you wept as time died, as your clothes were ripped apart and fell away to reveal this untold emptiness. Dancing.

Here I could no longer pretend to believe that everything was ok...
.....that the future existed ...that life had meaning ......that my dreams would be answered ......
that sadness did not exist.....
....that I would not die......

shadows bloom in the empty wasteland
You are the light that paints in color and beauty

You may think you're hearing the words of another but they are actually your heart song revealing your nakedness. Without effort or non effort your crown topples, your costume of jewels falls off and you find there was not even nothing there. You have been pierced by your own love and ravished by your own emptiness. All ideas of beauty and love crumble. All ideas of what life should be like eviscerate you. Consumed by the teeth of your own desire.
For what would you gain if you could choose to gain it, and what would be lost on the table? Your heart would lie empty, crashing in upon itself, only a memory of dust would

remain. Yet everything you have ever counted upon lies in that dust! Winds circle and swirl these phantoms into birds of prey that eat you and spit out your bones where you used to love. With no hands to grasp, everything is free to fall, including the falling, as it has ever done and will do without the sound of time, without the noise of reason.

This flood of love rips your feet from under you and pierces you with your beautiful shining sword. Eyes and heart glisten in its radiance and the cut is swift and sharp, and deeper than you thought you could bare. A thousand suns burst from your heart.

Unadorned love pierces through all defenses and the scent of admission is free as you slide into and through yourself. Oceans of stars feast upon your nakedness. Dragon breath steams the windows of memory, angels and devils slide down the glass, and every beat of your heart dissolves the gates of freedom. Leaving no one to be free or bound.

The sky was caught in your throat and your heart cried out as you drowned in this magnificent unadorned spaciousness struck by lightening. Morning sun streams through you. You spin and spin and spin and spin. Chasing after rainbows chasing after dreams chasing after ideas of what life should be like, and it dawns on you that you have been chasing your own tale. Spinning it into existence with every turn, and you fall through himself into your own shimmering. You sigh as 1000 rainbows dreams crash into dust. It is you it is you it is you it is you it has always been you. You were the empty jewel the unbearable magnificence. Vast emptiness exploding into everywhere and nowhere, and you weep the tears of eons of sorrow and joy and they sing a million shades of tears.

Empty footsteps fill with tears and the edges crumble into this supreme silence as it sings this sublime unspeakable water color dreamscape.

It's like you had spent your entire life like an empty kiss in the dark and finally you realize you are the kiss.

Your clothes are made of rainbows and mirrored gypsy skirts reflecting tears and laughter and delight in knowing there is no one spinning, no one under the pirouette of color. Dissolving sweeping through you as you. The dance the dance the dance. Life kissing you as you kiss it, this timeless dance spiraling ever outward and inward creating an afterimage of you. Every shade, every pirouette perfect in its own light. Uniquely you this centerless gem this sparkle that has no edges.

The center swallowed itself and the ripples ran through each other. Tears ran into the river of forgotten dreams.

Love songs shimmered in the emptiness where memories lost their footprints.

Storm clouds gather. Last light dances on the cottonwood leaves as shadow sweeps across the canyon. Rock falls as a young buck flies up the steepness. Hush reveals a tanager's song. Cool winds sooth my hot face. Tears last glistening yet still falling. Soon to be hidden in the rain.

I am nothing more or less than a melody carried on the wind whose words are never written.

I read all these people who believe in the true self and it's like that imaginary little lonesome frightened kernel inside of them so many has just taken on a more glamorous costume. There is often a denial of their beautiful humanness. Those teachings sound so wondrous to seekers, because that is what they're trying to do escape the pain, escape the loneliness. They say, 'oh I am not these thoughts! I am not these feelings!'
"make the world go away"......
And the teacher says yes just look just look and you'll find that you are perfect awareness
Unchanging
Solid stable fixed. Yet there would have to be separate things to have change or non-change, and there simply are no things or non things. We exist only as the dream of separation. Under the clothes there is not even nothing there. How's about them apples?
Oneness swallows Twoness swallows oneness
Oneness and Twoness are concepts
Made up
Every word every idea is made up. Anything you can think of is conceptual, it is made up.
Like love and beauty and you and me

Looking for peace is like looking in a mirage to quench your thirst
Even those little umbrellas in the drinks won't stop the rain

All your life you've been following smoke rings. Empty spirals promising nothing but more spiraling as the distant stars sing a name that you once knew but cannot recall beckon you.
The curl, the quivering tip of the almost falling, feels like swooning, yet even falling is a concept and it has never bloomed, and it always blooming into this deeply felt wondrousness of nothingness every thingness simultaneously silently singing.
The primal quiescence, a stillness beyond measure, beyond belief or imagination, without edge or center, fills you empties you and leaves you stunned with the obvious brilliant simplicity of what was simply not noticed.
An unending awe of dancing on the edge of a feather between the named and the wordless world
Lightly she twirls laughing in delight at her own delight
What you long for is far too simple for the mind to grasp. It is only when the illusion is seen through that the painting is known and felt to be made up. That sheer naked unadorned vibrant brilliant awareness recognizes that it is aware, yet needs the transparent window

of you to do so. How hearts weave and un-weave themselves in stillness, in sky dancing self sprung self releasing seamless spaciousness calling echoing wordless wonder as it blossoms into song.

How could it be that we never noticed this unutterable brilliance singing? How we longed to escape, to swim upriver, until we realized we could not. When we realized we are the river, and that there is nothing but the river, the flowing. We had never left the liquidity of home. The river holds its hand out to reach to touch the sparkling, holds its head up to look, and drowns again in its own beauty. Ripples bathed in sunset's glow

How many words fly over the bowsprit, they splash a bit of coolness on your hot face, so tired of squinting in the sun, ravaged by stormy winds, circling and circling the vast ocean of doubt and fear. Looking for one more place to rest, one more place to pull in, one more map to an imaginary destination. There is no safe harbor or anyplace to land nor anyone to take shelter.

Words fall silently on water. It takes more than ears to hear these empty songs that tell of tales never written or sung or ridden into the sunset. Like a horse galloping ever outward driven by the scent of lightening in the distance.

Tears reflect the song of the universe shimmering in your footprints. Magic footsteps in the dark You look around and see your face everywhere. Songs flow through me and paint my colors on the window, they wash away as soon as they are seen.

When the story of you isn't constantly reinforced, those tight threads may loosen, and that idealized flying carpet you've been longing to escape on may begin to unravel, and infinite iridescence that was confined to your imaginary wings begins to sparkle everywhere.

A chink in the wall of fear of unknowing let in a light so fierce so bright so piercing he began to weep, and the crenelated battlements of wind swept castles began to crumble. Fabricated walls of hope and fear and tomorrow ripped away at the seems as all he had believed he could count on fell away. Slammed beaten broken into infinitesimal pieces left to burn in the wake of desire, winds of forgotten memories and aches of future goals blew into timeless space. The crown had toppled off, the anchors let loose and bejeweled wonderment shimmered. Knowing he was but a beautiful dream a story a magician's tale, he no longer believed in anyone's stories there was never anything under the costume, there was no one having a life. He was a breath a sigh a star shadow falling into and through itself, brilliance unending beyond imagination touching itself through him as him.

Uncountable stars seemingly strewn haphazardly are our own immeasurable beauty. Lungfuls of light form rainbow winds that breath you shadow into shimmering sky.

Unspeakable vastness without end or direction flow through you like ancient heart songs you had forgotten, left on a lonely beach where only the moon remembered dancing. A sigh a breath a song left unattended merges with an undeniable aliveness that has no name but is recognized and felt deeply.

Feathered kisses of light reflecting in your beautiful beautiful eyes. You are the light and the reflection. Through your lips life kisses itself and sings its song. You are the shimmering mirrored reflection a brief window through which life catches a glimpse of its own majesty and mystery.

Time loses all meaning, yet in this dance with imaginary others, we speak of the future, we sing of the past, all the while never never does it seem real, yet somehow more vibrant and alive simultaneously. When there's no fear all the stories are beautiful. Like rainbow kisses alighting on my starlit cheeks.

Uprooted like a tree twisted out of the banks by a storm, swollen raging river careening down the canyon, roaring into the moonlit plains. You'll never regain those cement shoes. nor will you catch up with the moon.

Waves of grasses sparkling in mid day heat caress my heart as breezes cool my brow. The moon was caught in a puddle last night, yet leaves no trace in the mud.

we are memory's shadows

When somehow the brain which has created this phantasmagorical world sees through its own charade, it comes as quite a shock to realize suddenly that there are indeed no things nor non-things.

Falling through the mirror, sky swallowed me, earth buried me. There was no bottom nor end to nowhere. There was no beginning or edge to everywhere. Never always here nor there. There was never ever any other, I had been in love with my own love and emptiness! Oh my how I sobbed!

We are no longer an isolated lonely kernel surrounded by an alien world. The story of I am explodes into the stories of we are. We are everyone's stories we are the stories of all people who have ever been we are the stories of everyone who will ever be.

Like infinite parentheses, an ever blooming flower who's petals are hands, radiating light.

Infinite spaciousness vast beyond measure swallows you as you fall into, as, and through yourself. Like slipping into your own river of tears, love as an idea is often the last to go. A sage is the wake of love's demise

This is always the most infinite intimate embrace. As you are love the loved and the lover. An edgeless dance of one of two of none. A constant total swooning of everything into everything, of nothing into nothing, of all the lovers who have ever been and all the lovers who will ever be, like infinite parentheses of hands cupping and dissolving into an overflowing rushing roaring river of love. There is no one or thing separate from you, yet there are imaginary spaces in between us created by thought so we can waltz like the canyon slowly moving towards the deep bottomless ocean.

Your hands that grasped for other for better for more for next find themselves empty of even emptiness as they slide into an afterimage of themselves and ricochet endlessly like reverberating echoes that vibrate the strings to a heart song that used to be yours. You recognize the magic of the knowing there are no things, no ideas, not even love, that can be grasped as you dance this timeless dance of life, and life dances you. There was never a you to leave home nor a home to leave, yet you have always been embraced utterly intimately by yourself as there has never been another.

There is a sublime melancholy knowing you are nothing more or less than this infinite kiss kissing itself. That you and all you have ever known or hated or loved in this passion play have never existed. Yet there remains the water ballet singing your name and you pirouette into the flowing falling in love with everyone you meet. I catch a reflection of my own love and beauty as I swoon into and through your eyes.

We are Infinitely faceted Spinning centerless jewels reflecting reflections of nothing going nowhere create shadows of love streaming across and through the mind stream.

and if I could I would write you a love letter with your own tear o you could taste your own unutterable beauty

Climbing rivers to reach the sun, you fall again and again and again. Slippery sliding through endless oceans your tears become hotter as the planets and stars pour through you, and your heart bursts and bleeds as your very blood writes your story in sky. everything is lost, even the losing cannot be found, and all your hopes of even one more moment are dashed against endless blue. Shards of shattered dreams become ancient stars which shimmer in an unfindable vastness, yet are no longer sought. There is nothing to gain or lose, nothing to add or take away when everything is lost, even the tiniest secrets of what you believed life should be like cannot be found. Sourceless light consumes everything and nothing and imaginary lines of this and that erase themselves.

The desire for eternity, or even a next, vanished into the fathomless depths when a midnight song swallowed the day. Trying to grasp the meaning of meaning by wringing the moon of all its light, to drink deeply it's magic, only burned the hole in your heart into a vast recognition that the longing for magic was indeed magical. This empty Supreme spaciousness pushes away all ideas of this and that. Nothing has any more or less meaning than the wind dancing in the tree tops, an echo in emptiness, like growing a flower in space. this Timeless momentary, with no before or after, no better or worse, no other or next, reveals a shadowed veil of nothingness, a dreamscape of what has always been obviously apparent, simply life as it seems to appear, a dancing dream rippling across an edgeless empty sea. The echoes of after images dance as purely spacious magnificent dreams. And from the vast edgeless emptiness of space, echoes the sound of laughter and tears strewn across the vault of sky like ancient footprints, a treasure map that always led to this.

Moonlight floods my basement and I lap it up like wine. drunk on intoxication I flood into seamless sea, and kiss the saltiness madly. It pours into my teacup Unbidden, and I see myself laughing and weeping. The unseen unheard Ahhhhhhh... Swims to the forefront and kisses me on the mouth. the frog becomes a prince as it's crown topples and falls. I dance around myself and pirouette with my shadow. chasing after rainbows the horizon grabs me. I slip through the cracks in the sidewalk and join the dancing upside down. It's always love that rips you apart in the end and brings you back, weeping and laughing tears. What could possibly be more gorgeous than this rich lush immeasurable life? It's a ripple left in sadness running its fingers through your hair. butterfly kisses roar like a lion and howl at the moon. the dance of unknowingness is always on. It rides on unseen currents and floors you with it's brilliant beauty. The sky swallows you and you know the clouds deeply, intimately, as they are you. Your tears water the clouds that pour across the desert dream as you left looking for nothing and found the dream of everything sliding in you as you through you, of utter bereft lushness and richness, emptiness ever blooming ever wilting.

This symphony throws itself at your feet and you slip into unbound sea. It plays you as you play it, your fingers lost in the heart strings of a love that was never yours. your head lost in this uncontained melody of one of two of many of none. you no longer look for your part as there are no parts, and your feets always know how to dance.
Flower lanterns surfing waves of grass, soundless light ripples. colored murmurs bowing twisting turning and bobbing up again, always ready to play or to soak in the breezeless evening, and whether lit by sun or moon or invisible star dream, this dancing dances itself. Sliding down rainbows and up the other side we are catapulted into the untouchable sky, with butterfly kisses as wings. falling stars caress our cheeks with tears. Blooming, the dawn rises everywhere and nowhere.
Unabashedly I sing with passion and fury from limitless space where the wind rushes through me as me. Coming from nowhere going to nowhere, aimless and magnificent.

Oh! To all who care to listen to the stream of nothingness, this utter perfection is ensured, never beginning never ending, always beginning always ending. The zing of life as it seems to appear, this edgeless momentary is not separate from you. Your very breath is the whoosh of love! Your very heartbeat is the heartbeat of existence itself. Could you ask for anything more than everything itself? I show you yourself, naked, blameless, timeless perfection.

It was just a beautiful dream that you were the mover of clouds

Falling Into your shadow you disappear, sliding into whirlpools, only the whirling is left. In ever widening spirals of ecstasy, galaxies of wonder sing as shooting stars carry your song into the vastness. This place you looked for beyond the waves includes them in your beautiful liquid eyes as you have become this placeless place consumed with awe, constantly erupting into a flower of infinite beauty. Petals falling into themselves catch the evening light reflecting off the canyon walls, softness falling through softness. As rain pours down onto unused ladders and diamonds fall into the sky, you leave your chair of sheltering fear and gaze with wonder. The painting paints itself and you appear riding into the sunset on your beautiful pinto pony. Falling softly through the stars, your breath an echo of where you once lived.

I swam through moonlit ripples and tasted yellow through the saltiness. I sank in my own heaviness and looked for a shore to climb upon. Hand fulls of water hand fulls of air, tears could not comb through midnight. Hours could not erupt the day. Distance lost validity when it could not be crossed. Arms and legs and hands and lungs and hearts could not stop the floundering the flowering the lostness sank into itself. Peering into the vastness I could not see a thing, but I knew it was intimately beautiful, this infinite unknowing. An oboe wind filled my sails and I returned to the edge where everything kissed nothing and love recognized its own essence where dreams were made.

Like wax burnt and gathered at the base of a candle, telling tales of wine soaked evenings smothered in kisses spilled on the table cloth adding to the flowered print. Embroidered day dreams picking pinholes in the fabric of time that can never be stitched together yet illuminating a story of you.
The razor of thought cannot mend what was never separate. Its more like falling off the edge of reason, like seeing that the net of thought words can never capture the essence of wetness, of whatever is going on.
Ahhhhhh... The flavor of life

The unspeakability, the untouchability, the deliciousness of not knowing or needing to know to capture. Eau de life is life itself. It is unlike anything at all.

Love songs like spiraling arabesques forming and fading. Patterns rippling into and through each other basking in the noonday sun. Swimming falling teardrops I find you in my dream. Effortlessly beauty recognizes itself through imaginary separation. Through your beautiful beautiful eyes I catch a glimpse of my own beauty. Through our eyes life catches a glimpse of its own beauty and majesty.

Aloneness sings itself into a dream where lovers meet and fall through each other. Dream threads stitch themselves into a tapestry of unutterable magnificence. It falls away as tattered memories of love clothe the dream. Rippling bejeweled wonder sings of tapestries unknown. I fall through time and place. Dreams like shredded remnants of prayers lost themselves in the echoing blue.

Stillness sang of the ripeness of shadows lost and found, dancing in their own laughing madness. Plucking at my heart strings reaching reaching reaching. Plunging into the bottomless night where every secret was revealed and scattered across the vault of midnight. Turned inside out desire unabashedly wrung out every tear and more. Leaving only an edgeless brilliance singing to itself.

Morning wind rushes down the canyon telling tales of pine clad mountains clothed in swirling mist, unknown animals crying in the night, overgrown trails leading nowhere, and tattered sails wafting in the desert dream. Without these songs of love that are carried in the words and fly through our open window our hearts cannot be pierced with tales of promises of home. The spell of dreams cast by belief in a new dawn and a perfect love is broken, yet stories remain dancing our beautiful love songs echoing reverberating throughout the night and daytime dream.

You cannot hide from your own brilliance as there is truly no where and no thing to hide. There are simply no edges or outside to what is going on. Somehow I find that endlessly amazing, and sing of this unceasingly! Life simply doing itself. A constant explosion of the symphony of perception and the inseparable recognition of it.

there are no separate things or events or moments to have perfection nor imperfection, yet knowing that feeeeeeeeeeeeeeeeeels well, perfect, super saturated, naturally complete and at ease always, without time or non time or place or non place or anyone to leave or arrive at their own perfection.

It's like you're strapped info the confines of belief, an avalanche of concrete that has shut out the light. Sharp edges of black and white carving out your world, a two dimensional cardboard cut out of a life consumed with hope and fear of a never arising next. Suddenly the fabric of your universe collapses. The bottom falls out and you slide through the cracks of all the unyeilding beliefs of who you thought you were, and you discover there was no one under the costume of belief.

The reaching out fell into and through the reaching out as tears subsumed in their own wetness, light fell into light, space poured through space and a hush beyond measure embraced itself from the inside and out. There were no sides nor non sides, or a song without other.

Lost in puddles of emptiness, drowned in unanswered dreams. Reflection of the moon ripples softy across your forehead. Wind catches itself in the reflection of treetops dancing in its own shimmering shadow. Suspended jewels hang in this web of awe, flying into themselves. The loose ends will never be caught in the tangling.

This life this unbound love was longer yours. It soars unimpeded, unrehearsed, unbidden. This delicious unknowing settles in to your innermost being and transports you into the mist of unrehearsed forgotten rainbows. The imaginary lines that created this tinker toy world fall away and all that's left is a streaming sublime edgelessness. Utterly stunned by this boundless beauty, this utterly amazing dream, where love seems to be the heartbeat as it flows unencumbered by fear. Swooning in the ever new ever freshness the universe flows through your nakedness and a gentle breeze or a wisp of a cloud sends your heart skyrocketing.

Love songs echo in moonlit shadows never touched nor held yet embraced by their own kiss sliding into a sublime spaciousness where all your extensions of reaching out dissolved into pure stainless brilliance. Life a constant swooning into and through itself, dancing falling crashing into and through all names and ideas of a dream time song that has never left nor begun nor caught in its dance of utter awe of its own wonder.

A contrapuntal dream scape fell into a shoreless ocean rippling a soundless song of endless mirrored wall less canyons dissolving as mist in the morning sun. Bathing in its own essence a seamless ease akin to love and joy yet without edges or place to point. Moon exists only in its reflection. it cannot be pointed to, there is no one or substantial thing separate from this dream of light. It is all moon shimmering reflections of reflections. it is all gold radiating in all direction without direction or dimension or place or center or edge. Flung like jewels across all and everything our tears reflecting our own wonderment

our own beauty

our own love

Crickets sing their love song in the dark the moon silently shines. I'm just waltzing with the moon, rainbows in my hair, dancing in mid air on the edge of the dream..

How I love the feel of naked hearts singing

As sunset colors pierce the lengthening shadows in this

The first

And last

Dance

Beautiful tears stream through your bareback eyes

A song of silent sorrow floods in a joyful rippling of love shared.

In the end there is only the song

Singing itself

Echoing deeply in and through its own iridescent rippling reflection

He could smell the breath of midnight as the dance unwound, the first step, the last step... He could no longer tell and no longer cared. In the pause of a moonlit breath she crept in and stole her own heart. Like a stolen kiss left by an imaginary lover, all your world merges and falls into itself. I collapse as well.

A pile of empty clothes left on the bedroom floor. Under that rainbow raiment there was not even nakedness.

Stars and space, inseparable flowing naked as moonlight. Songs of lonesome shadows are strung upon the fence ripped apart by your own tremendous love. The moonlit road like a golden river carrying your edgeless heart.

Love is the center of the dream. This is where our waves collide and the only place we exist, between love and not even nothing, only the shimmering flung out into as and through everywhere and no where.

Night seas crashing on an unseen shore

Empty winds caress my face

Laughter from the shadows

Illuminated by tears

Splashes taste of love

Spiraling as ecstatic wonder into reflections of starlight exploding through your heart as your empty song is strung with moon and plays the breath of midnight,

Wind blows

Tears fall

No reason nor non reason is life's overwhelming beauty

and you find that what the sages have been singing about is simply this, your own life just as it is

We meet in the back beat of night where moonlight sways in its own perfect rhythm. Echoes pool in the clearing of reflected light and sing of the obvious beauty of light on light.

Howling moon winds itself in lovers hearts when all hiding places have been turned inside out. How beautifully the dream sings with reflected love light whether it is words tapped across this screen, or lovers faces slipping through my mind stream. This touch-less touch is all we can know, feeling the indivisible nature of all and everything knowing there are no things nor you and me to kiss.

This is all there has ever been and yet never was. Such sublime aliveness arising as the dream of you of me of we.

I'm not a philosopher
I'm not here to convince you of anything or nothing
I'm not a psychologist
I'm not here talk about your problems
or heal you
I know you are utterly perfect just as you think you are
I am not enlightened
I cannot give you anything
Or nothing
I am just like you
Except my brain has had a profound shift in perspective
So it no longer feels like there is a me a center doing life
Or that life is happening
To someone
All the imaginary edges have no one to cut
There is an overwhelming deeply penetrating sense of peace that is always on
And it is simply so stunning so amazing the feeling of awe is continuous
It kisses me awake in the morning
And I sing

Morning mourns the loss of night dreaming day into the dance of light. How beautiful when it is love's desire that paints the dance to no where. Long grasses waving on the meadow touched by long morning sun. Infinite shades of greeny yellow oranges dancing effortlessly for no one. No one knows what life is. We sing our love songs and share the awe and spin softly into each other's dream.

These waves of kaleidoscopic colors as sound feeling sensation merging into appear-ances of forms swinging swirling dancing. How wondrous our imaginary lines form as we speak, imaginary spaces between us form and love slides in. Only with our imaginary identity can our skins vibrate and sing when we touch, exploding into infinite colors and sensations that boggle the mind and are felt deeply and weave tapestries that as they simultaneously unravel we can call the song love as it sings itself.

Streetlights shadows pick out the crest of the wave a lonely tune on a tinny speaker rhythms the night into a song of skies dreaming. You cannot capture a drop of moon and put it into your heart. It is already there.
All your ideas and thoughts about what life is about, or supposed to be like is like opening an umbrella under water. They merely seem to obscure the light, the iridescent wonder on the surface. They don't keep you from getting wet. Trying to mine the treasure the treasure is missed, lost in a hole of darkness, crying, and my words are your words and you know this. My heart is your heart. No heart escapes the inevitable loveliness the inevitable aloneness
insatiable tears for no one.
Starlight the patternless pattern in unbroken sky. Thought and emotion blow like the wind, ease-fully without obstruction. Unborn and unceasing this magnificence appears as all things. Shifting light leaf shadows on the carpet. Soup boiling on the stove. Heartbeat in my fingertips. Moving fleeting intangible
Magic
Life unadorned, raw naked, beautiful beyond compare. This is it coyote, your one and only life, and it is not even yours.

There is no one who you really are
Not even no one

I longed to fall to loose myself and I simultaneously longed to be held. Such a deep deep fear of feeling all that love and have it wash away. What would I be without it? knowing deeply that there was no controller yet desperately trying to cling to hold onto life created a wall of fear, behind which a frozen heart longed to bleed. All that love that I held so tightly could never fill the emptiness I felt inside or fill that hole of longing. After a lifetime of tug-of-war, the imaginary wall between inside and outside melted away and my heart dropped as love bled into the dream. It was never my heart my love my life! The vast emptiness inside exploded and imploded into everywhere are no where, and ripples of loveliness shimmered in the evening sun, and I stepped out into reflections of echoed dreamscapes loosely clothed in a light gown of awe with not even nothing under this nakedness. love a dream like all things pools in rainbow clouds and soaring without belief in tomorrow, or hope and fear of life of death of love.

I tried to find the magic of an empty bowl, I heard the ocean and my heart song echoing on the freeway and saw the moon Whirling into a paper cup, but just as I tried to swallowed these Cloud reflections like castles under the sea, the sea swallowed me.

I swam and swam but could never reach this dream of peace of love of wholeness, and the waves reached down and grasped my hands and the bottom reached up and swallowed my heart and the radiance in between pulled me in. Every hope and dream crashed, and fear was no where to be found. I did not look for them, as the hunger of a lifetime was over. The search was over. The seeker was gone. I could not remember why I had wanted to fix the sky.

We are like the ocean without a shore. We spill into ourselves and it feels like love. We drown in ever present joy and sorrow as our hearts break open and never close again. they were never ours.

My heart sank as I believed I had missed the magic. That emptiness I felt inside that voracious hunger for what I knew not lingered on the evening breeze and hung on a heartstring, hovering... Into the still deep despair of a never ending night. Until day swallowed night and night swallowed day. Infinite permutations of wonder bloomed into smiles and tears. Hopes and fears and dreams of next falling dissolving like morning mist in the pure brilliance of clarity, Where shine and shadow are known to be illusion, yet color the dream of twoness with a feeling akin to love unowned, vast beyond measure or opposite. Thing less wingless soaring.

Sun and wind articulate these songs into soaring cloudbursts where they could be heard and pierced the hearts of only a few.

Her lips sang of an unheard untouched loveliness that pierced him to the core. His lips mouthed the words, longing to kiss what could never be kissed

A primordial song of vastness undreamt, a vibrant hum beyond everywhere and no where. A placeless place without edge or center spinning madly in vibrational hue. infinite colors bleeding into and through each other rippling contrapuntal heartbeats of this and that as emptiness overflows into and through itself.

Standing dancing soaring weeping drowning falling up. Dissolved in space and light and the winds flying down the canyon, as a sigh unsung yet felt deeply fell into and through a sigh. Softness falling through softness, space flowing into space, light into light. Brilliant uncaused baseless untouchable perfection touching itself through you.

There is no method or practice that allows you to be who you already are

You are a flowing thought dream there is nothing not even nothing underneath it or having it. No soul no source no true self no timeless awareness no pure consciousness. Belief in God or a soul keeps the self relevant. There is no one who you really are. Not even no one not even emptiness or nothingness.

True self source God timeless awareness pure consciousness these are all concepts that people turn to when they have a glimpse of their essential emptiness. It's really like a bigger better me.

It's like using the number zero as a placeholder so that the entire equation does not collapse. There is never ever awareness without perception or perception without awareness. It is only language that seems to divide it. Self is the belief in separation it cannot let go. There is nothing separate and apart from what is going on that can accept it or reject it or surrender to it or hold onto it or let it go. All trying or trying to not try simply perpetuate the most painful illusion of separation.

We are our beliefs and preferences, underneath them underneath the costume there's not even nothing.

and sun and wind articulated these songs into soaring cloudbursts where they could be heard...

and pierced the hearts of only a few

That there is someone to attach to beliefs is the belief in separation

Crashing through a tsunami of sea into infinite sky. Gazillions of mirrored shards of blue reflecting my tears as I was pierced and shattered, eviscerated by love's heart magic.

Knowing and feeling there is no next all hope and fear and need of a morrow disappear. Eyes licked clean of the debris of worry and despair.

Now these sublime liquid eyes gaze upon a world of many wondrous things knowing that there are none sings. Such tender delicate eyes gazing out gazing in self illumined wonder.

AUGUST SONGS

Morning delicately and tenderly unwraps her golden treasure of song that whispered your name in the dead of night. Blooming into the day dream of you and me and we, such softness of this caress of light and shadow creating a canyon of echoes where we dance. This unutterable warmth that floods the empty songbook when I greet you bathes my heart with a certitude of this wondrous intimacy of a touchless touch. I am not. you are not. We are not without each other

The unspeakable beauty of your sublime aloneness and the magnificent dream of love Swirling together into this life of a sage who swoons in love as love through love with a seamless ease falling through the awe of simply being. When someone says you're beautiful or I love you there is nothing here. Yet all I can say to others is I love you you're beautiful.

No longer wondering yet in awe of this magnificent emptiness of even love and emptiness, it feels like a summer love song streaming through every pore of my being that has no tags nor confines. The why's and where's and who's left the empty house as the floors and walls and ceilings vanished in their obvious transparency. Echoes resound through this brilliant unknowing, a flowing breeze pirouetting my mirrored skirts seems to dance me along.

I sing of what has no song yet sings me.

How many tears to wash away the wetness you seek? You were never more than tattered prayers, hopes and fears of your own undoing streaming in the wind. Words resound in the vault of echo's absence and sink into your heart of shadowed dreams. This death of certainty leaves only reflections rippling in the breeze caressing your beautiful tender cheeks with a love song that has no words yet includes all words. Even the wind sweeps itself away. Crashed into your infinite kiss, waves of shadows cannot undo this love that you sought but always were in this timeless embrace of nothing and everything.

A long camel ride under the desert stars strewn like memories across the darkness. You used to try to make sense of their patterns and capture their unknowable magic. Now you cannot find a space between their obvious light and magic and you.

It never had to made sense why starlight was so beautiful

Why it took away your very heart

Why this amazing life...

We are description. We arise in the thought stream, we are a flowing thought dream. All thingness is made up, including you. There are no things that can be glued together into some kind of place of rest or understanding or wholeness. Most mistake description for understanding. We are description. There is simply no one to understand and no things to understand. And that can't be understood

So sublime to listen to the heartbeat of existence of this and that swirling through the mind stream, there is nothing to attach or grasp and nothing is believed, not even disbelief is believed. This is a permanent end to belief in the dream of separation, yet requires the dream to be recognized.

Fleeting echoes of echoes seem to catch the wind but wind itself is merely an unknowable caress of a caress and requires a cheek to be kissed.

How many words between you and sky?

He saw the distant shore glimmering moonlight dancing and longed to escape his homeland, and set sail in a frozen ship of fear and hope. His desire burned deep and started to melt his imaginary vessel his heart started to bleed, and he realized that every league he sailed created the distance he was trying to cross. He asked me if he would drown completely, but there are no guarantees. There are many desert islands where fear can hide. Nakedness unwinds itself

Every secret corner of your being is ripped inside out

It is an excruciating process to be eaten alive

Before he could retreat, the idea of distance

And time collapsed upon him

As he drowned in the sea of dreams

Everyone is like radiant jewels strewn across the vault of sky, I am awash in their tender nakedness and beautiful tears. No words, not even a gentle touch can convey this undoubtable beauty that I recognize in everyone I see, yet sometimes there is a hint of an Oh My, that rushes through our hearts, as they catch a glimpse of how I see them.

Its all in the touchless touch, a sideways glance of what cannot be seen but it is felt deeply and recognized. Hair streaming, blood boiling, skin melting, tears flying, this fire raging within, bursting burning, spinning so fast! Trying to locate yourself you fall apart while falling within, collapsing into yourself, and find yourself caressing your own heart, smiling. Vibrantly streaming kaleidoscope dreaming, arising in the center of swirling thoughts handed down through eons like a string of Christmas lights reflecting in a mirrored hallway. Out of these learned words that seem to divide reality into separate bits you appear.

Voila! Yet the end of the sky can never be found as the edges of you are illusory, and there is no line around the sun, or a moment, or a breath, or your heart. All that you tried to avoid turns around and kisses you full on the mouth and rips your heart out

And love pours into everywhere and nowhere it was never yours

The lynchpin holding up the umbrella of fear collapses. A lifetime of light and love and beauty pours through, and no longer dying of thirst you bathe in the crystalline waters of home that you had never left. When this settles down down down into the very synapses that created the illusion of separation there is utter seamless ease and a simple joy of being. There is no fear that any heartbeat could be your last as your heart soars through the clouds clearing the wasteland of mirages that you mistook for reality. Your tears water the seeds planted long ago, the blossoms open with the sun of desire and the perfume of loveliness that was always here fills you and flows through you as you.

Shine and shade singing through moonglow, we are simply shimmering echoed dreamscape sailing on an edgeless sea.

You lean down to kiss your own lips, they sparkled so as they sang of love. As you fall into your own shadow you drowning in your own love your own tears your own reflection. You realize they had never been yours, and your hands your heart have no edges as they fade in the bloom of dusk

Your hands are empty your tracks dissolve. Footless we dance. Wordless we sing. No where to go this one note samba dances into the screen and explode into infinite beauty. Twirling in the island dream. Darkness hides the clouds that cover the sky.

Streetlights shadows anticipate my steps.

As I walked under the half moon through a warm and stone still night, oh how I yearned to warm my shivering heart in the gaze of a love gone cold. How many moons ago, I don't know as time has lost its edge. But to find my love song left unanswered was the final piercing blow, as summer's songs enticing rhythm moved me to the floor. I looked around and found no other weeping in the stars. I turned around and walked away and smiled softly at my memories of the dance.

Centerless brilliance saturated with awe. Nakedly playing in the splashing tides. Smothered with kisses drowned in your own love

Tears unraveling a thousand dreams. Mirrored reflections tumbling into kaleidoscopic colors bleeding through the lines illumined by awe. I look at the low light of orangy yellows playing through the leaves dancing shadows on the canyon walls and see infinite unexplainable beauty. What's going on expresses itself in infinite variety and some sing. Love and awe burst forth exploding in songs that are rarely heard. They flow through me

and I am like a bottomless edgeless cup spilling rainbows in the sky and most hear only the clouds crying
I am the horse the rider the desert dreamscape the rising moon. The dark breath of shadowy night sings me as I sing it.

Every last tiny belief in other, like a tiny shard left from the tip of a knife wound pierced by loves heart magic must surface and every one hurts like hell until it breaks open a festering wound that must be seared by your own love. Our tears flow washing away our very nakedness, revealing not even nothing.

Life does itself and is not made of anything or nothing not even god or emptiness or love. Knowing and feeling that there is no source and no things feels like love however but beyond any ideas we had of love before. There are no words for what has no words yet includes all words. This is far too simple for the mind of this and that to grasp. How could you catch that which has no edges or corners? Simply marvelous and superb.

without someone to listen I have no song, and there is no singer

You may find that the love you longed for and yet feared has turned around and kissed you full on the mouth. Reached down into the deep dark secret corners of your being that you did not know existed and pierced you and burnt you and consumed you. All that you thought you knew of yourself and your world unravel into tattered clouds raining endless tears washing through your delicate wetness. You may spin for awhile looking for a familiar face, a loving embrace, but you cannot find anything or anyone who will stop this ravishing pain, no idea or hope or dream will fill this astounding utter blankness.
The searching for handholds may stop and you will recognize everyone as your familiar face, and all and everything is your infinite intimate embrace. There are no reference points and no place to land as everywhere is home, yet no one lives there. Such a marvelous unknowing when there is no one to know or not know, no one to be confused or non confused, no one to be free or bound, no one to awaken or stay fast asleep. Gazing out is gazing in when there is no need to grasp life as it swims through you as you. Such unspeakable beauty in simply life as it seems to appear. This seamless ease this sublime awe this marvelous bittersweet aloneness of no one to kiss.

The dissolution of the belief in separation, in self and others and thingness can be scary. Hanging out on the edge of the known world. Intuiting that the conceptual worded world is made up. Here the longing outweighed the fear. And bit by bit, belief by belief, sometimes huge swaths of them would no longer be believed. I'd think, ' Oh my! I don't believe that anymore!' And ya know, I realized that I never had.

There is nothing you as a conceptual being can or cannot do to make this utter ripping apart happen. The nakedness of nakedness reveals itself on its own. The ravishingly beautiful evisceration of you and your world hurt like hell, but I never fought it. Somehow it felt just right.

We stopped by the old house. The garden was gone the grape arbor was gone. I ran up to the side and found that the grape vines were merely cut and growing on the ground. What are we but whispers of memories dancing in the dark?

You were the song beckoning in the night that told you there is something to get that was outside of you. The wall of fear of unknowing has to crack on its own, and when the light and love start pouring in, well, it may be terrifying at first, as they are the very bricks the walls of who you are. Most quickly repair any breach in that wall with new beliefs about how the way things are. But some are programmed to enjoy the fear and longing and the shedding of layers of beliefs about who they are and what the world is like and any ideas of truth or meaning or non meaning.

You were but a dream dreaming of a better dream, and looking for ideas like peace and love and enlightenment created and sustained the illusion of a looker. Round and round and round we spin, and the spinning creates an illusion of solidity. An imaginary center of the spinning cannot stop the spinning.

Somehow the longing outweighs the fear, and the imaginary walls between you and the world, between imaginary 'things' begins to crumble. The imaginary knots that tied a you into a world of things untie themselves, or knot How beautiful that aching heart that you used to think was yours!

What the hell

Who the hell

Why the hell

Where the hell

Are you?

Where here and there meet, where nothing and everything kiss and fall through each other. Where before and after dance in an atemporal symphony a placeless place that is undeniably sublime, yet like nothing at all. Winds of change you feared so much simply carry you away and with all your pockets turned inside out there are no more secrets to conceal. Velvet lips kiss your softness as empty flags unfurl, and catch your breath of the universe singing you.

There is no thing that you truly are. No true self underneath the dream clothes. There is no under or outside the dream. Not even nothing. You are I am simply beautiful echoed reflections. Infinite mirrored glances ricocheting like a gazillion parentheses, hands reaching and touching a seamless touch of touch itself.

It's like when the fullness rushes in

We return to an empty house

All the rooms are vacant and hollow more empty than empty

The shutters hanging by one nail banging in the wind

The doors and windows broken out

The cobwebs have blown away and they are swirling around on the floor with old leaves and dried flowers and primordial dust and he ashes of who you once were you

Now the ceiling and walls and floor are all transparent it's no longer feels like a cage, and sunlight and moonlight and starlight flow through you as you

And you find that old pile of clothes left on the bedroom floor

Those old comfortable shoes that know how to walk

And songs begin to flow through you

And write your imaginary lines

Just

Like

This

It feels like 3-D wallpaper swirling on the surface of deep sublime peace. Some call it love. Some call it life. Some call it madness, it needs no name as it carries you away. Ships un-manned are traveling through these wild uncharted seas and deep within loves sparkling gaze they penetrate your dreams. Clouds unleashed fly away and have no point to reach. Silver bells upon my toes I jingle as I speak, golden winds fly through my head and urge my heart to sing.

Happily the village idiot sings and flowers bloom.

Humans have the ability through language to objectify their experience into seemingly separate things or ideas with unchanging qualities and characteristics. A dog does not eat his own foot and through sensory memories including pain and pleasure seems to navigate his way through life, but he has no word for river. When we see a river we recognize it even though it may be in a canyon or plain or emptying into a lake or ocean. We have ideas about its flowing. We can even recognize a picture of one. However when a dog reaches the edge of water and land, he is not thinking river or lake or ocean, and that it why it obviously seems new and fresh.

We have names for ourselves that contain ideas of solidity and unchanging qualities and characteristics like extrovert or awareness or consciousness. These ideas or 'things' like river and tree seem to compartmentalize the flow of what's going on and isolate them.

That is cool as humans can imagine rearranging these things like making a boat out of trees for crossing a river.

However, this imaginary world of separate things and events is painful as humans imagine and feel themselves to be separate from the rest of what's going on and it some how doesn't feel right as they have a memory or a deep intuition that there is no separation.

So when this profound shift in perception we call awakening occurs all imaginary separation is known and felt always to be imaginary. Suddenly there are no separate things divided by space nor separate events divided by time, and the angst and fear of the assumption of personal volition disappears. It is felt deeply as a huge physical and psychological release. It is obvious that life happens utterly spontaneously without any effort and no longer feels like there is a you doing life or that life is happening to a you.

Life is infused with the joy and awe of simply being. It's like time dies. There are no more what if's or what's next. No more self judgment or self correction and no more trying to fix or change other imaginary characters or the world, as it is known and felt without a doubt that you or the world has never been broken.

So man is unique in that he has objectified the streaming perceptual input into seemingly solid and stable things. Ideas about what's going on. Some of these 'things' have a physical counterpart like tree and rivers, but also ideas like god and love and beauty. Only through this objectified perspective is there an imaginary knower of what's known. Only through this imaginary twoness can there be a recognition of unicity.

We as conceptual entities exist solely within this dream of separation. Outside of it there is not even nothing. Knowing that it is indeed a mentally fabricated pseudo reality and that your character is made up there is no longer any attempt to escape the only world we can know. There is simply no more hope and fear and angst of belief in separation in self in personal volition. It is known that through this brief window of life knowing touching feeling itself through you there is the experiencing fully the entire range of human experience.

She tried to find the ends of the ends so that she could lace them together and weave them into and through each other so that there would be no ends nor beginnings. Her fingers fell through light and space as she reached for the reaching.
Out through in
In through out

Up through down
Down through up
She fell through herself
Laughing
Weeping
At the utter enormity of spaciousness. The astounding weight of lightness. The total magnificence of vast emptiness. Beyond lost and found. Nothingness fell through not even nothing. There was simply the hush falling through itself. A sigh swooning through a sigh. A freedom beyond any ideas of freedom breathed her into a blossoming effervescence without place or time. As an unowned sparkling dances.

She was the wind and the clouds sun and light streaming roaring echoing down the canyons as they soared through her. Clear skies and storms and lightning and thunder and the ease of deep green pastures and the ache of mountain streams tripling through Rocky meadows into long endless deserts heating in the midday sun swirling mirages rainbow dancing almost forming almost kissing and yet never touched never grasped.

The kiss falling through the kiss
Beyond time and non time
Just this
Life kissing itself
Through us

Life cannot pass you by as you are not separate from it.

I have been wearing rainbows since I first discovered them when I was eight. For so long I hoped that they would rub off on me, and lo and behold I found I was it. The prism the unique lens that creates color shape form love and beauty out of not even nothing. We are the sparkling reflection
Uncapturable
Unfigure out able
unfettered
uncaused
unbidden
Rushing wiggling twisting turning into unfathomable uncatchable shapes that disappear as soon as they seem to appear.

Out of the inky blackness shimmering rainbows echo the ripples on the surface, merge and explode, into a brief shining shimmering iridescence. Always the sunset colors flow, adrift on a sea of dreams. Sun slides across the sky falling effortlessly through an edgeless fathomless ocean, dissolving back into greeny blues, leaving ripples of echoing memory floating on the sparkling that fade into nothing.

It's a passion play that writes itself with invisible ink in the vastness. Dissolves into itself just as it is written. By no one. For no one.

Ribbons of wind flowed infinitely petaled blossoms through my mind stream. Playing as rippling showering love through fields of color.

Every moment is like finding the magical butterfly ring that you thought you lost when you were a child.

What you have been longing for is right here right now and has never been separate from you. It is not some special state of peace or bliss or happiness or the end of sorrow. It is not expansion of consciousness or finding a magic key that will open the door to a place that is not already everywhere and nowhere.

It is not discovering that you are some rarefied thing like pure consciousness or time-less awareness or a true self that is separate from the symphony of life that plays itself. It is not about finding your rainbow body. It is simply the recognition that you already are awareness aware of being aware through this passion play of you of me of we.

For when have you not been aware? When have you been separate from awareness, or the stream of perception? When have you been separate from your tears or your joy or your sorrow? When have you been separate from the feeling of the wind on your cheek or the wind? When have you been separate from thought? When have you been separate from the feeling of your feet padding on the sidewalk? When have you been separate from the perception of moonlight dancing on the water, rippling so lovely in the warm summer breeze? When have you been separate from life? Has life ever been separate from you?

Hasn't this vibrant aliveness always been on? Have you ever been separate from it? The slipstream of life flowing through you as you? Truly all of this happens by itself, like your breath at midnight whilst you sleep. Like your heart beating, your eyes seeing, and your brain recognizing what it is you see. The seeing and you are not separate are they? The sound of the cars motoring down the street is not separate from you. All spontaneously occurring without any effort or non effort.

How amazing! Life has always done itself and you thought you were doing it! The thought that you were doing it arose perfectly and seamlessly as the thought stream of all this and that. Indeed all perception and the simultaneous inseparable recognition of it, self arising and self releasing, without time or non time, arise evenly and equally without any effort without anything needing to be done.

Wow! It is truly beyond belief or imagination this edgeless life, for I cannot find an outside to what is going on, can you?

Truly this is all I have ever longed for yet beyond anything I could have wished for. Always on always perfect, never ending never beginning always ending always beginning, seamlessly life kissing itself through your beautiful lips, life seeing itself through your beautiful beautiful eyes.

You have never left your infinite intimate embrace.

You are a story writing itself with disappearing ink
Tears slide down a river

All we can know or understand are conceptual bits put together into frameworks that seem like they make sense into some kind of understanding. Like exploding the sky into a gazillion shards and gluing them back together.

Yet the feeling of fluidity of unicity, the knowing feeling that all these little bits are indeed conceptual, allows us know that there truly are no separate things to know or understand and no one to understand them.

No one really has any idea what's going on, yet you can know that you are an idea.

All looking seems to create ripples that obscure the transparent clarity of seeing the ripples as imaginary, a self perpetuating loop.

We are imaginary painted thought dreams recognizing our own love light reflected in each other's eyes...

shimmering echoes in the dream

She looked for the meaning of sadness in the wetness of her tears
How many oceans would she have to fill
In order to feel whole

Tattered sails in the midnight sun dissolving into nothingness...

How many tears were left uncounted as Dragon clouds scratched sunlight into your mind?

As he fell into and through placelessness. the lyrics of the onion ripped off and he discovered there has never been anything there. An empty jewel, leaving only shimmering reflections.

Empty flowers bloomed into a radiant song that was heard by no one, yet the singer cried a love painting that pierced his heart. Colors merged into midnight dawn and sailed away on a rainbow ship. He chased the beauty until it pulled him in and through this centerless center. Awe seems to explode like a fountain and songs flow though us into a tapestry as this rainbow dream paints itself.

Words rush around this empty room and can never escape the lines they are written with, tumbling sweetly, turning on a dime. Dancing breaks through the barriers of silence, and roaring thunder rips down the canyon splitting a path to your heart. Love cleaves you into a gazillion pieces and you just can't and don't care to put the pieces back together, your hands refuse to move as they are dissolving into the dance. Like a suit of armor stung by lightening, brilliant light is revealed. We emerge utterly naked vulnerable tender unafraid, new like a butterfly, wet with tears. Such beautiful utter nakedness of life unencumbered with hope and fear.

Moonlight floods into your nakedness, and you swim into yourself into the cool clear waters, liquid luminosity, where you never left, of home. Every drop of rain reflects infinite rainbows

smiling.

Bejeweled tears dripping from every interstice as the fabric of the dream weaves and unweaves itself from moonlit shadows under the beckoning sky.

Words slide off the mirror as it shatters into infinite shards and you are ripped apart, pierced and shattered, falling though all images you have ever thought you had grasped about the world and yourself. On the other side of the mirror there is not even nothing, you have been devastatingly beautifully breathtakingly ravished. There is not anyone to have hopes or fears or religion or preferences or a future or a life or love. Under neath the costume there is not even nothing.

Yet you cannot choose to loose the tattered skin you've been living in as you ARE it! How I longed to rip off my cloak of hope and fear. I spent a lifetime trying to run away from sadness. I believed I was looking for love, but I was really running away from that true intimacy and honesty and the knowing deeply that there is no next. I had felt that I had been trying to hold onto life, and that there was constant tension of trying to 'hold myself together' surely if i let go for even an instant I would fly apart into a gazillion pieces!

After this most painful personal Armageddon that most go though before this uncaused profound shift in perspective happens to their brain. You re-emerge, yet it is always known that all thingness all separation, and you, are a made up story, feeling deeply yet impersonally.

Life as a human being is filled with great deep deep sorrow and unutterable joy, and love, and love lost, and all of it is wondrous. How magnificent that anything at all seems to be happening!

This is it coyote, this dream of separation that we are.

Knowing it is made up and feeling this seamless ease

is marvelous and superb beyond measure.

And so you were raised with a bunch of beliefs that no longer ring true
and so you search out and find some other beliefs that sound more plausible but basi-
cally it is a searching a reaching for something solid and stable and fixed that you can
hold onto
And you want these beliefs you need them
for what would you be without them mostly they are a mental construct about time
and how things are
How they used to be
And how they may be or should be in the future
There's great hope associated with these beliefs
About how someday perhaps you may feel better
Or perhaps the world may feel better and the universe
Your friends and your family and your loved ones
But in truth you have never found a next or another or a better or a more
And it's starting to gnaw on you that most assuredly you will die
And be forgotten
And you know where did you get these beliefs
Where did you get the first ones where did you get the new ones
They are all hearsay
They are all learned
What is the most terrifying thing to you of all is that possibly underneath all of these
beliefs there is nothing there
And so you will keep grabbing and grabbing grabbing at straws
trying to construct a home a place where you can live and where you will never ever die
Under these beliefs there is nothing there

Just imagine a wide expensive universe filled with vast deserts and towering mountains
reaching into the sky and sky reaching down to touch the inside of the valleys and rush
down the canyons and kiss the shoreless oceans and shimmer across the sandy desert
dream, with no edges nor non edges no outside nor inside. Seamlessness is unimagi-
nable! Imagine the whole universe weeping and smiling and laughing and sobbing at the
same time, imagine everywhere you look you see your own face, or perhaps it's someone
elses face. A faceless face recognizing its own kiss. Intimately familiar and yet wondrously
mysterious.
You smell the flowers that flow on your gypsy skirts swirling in the wind, and you are the
dream caressing itself as softness falling though softness. The tightly clenched fist had
opened, as if tied with knots that unlaced themselves and even freedom flew away

ahhhhhhhhhhh this unbearable light, this wind kissed dream, languid liquid, an edgeless flow of starlight sunlight moonlight streaming from everywhere and no where.

Traceries of patternless patterns strewn across the rippling sees, shimmering echoed glances shadow play of memories and moonlit dreamscapes trembling soaring vibrating into song silently whispering your words across the staves of spidery nets that never caught a sigh

life sings us......... and we sing

Songs flow through us and we watch astounded as our imaginary lines of awe seem to paint us into the dreamscape, flowing glowing wind and sky pouring through us as us. How spectacular this knowing feeling of inside out turvey topsy living, raw naked skinless, flowing fluid unfettered streaming transparent being.

You found you were an empty shell of memories. You could hear the surf your heartbeat the world surging whirling spinning the lacre embossed starlight singing. Light streams through your prism window and colors of infinite hue and timbre bloom on your doorstep. Stepping lightly delightfully bathed in your new lightgown of awe spinning whirlpools where ever you step on the groundless ground. Your footfalls had always been empty, just shadow play dancing. Your arms had never needed to hug the universe as you were always hugged by your infinite intimate embrace, you all are all encompassing, the inside and the outside of a gentle caress. You found your tears that seemed would never end had no end. The warm liquidity of home welcomes you, "hello, I love you" you hear your voice sing. You had never left.

Lets go sit on that bench by the sea and watch the sun streaming falling kissing the orangy reds reaching up to swallow its own reflection...

only with imaginary twoness

can we fly

Butterfly wings and nighthawks in the dark of silent stealthy footsteps that you reach out to grab and find they are your own. There is no other but it is not the you that you think you are, yet includes it.

Ahhhhhhhhhh

The fullness and richness of life just as it is

the longing for the longing

for the longing

for the longing

all of it always was simply a pretense

An ignorance of the beautification's of life

Trying to rig of the sails

Adjust the winds of time

Desiring an outcome
Of no desire
And why pray tell would you want to lose your beautiful humanness
Does it hurt so much
Do you long so much
To be dead
Tristess in the dark
Cricket song
Midnight dances... fairy rings spinning into song
Feather light sun streaming through you as you
Butterfly Kisses in the night
Simply a beautiful ache in your heart
.....and it is no longer yours
It was merely a dream of you and me that we could hold each other touch each other kiss
each other, that we could hold the sunrise in our beautiful hand in our marvelous heart...
a moon dream
like a treasure in your heart that need not be opened
Because it is you
Your name is written with tears on the river and you are pulled along as the great flowing.
You began to see that you name is a flowing echo of this unknowable scintillating alive-
ness rippling streaming without interruption.
The delta of your life approaches and you no longer look for the winning hand. Your
pockets your sleeves are empty. The magic card is no longer searched for. The silence
was always singing of this unknowable magic that could not be found or lost as it was
everywhere and nowhere. A deliciousness of all you had feared had become the non
holding of emptiness and fullness as there is no longer an empty hand...
You see the sunset and smile, tears reflecting you unutterable wonder at this brief beauti-
ful human life...
In the vast trackless wilderness faint suggestions of trails appear, and soon you are learn-
ing to color within the lines. You learn how to draw the birds and flowers, and you draw
yourself in, a paint by number set, where every color is known....
Yet the beauty pulls you in as you are lost in the redness in the light in the flowing. Light
runs through your fingers and your tears and wonder drenches your heart until it is no
longer yours to give or hold
found and unfound in a shoreless ocean, and you are left with simply magnificently plainly
overwhelmingly marvelously
this

My heart beating madly it flew towards the end of the sky, looking everywhere looking nowhere under the stars behind the rainbow for a place to rest. Finding nothing, searching for love, I found only my reflection in your eyes. It slipped between the cracks and I chased after it madly. The journey wore away my edges as love grabbed me by the throat. Choking on my own tears I drowned in unowned sadness. Beautiful shimmering wetness caught the sunlight as they fell, weaving a path to nothing. Carried in the bowering heights of my sweetest dreams like a crown they toppled and left me naked and bleeding, unafraid of the piercing unknowable brilliance that I am. Utterly empty skies reach down and capture my heart. Wrapped in tears rainbow rippling iridescence, never not sung, this profound unknowingness is always on.

Empty mirrored skirts dance in ocean breeze as nighttime descends upon the island, and no one knows when day turns into night, no one can catch the day. Opalescent clouds feather the moon. Slumber closes her eyes. She dreams the dawn. Cricket song fills the night air. Soft footsteps echo. It is me I present to myself. I listen and wait. A night bird calls. I am a song no one hears.

Unfathomable beauty everywhere through these liquid eyes

Midnight flowers close at daybreak and droop by early morning and only the moon caresses their tenderness. Yet their essence sings in my dreams as a clear sweet stream meanders through this canyon in ripples that reflect morning light, sun sliding over high red walls. Watery designs repeat themselves on the sandy bottom and echo in sky. The sun is never caught and the bottom moves slowly. Footsteps softly padding, walking in wordless wonder, swirling unseen ripples flying back into sun. Forever opening, forever brightening, inexhaustible love. We envelope the universe as the universe consumes us. Waves wash through you revealing a brilliant vastness beyond comprehension. Immersed in your own kiss the sky and sea reveal a silent echoed shimmering song. Mirrored emptiness dances, fills you empties you, flows through you, is you. Vast beyond measure, all encompassing submerging subsuming all and everything the song of one of two of many of none.

Spirals of light stream through light, I am enveloped consumed subsumed flooding washed away into light itself. Folding and unfolding a weaving unweaving itself, of endless beginning and ending, space soaring into a tapestry of dreams sliding into and through itself. Simply stillness kissing its own kiss.

Without other self is not so. We are magnificent reflections of each other. When the ends meet the timeline spins into itself and disappears. There never was a center to the swirling. We are simply and most marvelously the imaginary transparent lens through which the unknowable unknown catches its own reflection. And sings.

Beyond that which we think we know there is a wall where thought cannot go, and we fear not knowing. We use others descriptions to whistle the darkness away. Aliens, dragons, god, grabbing anything any concept no matter how absurd to avoid recognizing our essential emptiness.

That avalanche of fear. Oh! How we suffered in the darkness, frantically searching for the light switch. Grabbing and following every Map we could find. As we are the walls we cannot climb them. Thought cannot see beyond the known worded world. Yet there is knowing of this edgelessness, and to speak of this wonder we can only use the tools that created the imaginary lines in the first place.

It is fear of unknowing that seems to create a wall around your heart and it must crumble on its own, as you are it. Where was your heart when you last saw its edges collapse into the flowing? How could it be that life was meant to be held or the sun sliding across the vault of sky? Or that waterfall of beautiful tears? Or the wind? Or love?

No one can touch your salty tears, everyone is drowning in their own ideas of sadness, like ladders scaling ancient walls where treasure lies bleeding, searching for another path. Trying to drink the ocean with a teacup, tears pouring, heart despairing, you may suddenly see your reflection and swallow yourself. drunk on love, and that great hush before the dawn never leaves when there is no more waiting for light, as all is light.

You are the imaginary line between this and that, Inside and out, you are the dream that you are trying to escape from. Knowing there is no escape this transparent shimmering mirage becomes wondrous beyond measure. A transparent window of chiming overtones of awe.

Crystalline ships of forgotten heroes cast shadows upon unseen lands as your footsteps are forgotten where you believed you were treading. Love cracks the edges and rainbows slip into the flowing, and there is no doubt that this is home. Stretching quivering tenuous feathered fingers stretch out,

simultaneously reaching in. Folding into rushing streaming through each other, opposites collapse, your heart drops. there is no middle or ground in which to hide or land. soaring utterly amazed in a sea of dreams where earth and sky have kissed you from the inside out.

Your heart has exploded into infinitely colored and hued spirals extending through a vast untenable spaciousness without end or source, singing a chorus a symphony heard by this unknown vibrant alive super silent stillness that sings it and sings you. You are the vastness between the breath and the song and the breath and the song. The wetness of your eyes betray that you know this deeply.

Imaginary distance is only needed to feel the lips brush each other. Feathered hearts dance slipping into and through each other. It is always a perfect fit. Your song was in my heart before I met you. Whose love pours through me. Whose songs flow, I no longer care to find an imaginary reference point. For all love songs are written with the same words. Reverberating echoing from within from without from everywhere from nowhere. Always the first and last kiss.

Is not magnificent we can feel so deeply? Aren't they the same feeling love sadness longing joy... All such a beautiful ache. It is our very humanness that is so wondrous.

We are threads of gossamer light dreams weaving themselves into a circle around the sun. When the feeling of trying goes away, when that gripping stocks and life goes along simply as it always has easily without anyone doing or not doing anything and nothing to do, no where to go. No other better more next. The center was imaginary. it is everywhere and nowhere at all.

We are a patchwork quilt of learned and shared beliefs and the brains natural preferences, a truly infinitely intricate stained-glass window coloring in the dream with reflected unbelievably beautiful light. Rainbow colors of every hue of every timbre of overtones and undertones resonating vibrating into a frequency a song of I am. Weaving into the song of you and me and we. Unraveling at the seams as the tips of the threads dissolve into pure space leaving only a shimmering ripple in the air.

You stretched your hand into the rippling iridescent light and sound kalidescopic dreamscape stunned by the utter beauty sparkling shimmering reflecting your beautiful face and sky and unknown vastness.

Trying to catch the rippling waters was the rippling. The dream weaves itself, it cannot be caught as there is no outside to this infinitesimally marvelous sea of dreams. No shore. No escape. As outside and inside is the dream. looking for the magic is the magic...

Where always and never fell into and through each other. Place and placeless Ness. Meaning and meaninglessness fall into a vastness without edge. Space and emptiness and nothingness are known to be the dream. There are no reference points whatsoever. You no longer long to fall into the stars as Suns and moons and starlight pour through you as you.

Coalescing in a timeless breath to sing

These

Tears

The air get so thin as the view gets higher and higher.... And the breath the songs cannot flow..... you reach the edge of the known world and realize the dream is all you can ever know. You find one foot in the dream world so you can dance and sing and kiss. As all ideas of movement and non-movement are made up, you simply disappear into the flowing as the flowing. After the shift it is easy to for the character to continue the passion play that was already there.

It's like you find a pile of old clothes by your bed and you put them on and the shoes are comfortable your feet fit just so. They are your dancing shoes.

How can I sing of what cannot be sung? The hand looses its grip on the pen and words flow like tears as the saltiness longs for the edgeless bottomless ocean where dreams were washed away and only this light this light this wonder fills the ever present falling through the falling.

There is no such thing as a mind much less a still one. Like a still wind, mind exists only in its movement as it is the thought stream . As you are a streaming thought dream, you are painted by thought. You are not separate from it. All seeming separation comes from it.

By naming it emptiness or mystery or magic the mind feels it has put what is going on into a box, and one believes that they are someone who has understood that there is not even nothing. Yet there can arise the deep feeling that all the boxes are empty, and tears melt the cardboard.

Your trying to catch the magic becomes the magic, and trying to catch the rippling iridescence in the stream paints the rippling iridescence in the dream.

As the hand reaches out to grasp the fingers dissolve, and all pretense of knowing is subsumed in the wonder of not. There is nowhere to rest and no place to land, and no one left to look for a place to hide. There is nothing to hide.

Simply an all pervading brilliant stillness pervading the rippling iridescence. You are but a dream, an echo, the imprint of a memory on a breeze. An afterimage of a dream. Overtones of a soundless sound.

Wondering at the wonder, in awe of awe, delighting in delight. The magnificence of imaginary separation!

You are the jewel you have been longing for your entire life!

Chasing after more colors in the rainbow only left you with sky tears...

How effortlessly clouds form, and how effortlessly they weep. How the rush of love silences your looking for other. How naturally the universe dances itself, unfolding riotously, without any pushing or pulling. Never done the poems are unfinished and sky erupts in your heart.

The outline of the sky and the inline of the tree shimmer into and through you, as you, and leave nothing but the rippling of a feeling whispering love songs into your heart.

There never was a key there never was a door, you are an imaginary window. How many years and years of tears and tears did it take for the painting of the sky to wash away and reveal your inherent vastness, exposing the fraud of tomorrow.

It is realized that you have never left home, and that there was never anyone to leave or arrive. No one to ask how do I get out of here? No one to look for a map or ask for directions

To nowhere. To everywhere. No one to ask where am I? There is no more where.

No one to ask who am I? As there is nothing outside of you, there is no outside, nor in.

No one to ask when am I? No time can be traced or found, no past nor future nor now.

No one to ask why am I? No movement can be traced, no path to be found, or goal.

The very ground has fallen away, earth has swallowed you, sky has embraced you, space has fallen through space.

The questioner himself has gone away. He was simply a misconception of separation. A belief in other better more and next.

This passion play continues to write and erase itself. Dream Castles painted with light in light. Air in air. Space in space.

Even oneness is the dream. Anything you think of is made up.

....dancing naked in the rain without any notion of how wet you are...

How can you catch a sigh
how can you capture a hush
How can you cast a kiss
Without anothers lips
How we ran chased by un-named terror, desperately frantically down every promising alleyway, around every secret corner. Somehow believing that there was light at the end of that tunnel, a place where we could rest and find the end of fear, but not realizing our hope was the same as fear. We fervently believed there was someplace something other or a magic pill or a certain book or phrase or philosophy or something we could do. Something we could catch or grasp to stop this hurtling into death.

Every pathway turned out to be a dead end... rushing headlong into a brick wall. Somehow someway we turned around, headlights pinning us to the wall, exhausted, realizing that no more running could be done, facing ourselves we collapsed into ourselves and we lost ourselves. We lost everything and found nothing. Yet it was all we ever wanted.

Words like tattered raindrops sweep across the dream
Magnifying and erasing that which cannot be kissed
With lips with teeth with eyes with minds
With tongues with language with words of love
Whirling and whirling and whirling
Like an echo chamber where love bounces about and never dies, yet always hears its own song beckoning waiting for deep release into itself. Into a constant union of what has never been apart and that has always been, without time or non time.
An unending sigh a river of tears uncounted unowned
Merging in as of and through you
life itself
dancing
Her tears were dipped in rainbows and sang in the wake and the fleeting memory of iridescence that once touched you. A butterfly kiss in the dark. A song you sang when you were young and had never heard.
Once this love is known this infinite beauty that cannot be captured as we are all poets with deeply unprotected hearts.
Yet the imaginary separation is what makes the reverberation, the resonance the dissonance the imaginary lines that let us know where we are so that they can disappear and we can fall in love again.
You fall into and through yourself and disappear and reappear with magic in your lips and smile and tongue and heart, an unending sigh a constant union an ever knowing of. YES.
You realize that what you have been searching for so desperately so adamantly so frantically your entire life is just this
As it is
Nothing other nothing but never anything other than this
As it is
simply so

Searching endlessly for love, hungry for an idea of love, once tasted the scent remained in my heart. There was always a glimpse of this delicious unknowing luring me, I was trying to capture it. The orb untouchable setting on the horizon, and failing again and again and again and again. My hand coming up with nothing, crying despairing deeply. Oh! Everything I'd heard read dreamt faded into silent ideas, dissolved into meaningless patterns like last night's rain evaporating into untraceable sky.
Walking in the burning desert, chilled to the bone, footsteps filled with blowing sand. There is no retracing your path and no map to the imagined palace where fountains

quench your thirst to know, to love. The mirage of ideas plays across your mindstream and creates shadowy arabesques out of mountains of sand. In the moonlight they look like a place you want to be. Your camels balk at the darkness and your journey becomes lonely.

The thought that there really is a pot of gold, so many grapes you can dance in them and rivers of intoxication will flow endlessly! It's an ear worm that will not stop singing, until the sand and the sun and your heart burn, and melt, and the diamond is seen. Myriad facets reflecting a kaleidoscope of tears is recognized to be nothing separate from you. Utterly exhausted I fell, and all that remained is this endless swoon into the ever forming ever dissolving seamless spontaneous brilliance seen through. A crystalline lens of life looking at itself and moved deeply by its own magnificent beauty.
Colossal winds spill through the rips in your curtains of make-believe where you had projected your ideas of reality. The old images fade like fabric in the sun as your cloak of fear unravels, and three dimensional aliveness bursts through the flat life you once knew as a flood of un-utterable awe consumes you.
My own love turned around and pierced my heart, stabbing me deeply. I was irrevocably shattered ripped apart utterly wide open raw skinless.
Haunting melodies slide through tears, kissing your own lips, tasting your own saltiness. It has always been your own love dancing. As you pirouette with yourself you become dizzy with love, your fingers bloom...
....and sky bursts out from your irrevocably broken heart and dissolves in limitless blue...

It may feel like you're on a path. There are many others climbing this mountain with you. You may feel like you're gaining ground, you feel lighter, less stressed, your friends notice. You're having insights, and glimpses, like beautiful gleaming jewels you gather them and string them on a necklace. One day it feels like you've arrived. You put the necklace on and bathe in the glowing brilliance of your enlightenment. Your serene face draws others in, and you teach them how to make their own necklace, and you may wear this for the rest of your life, or...
You recognize one day that the gems are actually skulls, and their teeth are huge, and they break apart as they dig into your neck. The tiger finishes his job. It was never about you....
This most precious of jewels is living breathing and can never be caught or held.

The future seems so dream like after time dies, impossible really. The past simply random memories, like us. Although I just bought a ticket to Florida. Dream tickets to dream shores. Misty shades distant peaks are so beautiful, but there is no one walking there. There is no here or there. Simply a swirling diaphanous dreamscape coloring in tears.

We are simply a swirling bit of learned labels and haphazard memories. A ghost a shadow a forgotten song an idea an afterthought a phantom a magician's tale.

Unutterably beautiful, this dream of you of me of we. You are as real and unreal as me. As love. As truth. As meaning. As next. Empty shadows waltzing in the dark. Like a song you sang long ago but hadn't heard, it's far too marvelous to capture as the magic is you. You cannot have it. Its inexpressibility is its beauty. Marvelously indivisible this wonder cannot be put into a present. The very uncontainable nature of transparent seamless beingness simultaneously fills you and empties you as you are the wide eyed wonder knowing of your wondrousness

It's a trick of the tale, words seemingly creating this and that. We simply cannot find ourselves without others.

...and the mud laden river roars down the canyon carrying the mountains to the sea....

...the pines of the high peaks send messages of forest dreams...

...and the knowingness of the deep current of silence that needs no words is never lost .....
it merely seemed to be forgotten ...the water is always wet no matter how dirty ...and the sky in your heart is always clear even when lightening seems to cleave it into pieces...

And her clothes were the essence of falling blossoms her house the wet iridescence of waterfalls of tears

Her song rushed down the canyon and across the burning desert

And soothed a heart and tore another

And dissolved into rippling wonder

I walk on this path my hot black telephone in my hand speaking into the white smooth glass screen, the softness of my feet and my wonderful running shoes padding along the path. Shadows getting longer my feet walk through them. The sound of my voice my breath the sky so blue it swallows me, winds caressing my hot sweaty face, my hat blowing, but not off. My shadow to my side, mountains so vast so red with innumerable features that can never be described as there is no reference point. It's my gaze takes it all in. There's a symphony of perception simultaneously recognized and then description happens utterly naturally.

Yet what is going on can never ever be kissed with words. I can write volumes and send you a video, but you will never ever have this emerging momentary. All description happens with shared learned words, this is the dream painting itself. Once it is seen and recognized it has passed. Yet time is the dream as well, just like you and me and all separate things seemingly created, an illusion made by thought.

Knowing it is a dream, the un-capturable un-pinpoint-able marvelously indescribable un-figure-outable fleeting transparent beauty is always on.
It always feels like the first and last kiss

shhhhhhh she whispered, there was never a mountain nor you to climb it, but we can swim together as starlight

All the castles built of dreams echo down the empty streets where you once played and sang of love's good byes. They have no meaning these empty tombs, yet they ring of tears and laughter and deep kisses when you tried to suck the love out of a glimpse of freedom. Tracing the path of stars, looking for a way to fall and be held simultaneously. Summer rains streaming down the windows catch your movement in the droplets. Reaching out to grasp the beauty your hand slid into its reflection. Life is ungraspable and it will let you know every time you try. The broken shards of your life will rip you to shreds as the pain the sorrow of untold fortunes of shattered dreams of all futures and all pasts breaks away, and there is no more effort to try to be.
Dogs ripping through the garbage as shadows lift and the midnight flowers fade. Morning sun brings a song to my heart. I could never hold onto the day, or catch a shadow. The moon ripped through me when my hand came up empty every time, and life became rich as it was no longer mine.
The words slid off the mirror and we fell though. Falling though time, out of time, out of reason out of rhyme, falling through the falling. No longer trying to rearrange the sky we fall into the blue. No longer trying to count the stars, starlight floods us with raging simple beingness. Light flowing everywhere and nowhere from everywhere and no where, this unbearable brilliance rushes through you in you as you. It is overwhelmingly wondrous! We sing, yet every word a razor cutting up the sky. Knowing we cannot touch the beauty our songs slide into it.

It is all your wondrous beauty... these liquid eyes behold their own wetness and weep

There is nothing happening within without this Space time dream. It's over the top flipped in the middle stretched outside of the bandwidth of sound, and until your heart is broken the needle will skip and replay the old groove. Singing the same old love song. An endless replay so loud you cannot even hear your own breath, the heartbeat of existence listening to itself.
This magnificent dance of unknowing twirls around itself and touches the middle, yet words flow never catching the rainbow. They paint and slide off the colors dispersing pure light, glance off the wonder, pouring through the emptiness and dissolve back into

the flowing. It's a symphony of perception, one glimpse of life un-owned can enrich a lifetime, yet you will never stop searching for that forbidden taste, until you realize you are it.

Those glimpses of moonlight pierce the utter bereft darkness, through the impenetrable walls of self, of fear, and lightness pours through the tiniest of cracks. A thin place reveals a silhouette, a memory of the big wow slides across the steel doors surrounding your heart. Every taste only makes you want more, so you try harder search further, perpetuating the illusion that you have left your own embrace.

How or why this seemingly impenetrable facade is seen through, no one will ever know how these glimpses turn into a lived reality.

Your head's on fire, stories are seen through, words become meaningless air blowing through, letters merely lines and squiggles. The hot breath of emptiness calls your nameless name. You've thrown the ball for the last time, and no one catches it. It ricochets back to you and sinks your bleeding heart. Only when you've been ripped inside out can the light reveal itself, and nothing can ever hide it again, as there are no separate things. It all is illuminated as from within and without simultaneously. And a hawk soars by through the clouds clinging to the cliffs left by the afternoon storm and catches the last rays of sunlight as he emerges, not caring why or how or where he flies, and not eager for anything other than this.

Songs flow through this edgeless empty heart and waves swell and bloom and soar like wings as this fullness bursts. Surfing the fleeting light and shadow, of painted dreamscapes reflected in moonglow in a sun star'd shadow dance. Feathered glances sing of filigreed fingertips reaching reaching reaching and constantly touching themselves as in line and outline seemingly appear. Reflected in still still waters a hum a vibration a reverberation of echoes that were never sung, but felt and heard deeply. Deeper than deep, stretching higher than high, touching greeting meeting and collapsing into and through each other, the dance of this and that of you and me magically appear.

Always on, this kiss of this and that. Merged submerged consumed by this all pervading untouchable knowingness that this is indeed the first and last kiss. The only kiss we can ever know, and yet knowing it is us kissing ourselves. We are the imaginary space between the breath and the song. We are the dream of separation, and the knowing it is a dream Is sublime.

Through you I catch a glimpse of my own love and beauty

Without you I am not

Oh! The wonder of echoes, singing with themselves, a symphony in the dark.

What you were looking for dissolves, as the looking itself cut your name into the sky, and it all collapses into itself leaving just the whoosh falling through the whoosh. Drinking deeply this sublime thinglessness. Bathing in utter wonder and simultaneously spinning a two step while a whirligig constantly blows you away. Like a wish blown out, only ripples of a song hang suspended for just this kiss and dissolve in the touching.

Starlight thrusts its shadow into your heart and you explode into everything and nothing. Colored by sadness filled with joy, there was never a gap in between what has no parts or pause. No longer trying to rearrange the sky we fall into seamless blue. No longer trying to count the stars, starlight floods us with raging simple beingness. Sky swallows us, spits us out and we are always part blue.

Never found a future and your life and you are based on a fiction. Desire is the movement of life. You will not escape desire.

You are it.

Surprise

Sunset spills into the darkening canyon bouncing off rivers of rock, alighting like drag-onflies on trembling leaves, kissing cascades of roaring falls, sliding off my shoulder rip-pling down the path, bursting my heart on fire. Evening winds rush down the mountains as daytime heat loses its grip, awash in the glowing, breathing, softly walking bathed in, dancing as and through the lines of shine and shadow.

She tried to add more darkness to the night and tried to pick shimmering moonlight off the waves, but the wetness of her fingers and her face couldn't undo the clouds! Trying to ignore the magnificence knowing it would slay her and reduce her to only tears that would pick up the unbearably beautiful shimmering moonlight. She lost her self in between the in between.

A gazillion points of light shining in the darkness. Trying to figure out which one you are and how all of the rest of them go together. Searching for patterns searching for mean-ing searching for ways to rid yourself of this feeling of separation. It's the very whirling that looking for other for better for more for rhyme or reason that builds dream castles in mid air. Ripples weave themselves into rainbows of fantastical proportion and create an imaginary center. Yet they may crumble into and through themselves and only a mist is left. An imprint of a memory of who you used to be. The shroud of fear and heaviness dissipates in the dawn, and all of the points of light become a light so brilliant so all encompassing flooding through you as you, filling you emptying you. All ideas of love and peace and fulfillment and wholeness and oneness and unicity are attempts to touch this but this really like nothing at all.

All along you have known this deep down in unfathomable places, like a forgotten dream or song you sang long ago but you have never heard it. It is you. You have never been separate from home. There was never a you nor a home to leave.

Self is belief in other better more next. Trying to regain that feeling of wholeness perpetuates the feeling of lack.

We are the twinkle in each others eyes. We are the love in each others hearts. We are the song on each others lips, we are the kiss that has never been kissed. We are the pain the ache that we all so deeply feel. Life is so beautifully doing itself. A constant consummation of itself. There is never anything other. There never has been or will be. The beauty of this simply blows you away, down the canyon, wind dancing in the treetops. A waltz tango a twist a two-step. Only with imaginary twoness do we know of this aliveness that we are.

Life simply cannot be figured out. It is beyond reason and rhyme. How can there be two and one at the same time? The spiraling seems to create a trail of tears reflecting the wetness through others eyes. Total consummation in each and every inseparable moment. Light rushes through you and rainbows explode, appearing as anything at all, yet without any independent nature, fluid and vast beyond comprehension. Feeling deeply we drink this aliveness, swallowing ourselves dressed in tears of wonder, we are love's reflection, dancing. Shimmering echoes flowing across the desert sun. Words like crystal ships sailing on a breath of love, painting dream's reflections on luminous wakes, disappearing into inky blackness.

A life without memory is not.

How can I sing this overwhelming song that has no words yet has moved me, ripped my skin off, torn out my heart, even the very idea of an essence of myself? Every dream of next, every shred of hope and fear shattered like cloud castles dissolved in sky and me, left breathless and wide eyed and living in an unending swoon. Dragon clouds swallowed the moonlight deep inside my heart and exposed the brilliance of a love dance that was never mine to find or follow yet dances me as I dance it.

I am simultaneously a vast edgeless centerless spacious emptiness extending infinitely without direction, utterly vacant, more empty than empty, and simultaneously infinite color and hue dancing singing a passion play of all and everything. Delighting in utter awe as both. Life flowing through me as me. Light dancing into and through itself. When songs are not flowing through me and painting wonderment, there is only flowing rippling shadow dancing across its own reflection. Soaring skinless in a warm summers breeze falling into and through my own embrace, my own love my own intimacy infinitely exploding. I am a song without meaning that breaks my heart every where I turn. Like a kiss out of nowhere from the inside and out on a skinless heart that never ends or begins and is always the first and last. An unowned river flooded its banks and roared, its very depths the thunder of godless brilliance playing.

The current of the river continues but time died after death lost its meaning, yet the orangy reds of sunset are so beautiful on our beautiful faces. never here nor there it is all in one fell swoop an a temporal back-beat where contrapuntal flavors spread like buttery sunshine on my heart. walking in wordless wonder, ripples flow through shadow'd dreams of what I once was. alighting on fairy tale paths where I once walked. Illuminating golden treasures I tried so hard to capture, but my hands could not grasp the shimmering, and they dissolved into the imaginary spaces where empty love songs echoed. A lone shadow walked into the light of his own love and dissolved, the noon day waltzing. Yet songs pour streaming flowing through me as me from the tippy top coldest mountain peaks, my breath rushes and roars through the canyons across the burning desert and into the salty sea of tears. Surfing gliding floating as the river of song we look around and weep at our own beauty as we swoon into each others eyes.
There is no space nor emptiness between the breath and the song. Between light and color, rippling between shine and shadow, between the lips and the kiss where here and there fall through each other. Where falling turns into soaring. No longer trying to find it we see we are it.

Light dances and skims and soars through light and paints the name of dreamtime wonderment reflecting across the canyon singing I love you. Your beautiful face is mine is yours is ours. How could you not be naturally sublimely perfect, being obviously supremely human? A life without memory is not.
We are indeed
Not connected
Nor one
But the same still wind that sings our footprints in sky

The night time dream stretches its toes into the day time dream. rivulets of water colored thought paint echoing reflections of insubstantial silhouettes that play across the theatre of my mind stream. There have never been any things and never will be. Not even non things exist. The physical world is real, although real and imaginary are imagined. Nothing has ever happened yet it has always been. Rich and full beyond measure this life is super saturated wonder, a love dance exploding and imploding into song and silence falling into and through the blooming blossoming and wilting as I exist as love's reflection weeping at its own beauty.

Morning sings itself through my synaptic gaps ripping a world of light and shadow into streaming tatters of memories and thought twisting and twining and pirouetting themselves into this magnificent wind ballet. A sonorous light dance heard always yet never sung by no one by everyone, our voices silently weeping and laughing the stores of sorrow and joy, of a love unencumbered by words yet like rippling colors streaming across the vastness only words can paint us into the dream time dance where sorrow weeps a song of empty shadows lit by mirrored shards of broken hearts.

A kiss just missed. Tears never filled your empty shoes. Sodden moonlight swims through your heart.

His entire life he had been enchanted with the idea that he might one day capture the magic he just knew was around him, until one day realized he had been mesmerized with his own reflection...

Gazing out gazing in, liquid eyes lost and found in the beauty of the wetness of wetness, of light and shadow playing rippling kissing edges into a meeting of nothing and everything. Bedazzled by the beauty of beauty I gaze into my own reflection dancing in your beautiful beautiful eyes.

A seamless touch of touching nothing other than the touch itself. This kiss of this timeless ever blooming ever wilting kiss bathes a soft piercing brilliant all consuming light that dances without time. Flooding soaring stretching reaching in and out everywhere and nowhere without direction or purpose, simply nothing other than this kiss of life kissing itself through your velvet tender kiss.

We need our eyes to see, but it can be known and felt that we are baseless reflections less real than even the moons shimmering streaming across rippling waters. Thought sings and paints things to fill in the utter devastatingly beautiful emptiness with arching color and moonbeams that kiss their own reflection. Wordless wonder sings in silent shadows and erupts in the moon glow to revel in its own nakedness.

The limits of imaginary edges feel hard when believed. Sky has no reflection in water without your eyes, yet you can feel its vastness. It cannot be caught and poured into an empty glass and drunk, as it simultaneously drinks you. There are no limits and nothing to be contained. No infinity nor eternal nor limits without limitlessness, Empty beyond empty the vastness crumpled into a paper cup is ripped beyond recognition as even words like limitless and emptiness have lost their footsteps in the broad endless night.

There was never anyone to reach out and grasp the day, there is no light or dark without you.

A song that sings itself, trembling tenuous vibrant fleeting kiss of aliveness kissing itself. We are words whispered in the wind. Everywhere you look there is the melody the symphony of you.

Moonlight dances with the shadows of my skirts. Waltzing toward another streetlight I cannot find myself, yet I am everywhere. In the pouring of the pavement, the crying of the night hawk, the tears of unheard shadows, the tongues of foreign hearts, the ones who hide their longing, cricket song lost and found in the rumble of the cars, and stars hiding against the distant brilliant summer's dawn.

This dance without a name, this one without a second, not one not two not none. This raging calmness for nothing other than this.

I dove into the river and tried to swallow the moon. I cried out as the sun burst from my chest, raining stars. I crashed through the mirror of my own reflection as every shard ripped and shredded every idea of who I was and were and should be, until there was no one left to be free or bound. I was nothing more than a reflected image, an echo of an echo, an after thought, an after image of not even nothing shimmering through the mind stream.

Rushing gently the tides sank into sky. Infinite starlight swept through my heart when time died. I fell into this edgeless vastness where songs echo infinitely, reverberating ricocheting, creating imaginary rhythms in the dark, and brilliant clarity beyond measure without source reflects a boundless heart.

Knowing the only dance in town is in the imaginary spaces in between, there is one foot in the dream, dancing footless, and the other is constantly dissolving. Amazed at the beauty of all and everything as well as the unknowable unknown. There is a sublime unknowing of this unspeakable vastness. This unfathomably beautiful dream has nothing under this infinite nakedness, or under these mirrored skirts. This fantastical gossamer light fabric weaves and un weaves itself simultaneously. It was merely an illusion that seemed to separate me from starlight
Or tears

I remember feeling like I was chasing my tale, like a hamster in a cage. Truly not knowing for what I was looking. Perhaps some kind of peace or ultimate love, or an unending wow. It seems like the spinning was a life of fear and effort, running away from pain and yet the running itself was painful. It seemed to create a solid center of the spinning, making it feel like there was a me inside all the spinning. A thinker, a feeler, a do-er of life. That palpable feeling of being separate from thought feeling, action and life, quite simply hurt, so I ran faster and faster and faster...

Sometimes I tried to replace that frantic spinning with a slower spinning, like watching the breath or other types of meditation, or drinking. But it was still a life of keep spinning the plates or my world would crash and fly apart into a gazillion pieces.

Somehow the endless futility of this hit me like a sledgehammer. All spinning stopped. And as it did, yes, my world did fly apart. I did fly into a gazillion pieces of tears. And Oh! the heartache of losing absolutely everything I thought I could count on to keep my world intact. Every tool in my toolbox burned into ash, and there was no where I could turn. Until the turning finally stopped. It was like life stopped and turned around and kissed me full on the mouth and my own love plunged its greedy head through the skin the lips the teeth the gut the heart and eviscerated me.

There was no where left to hide by the time there was nothing left to hide. Every secret corner of my being had become undone. Ravaged and left to burn, the ashes blew away so beautifully in the winds. Trailing multicolored streams of every hope and dream and fear of next, time died.

From the ashes a dancer arises, a dancer of the winds. She feels she is the wind as the wind flies through her. Life kissing her as she kisses life.

Then the winds sail off the edge of even wind itself, and light replaces any feeling of solidity as there is no balancing required. Light pouring into and through itself singing of its own brilliance. Transparency slides through transparency. Not even shadow dancers remain. Not even a footprint in sky...

You are the longing to return to a song you dimly remember. Yet by naming it oneness, you feel separate from it. Always on the tip of your tongue as you are trying to mouth the words to a song that has none. Trying to figure out a dance that has no steps. Trying to figure out where to place your feet when there is no path no ground and no where to go. Trying to patch together a gazillion shards of blue, your fingers bloody your heart aches for what is already a clear blue sky.

Without words there is no unique perspective, this and that created by the razor of thought creates this point of view that we are. The two step, the dance of this and that beckons, and the figure is looked for on top of the ground. Some long for the silhouette to change places with the ground which Is Merely another imaginary place to land. All an edgeless dance of shadow puppets looking to destroy their shadow.

The light the fire the longing to burn to die into oneself, to shed the skin, looking for wholeness, oneness, unicity within a twostep is impossible. Yet imaginary twoness is required to know that unicity.

He was enchanted with the moon trying to hide between the clouds and longed for rain to hide his tears. To reveal his heart and lose himself. Yet longing to be held simultaneously.

Shadows glide on the empty pavement they have no source other than an echo of a memory of a song sung by no one, and leave no trace but an imprint of a tear that dries as it hits. A shimmering of a heat wave in the desert that beckons refreshment, yet cannot fill even a whispering tongue with words to speak of what has never been sung. Yet always longs to
Sing itself
As it does
An unfold able tearstained page in a book without covers
Twirling into a picture of you. A composite of stills that were never taken. An afterimage of pure un stainable brilliance.
Like a wall crumbling melting into the sea, the place where this and that meet and fall through each other. As all dreams die the light floods in. unadorned life flows as you, the unowned dance. A placeless place where time dies, an unknowing knowingness settles softly into the dream, and the wind flows through you caressing your lips your teeth your kiss your heart, as you are the wind dancing flowing everywhere and nowhere there are no limits to your nakedness. singing is your very breath.
Where do everything and nothing kiss and where does here turns into there and when does now fall away?

It is an edgeless point a shadow cast by an unknown dancer a prism a lens of unutterable beauty turning spinning uncatchable magnificence into all this. Splendor breathes and you appear.
A shock of reality, this pure wisdom magic Forever blends effortlessly into Pure Space when we are pierced with love's heart essence. Like a never-ending blossoming flower of love, all petals divinely illuminated as one undivided expanse of freedom beyond all ideas of freedom, we are forever moved from the painful life of this and that to the dazzling all-pervasive expanse of pure heart magic. Vacant beyond emptiness. Yet there is dancing. You see yourself reflected In between everything and nothing.
Never feeling like there is a you are doing anything or nothing, this is always an indivisible streaming. How can one use words to kiss what cannot be kissed as it has no surface or edges, and you are the this kiss exploding and imploding. As an imaginary character I feel the aching heart of others it is no longer their pain nor mine yet felt deeply. My mouth opens and songs are sung. there is no listener but the canyon echoes so beautifully as songs roar through the dancing treetops and fade into the shimmering desert. The song sings itself and breaks your heart in its terrible beauty its ultimate sublime

aloneness, and the harmony is your very own breath your very own heartbeat your very own embrace of edgeless love that opens its wings and takes you in.

You have always been this, nothing and simultaneously everything. there are no things no two, yet without dancing we cannot find ourselves.

whats going on cannot be figured out or touched as there are no things to touch nor no toucher. yet the apparent toucher the apparent kisser the impossibility of a twostep sliding along a dancefloor that does not exist. like a hologram like a dream like a hallucination an illusion a mirage shimmering across the desert of ultimate aloneness... and we drink deeply this impossible life of utter awe.

This bottomless treasure chest this passion play writing itself and simultaneously erasing itself as it is recognized, the point with no edges....

a song with no words.....

a dance with no steps....

Ahhhhhhhh

that beautiful aching heart is it sadness is it joy is it longing

Is it love

Who can say

tears arise for many things not just sadness

Here I no longer know and no longer care to find out and never really even take my happiness temperature anymore

It's all a beautiful current of unowned unnamed emotion

And it seems to soar and pull me along

Without memory we can't even know what anything is. There is not knowing that we are!

The imagined past is where we exist really. Just a millisecond behind perception

The stories are written.

We are memories and they are always fading flowing changing no one knows what memories are forming at any moment

I fly to Florida and I get off the plane and I walk around in the smell is intoxicating

Maybe because I came here as a child

I don't have a memory of it but the smell is superb

Like a pool of shimmering reflections rippling through over and under each other

And underneath a deep deep stillness and inky blackness where the deep greens and blues begin to rise mossy caves catching bits of sunlight

Seaweed flowing

Currents rising and sinking

Whirlpools...

Truly I cannot find the future or past

But I am indeed memories

They are not owned. Sometimes stories are written in tears. I am everyone's stories now as they weave them selves and unweave themselves in this magnificent three D light tapestry.

Heart songs echo in the canyon

Recognized as they paint our pictures soaring in the winds

Ahhhhhhh ..... so rich and lush this indeed love. Gob smacked mouth agape in utter wonderment.

At first I used to ask myself constantly how can it be how can it be how can it be but I was not looking for an answer

And it was not a question

When some sages say that there is no death they are not speaking about living forever they are merely referring to the fact that no one ever lived

The self never existed so it cannot die

many mistake that as a confirmation for living eternally

After love burns it's name in your heart you will settle for nothing less than swallowing the sun. River of tears cleave the canyon, mountains of rock pour to the sea, their shimmering brilliance leaves no footprint on this ribbon, heron flies low and a single feather falls.

Footfalls longed for, safe and sure, slide under what's known. The whirling dervish slips, and you see your face in her footprint where your tears pooled in her love light. Swooning into yourself the moon carries your heart under it's sleeve, weeping through its smiles.

It's like living between the cascade, falling, and merging with the river, and the mist rising, evaporating into seamless sky.

Trembling traceless shadows dance and carpet the world with shine and shadow, flowing everywhere and nowhere, they lend their silent chorus to the slow surreal waltzing of the trees high up on the hills. Suspended without time or direction I flow as the wind through my own heart, breathing altitudes of intoxication. Summer heat rises.

Castles built and toppled by summer nights dream. traffic pursues it's ever winding tale. My heart breaks. I cry out! I loved you once and it ripped me out of my heart. I have never found myself again. But this love was my own love, just a rippling idea on a sea of dreams.

I called my lover in the dark ...

and all I could hear was my echo in the stars

Words sing rainbows and clouds and sun light hiding in shadows of tears. Through the language of love life sings itself. Watching my hands crochet sunlight into song. You are the universe kissing itself through your very own lips the universe sings you as you sing it. Always without time, there is no here or now or you to transcend.

...and in the weaving we shimmer and glow in each others brilliance, and recede into the wakes and streams of love remembered... I have swooned into the rippling fluid light fabric of we are...

Was there nothing true? Was there no place to land? Were there no paths to traverse in this empty edgeless sea? He could no longer find a place to set sail, for a safe harbor. He looked and his anchor had disappeared. Where was the sun where was the map where was the starry night? Where did his tears go after they fell into bottomless blueness what was under the weight of knowing?

The pendulum swings to its highest point, the conductor raises his baton, the canyon stops in a darkened hush... A pause between falling up and falling down, as thunder crashes in the canyon echoing loudly in my dreams like cymbals in my head. Lightening burns my eyelids, there is nothing outside this obvious brilliance. I cannot escape this storm as it is me. Rain washes all color from me as the river crushes me like like a freight train and dashes me upon the rocky cliffs. All my dreams of happiness and all my fears of sadness are forgotten in the deluge. How the moon became bigger and bigger as I fell into it! No longer enchanted by stories of moonlight dreams we are stunned by their absence. This vast immeasurable emptiness sings us.

Its like every book you ever read every word you ever heard every idea belief of what you are and how the world is and should or could be is ripped apart and burnt. Every secret corner you used to hide in your deepest darkest secrets are turned inside out, many or most you had no idea existed! The ripping and shredding and burning is you. Those ideas painted your imaginary lines. It hurts like hell.

Darkened seas lose the horizon under the weight of sky. What was lost? Everything. What was found? Nothing. Not even a seed of hope a scent of rain or a dawn that may arise.

Yet after the tempest, rainbows paint themselves in the glimmering late sun and shimmer in the filigreed remnants of waterfalls dancing, and the hush, the pause, the sublime peace remains. Underneath the storms and rainbows always bathing in the warm liquidity of home.

It is like being dead at the end.

There is not even nothing left. Suspended as emptiness. Not OK nor not OK. You and time and others and all thingness is gone. And preceding that there was so much pain! The lifetime of searching is over. Your eyes are licked clean of hope and fear of a never arising next.

That was you, the desire for other. Now it is known without a doubt that there is none. You are utterly sublimely bittersweetly alone, and yet there is no you. The path the ground the sky has collapsed and you return to an empty house like a soundless footstep, like a torrent going nowhere, a shoreless ocean with tides
A wind singing
In an empty breeze

You are the garden of earthly delight
Spreading its wings the heavens unfold you, and suddenly you are the inside and outside of the caress of everything and nothing. You are we are this is where fullness and emptiness kiss. Your lips mouth the words, as songs flow painting a water ballet of sound and light and rainbow tears.
A thousand hues of now slipping into a kiss unending, innumerable stars swooning breathing your song into the night. strewn scattered rainbow leaves floating flowing suspended on a mountain stream. This rush of almost verily appearing yet dashed into nowhere before it blooms into two, as infinite petals thrust into the sky and melt into blue once they catch a glimpse of their own magnificence.
Floods of tears flooding through bottomless shoreless oceans. Ripping raging flowing sighing tiptoeing a kiss beyond measure,
always the first and last.
I can no longer find my voice in this symphony, neither close nor far and no longer caring. Not my words not your words, not my love not your love. Simply love beyond all ideas of love.

The words of a sage slide through you and envelope the emptiness. It radiates into your heart song where it had never left.
The mind looses its grasp
Just for a moment
A hush falls
Your hands off the handlebars for a breath
Like when you see beautiful sunset for just a second before it is starting to be compared to all the other sunsets you've ever seen
That mesmerizing awe
It's like a beautiful stillness a hush when moonlight floods the canyon
The lack of color blankets all and everything with an unspeakable wonder

Waltzing a footless tune across your rainbow'd eyes. Movement within non movement, edges within edgelessness, iridescence shimmering from everywhere and nowhere, no cause is looked for no answers or questions. There is no one to be confused or non confused.

Ahhhhhhh

When meaningless was seen to be meaningless...

It's a delicious unknowing and feels like space pouring into and through space. Life and light streaming through you as you, my mouth kisses the words into song and the song sings me. This touchless touch breathes and symphonies of exquisite unfathomable beauty seem to appear. A diaphanous light ballet swirls in dreamtime wonderment and smiles.

She sang of rainbows and elegant trails of color rained through the dream. She waltzed in splashing puddles and adorned only in her nakedness with joyous knowing that there was not even nothing underneath her watercolor tears.

I am a reflection of an echo of an echoes reflection. The universe calls my name yet I have none. Like blossoms falling in a midnight rain, their shadow imprint dissolves in morning sun. Falling endlessly in love as love through love as this mirrored dreamscape shimmers and sings a strange and familiar tune, I am lost as your beauty sings me.

Dancing madly in rainbow raiment in a constant state of disbelief.

The ever-present wow undisturbed

I sing I dance I fly this song of freedom. Heard only by the heartiest of tender hearts...

Love overtakes you and slams you to the dance floor and you lie there bleeding. Overcome overwhelmed over taken. Utterly slain by the beauty that surrounds and engulfs you, and needing no more barriers. No more walls. No more explanations. You are utterly and completely free of even freedom itself

undeniably supersaturated with all pervasive love and awe...

no more wondering if there are Christmases yet to come, life is always a wondrous surprise smitten shaken swallowed and spit out again. utterly free, unfettered., untied, undone

And you lose yourself and reappear, simply an amorphous unfindable non reference point. Ever shifting like sand dunes. Like a whirlpool in a river it seems constant, yet is merely patterns that seem to repeat. There is no caring if there is anything substantial whatsoever as we fall through the looking glass. Never finding anything but fleeting reflections...

And petals of musical laughter blossom endlessly and rain diamonds in the treetops...

Words are like painted tear drops pretending to quench your thirst to know, yet they are silent imaginary handfuls of air. They twist and turn and seem to weave rhythm and rhyme and slide into the deep dark fathomless embrace of time and timelessness. The tale can never be told, as it sings itself, every word is the steam rising from my tea that whispers tales of morning. Never catching space into its twining, into the fabric that is simultaneously ripped apart. This magical flowing web of description never catches anything, yet seems to create them, painting our watercolor silhouettes in sky. Blue on blue has no beginning or ending, yet is always beginning and ending, ever blooming every wilting, all and everything wrapped in its own infinite intimate embrace. Simply tattered reflections of ancient melodies that swim across pools of memory rippling infinite songs of every heart that ever breathed and every hand that reached out for love. Utterly without substance, this amazing display, this magicians tale. We are life singing itself breathing itself kissing itself through our very own delicate tender lips.

Our own warmth and light is kissed into being by this song that sings us as we sing it. Skinless nakedness penetrates more deeply than imagination can go. How unbearably intimate and wondrous and raw! We are revealed to be an edgeless centerless infintely faceted gem reverberating into and through everywhere and no where. It's the dissonance the overtones that is the richness of life, this lushness is the vibratory contrapuntal heartbeat splitting into magnitudes of forces that have no edge or name. We call it love as these intimate soundless melodies merge and and dive into and through each other, an ecstatic love dance of one of two of many of none. We are plunged into and through the tsunami of ourselves and emerge as the song of we. As the song sings itself it needs imaginary intervals to be heard as a melody. This sea of dreams needs imaginary separation to be seen. For wonder to be wonderful and love to be loved. I look, submerged, consumed, burnt on the pyre of my own love and life explodes into all this!
Shadows slide around my feet as cars flow down the street. Weaving a dance with headlight magic, this many petaled flower paints an ever changing story on the sidewalk flowing over and through my footfalls. These shadow leafy curtains weave an untraceable magic spilling into an after image of what has never happened and what will never be. Some of us who taste this ultimate unspeakable flavor of unending awe gather near the doorstep like butterflies sipping each other's nectar. Some swim in pools of moonlight delighting in the summer's breeze as light and wind soar through us, we exist as reflected light. Merged submerged drowning in tears, lost in madness laughing softly. Wandering nowhere, we sing.

MY STORY

I could never figure out why there was only one green in my crayon box and where blue green turned into green blue. I learned early not to ask who in the hell chose which was which, and I used to wonder since my right eye saw color differently than the other, one saw a yellowy green the other a blue green if others saw color perhaps entirely different from me. Perhaps what I called yellow they called red. I began to feel that great aloneness, and I would hold onto the grass for fear that I would spin into space.

I remember clearly hating it and trying to avoid being forced into boxes of this and that like, "whats your favorite color?", "are you an introvert or an extrovert?". It felt like a straitjacket. Later, however, I remember looking at people and trying to figure out what type of person I wanted to be, as I wanted love and it seemed only formed people were loved. How could I make myself loveable? I knew I didn't want to be like my Mom or Dad or anyone else I met as they didn't seem happy. I didn't want to be a man or woman, I didn't feel like either.

It wasn't until I was eight that the pain of separation hit me like an avalanche and squashed all the light out of my world. I spoke about it with my parents and they laughed and told me that little kids don't get depressed. A few weeks later my mother came into my room one evening and said that it'd get better when I went to college...(wha?)
Soon all the other little girls were talking about how many kids they wanted, girls or boys and their names. I knew without a doubt that if I had a child it would most likely feel this pain of life as I called it, and I knew I would never have children. I don't even remember a lot of my teenage years. Wrapped up in a fog of depression and layers of fat.
In my early 20's I took acid and the light of the world started to shine in. I remembered the laughing child I had once been. So I decided to be happy come hell or high water, shoving all the sadness under the carpet. It was a life of painful pretense. Self is pretense, the belief that what is going on can be known and the terror of not knowing.

To try to fill that hole in my heart, I over ate, exercised, took drugs, drank alcohol, traveled, read psychology, philosophy, I looked for it in romantic love, read books and daydreamed to try to avoid it. Pretending that I was happy was a constant. Fear was the constant. Fear of myself and others. Fear of admitting that I didn't know. Fear of loving too much, and losing love.

Pretty much every perception was judged as helpful or harmful. Every moment I judged what was I feeling. If I liked it, how could I keep it or get it again? If I didn't like it, how could I change it or get rid of it? It was exhausting and painful.

I had an intellectual understanding that there was no free will decades ago. We went to a Hare Krishna joint for a free meal as we had heard they were not too pushy. Well, I was obviously entranced with the girls beautiful butterfly winged saris and it must have showed, so one of them came over and began to try to sell me her thang, I kept just trying to run her in circles to continue eating.

When it came to free will I said I didn't believe in it. I said ya know you can never go back and see if ya coulda done something different. That ended the conversation. However actually I did believe in choice and someone to have it, as well as separate things to choose from.

Beliefs are like that.

We are convinced that ours are right. We will fight for them. As we ARE them. As all beliefs are accompanied by hope and fear, hope that it's true and fear that it's not, or hope that it's false and fear that it's true. (Like the guy who says he doesn't believe in horse shoes for luck asking where and in which direction to hang it).

It's truly obvious that there is no next, and many agree with me, but they believe there is. They hope and wish fervently that there is a next, because that belief is what they are.

I remember the first time when it occurred to me that cause and effect was a belief. I could say well what was the cause of this tea cup breaking
The falling
The newspaper I was reaching for
Or the day I bought that dam table!

I had read that a hiccup was the same as a lightening bolt, and intellectually understood that all things were interrelated or interconnected, and I longed to grok that. I longed to recognize the sameness of inside and outside.

I read many books that last couple of years, and found watching breath meditation. I did it almost all day and I was pretty high! Contriving this feeling of ease. In the end I was trying to get rid of thoughts. Even the music and pictures like vivid day dreams that filled in when thoughts were absent.

I used to meditate, "My blood flows the wind blows". Trying to truly get that inside and outside were the same, but to no avail. I was waiting for a bolt of lightening, and it happened as soon it was apparent, like a bonk on the head, that nothing I had ever done nor not done had ever brought me what I so longed for, even though I had no idea what it was!

When it dawned on me that I could no longer pretend that everything was OK, and that all the methods and practices I had used to achieve well being were not working, I was utterly stunned for a month. My practice was to recognize awareness for short moments but by the end of the month it was obvious that awareness was always on, although I still thought of it as a thing.

Then there were four days of unutterable joy and awe. It was a beautiful powerful free glimpse of the utter perfection of things, yet it was not a seeing of no-thing-ness. That shift in perspective would come in less than a year, and it was permanent.

One method I was supposedly using was to let thought and feeling happen without trying to change or get rid of them, but I have to say that I never ever felt like I was doing this, it felt like this was happening to me, there was no choice but to feel it all fully. As the entire structure of the beliefs of who I was was crashing I never tried to fight it even through the most excruciating pain, as it somehow felt just right. The first big belief fell. I had used a particular diet in order to rid myself of a disease and I had always wondered if it was the diet or the belief in the diet that had cured me. Suddenly an intense fear gripped me. I felt it physically and psychologically. If this belief left would I die? I lay on the couch powerless to even try to escape it, and just as suddenly the fear and belief fell away. I suppose it was the beginning of the end of belief in belief as well. It was like an avalanche of what I had feared ripping through me.

After that there were six months of extreme sadness and intense despair alternating with unspeakable joy, peppered with sudden bouts of impending doom. I noticed beliefs about who I was and what the world was like catch fire and burn and become transparent and fall away. I felt lighter and lighter, and noticed that memories and thoughts of future and even what was seemingly going on was losing its grip. Quite suddenly after six months I noticed that joy and sorrow had merged and I truly could not tell the difference!

I remember as so many beliefs popped, it was scary at first but also enjoyable as many of the beliefs that were leaving were the beliefs I didn't like about myself or the world, that I was unlovable etc., or that others were. But I remember it suddenly hit me oh my all these things that I believe in that I like will also have to go, that I am lovable, or that there is something called love!

After that there was a period of intense anxiety, I would lay on my bed of nails every night, sleepless, gripped with unknown terror. There was a point when I realized that I had thought of myself on a path, and that I was 'getting' somewhere, and I just knew that that belief had to go. I remember sobbing hot hot tears. That too was absorbed somehow, it was obvious that phenomena were uncaused.

In my tradition the 'goal' so to speak was called 'going continuous'. I had no idea what that was but I wanted it. I was trapped in that most magnificent conundrum of everyone saying there was nothing to get yet that you would know when that happened.

At one point my desire consumed me. My chest hurt and I could hardly breathe, it was worse than when my mom had died, and I kept trying to talk myself out of my desire. It finally burst and morphed into a marvelous overwhelming love as I saw there was nothing to get. I realized many years later that this was a mourning of my own death.

I had the very clear picture of myself before the shift of trying to grasp something that had no edges that was very slippery and there were no indentations there was nothing I could get my fingers into to hold. The other vision that kept happening was I was in the backyard with a butterfly net jumping very very high and trying to catch the air I didn't know what I wanted but I knew that I wanted it and I was beginning to realize that I could not have it.

I started to recognize every face as mine, not in form or substance but an undeniable recognition. That has never left.

Two weeks later I was cleaning a stove and suddenly the rag became my hand became the space became the stove, as all lines between things between moments and between myself and the world dissolved. There were no separate things divided by space! It was like the scales had fallen off my eyes! I was astounded that life happened without a me doing it! There was a palpable incredible bodily and psychological relaxation that accompanied this shift in perspective. I felt that I might pee my pants or my body would crumple to the floor, yet my body continued to do what it was doing without effort. All ideas of effort or achievement were gone. It was obvious that there was no one doing life, and that life wasn't happening to a me. It was the end of a lifetime propelled by hope and fear and need of a never arising next. It was as if time died. It was as if I had died, yet it was obvious that I had never existed.

I wondered if this was a 'special' state I had read about, yet could not believe that one could put the blinders of separation on again. After three weeks I marked the date. It was easy to find as we cleaned that house every other Friday. There was no fear associated with this new way of seeing, I knew without a doubt that this was what the famous sages had been singing about. I really never looked for confirmation or avidly sought others who knew this. Who could I tell? I also knew without a doubt that most others I had read had no clue about this no-thing-ness. I called it 'falling into indivisibility'.

Yet, somehow there was a belief that this had happened to a me. So the next two years were smoother. Just watching as more beliefs of who I was untied themselves. Through out these years I watched many beliefs fall away, either as they popped, or after, I'd think, Oh my I don't believe that anymore and never really did!

I sang about this incredible stunning no thingness on facebook for over a year and a half and finally I met another who echoed my heart song, not just speaking of no self. It was such a relief! We sang together on a forum until it folded.

It seemed that the 'gauge' during these two years was self consciousness, self judgment and self correction and doubt becoming less and less, until there was nothing left. Not even nothing. I never knew there would be nothing!

Suspended as nothing I felt I could steer the car into the oncoming traffic and it wouldn't make any difference. I couldn't say it was OK or not OK. I had no group or no one to share this with. I can't even say when it happened as it was such a gradual falling. I did remember that friend saying once that it takes years to get used to this.

About a month later, one day I was speaking with this friend about how it requires imaginary separation to recognize unicity and I said, "oh I will dance with you anytime". He said, "We have been dancing for quite awhile". Suddenly it hit me. The enormity of what had happened. and that he had been there those last few months. Love had been there. Not a psyco-sexual love, but a true Sage is a beautiful clear reflection of your own love and emptiness.

For some the fullness trickles in, but here it was all of a sudden.

It was like he gave me back myself. It was love that brought me back. That's when the weeping began. For no reason. For every reason. I was back. But I was dead. Both. A story knowing I was a story. Like being a character in a movie yet knowing you are made up. Like a hologram, a dream, a magicians tale. Dreamlike yet somehow more alive and vibrant, wondrous beyond measure.

This is an entirely different way to experience what is going on, free from the terror and pain of looking though the window of imagined personal volition. Somehow the window looses the painting of what you have imagined life to be like and ideas about what it should be like. All ideas of truth and meaning and non-meaning fall away.

The imaginary clouds clear themselves and there is no more longing for an idea, no more longing for that which is not. It's more like a longing for what is and there is utter ease. There are no more what if's or what's next. It's like time dies.

No longer does it feel like there is a me doing life or that life is happening to a me. There is an untouchable profound peace underlying all and everything a seamless ease that has embraced the mind and always an unutterable sense of awe.

Self remains but it has lost its relevance.

Life is passionate full on yet impersonal at the same time.

Whilst not singing here with you, I slide into the vastness. Suspended as nothingness. Just a constant wow. But camping with friends and family I felt like transparent light sliding into and through the dream. I Appear and disappear into my own beautiful reflection through their eyes. An ecstatic love dance of one of two of many of one... as love, lover and beloved, a constant union a swooning into the swoon of what was never apart.

It's like before I was wind dancer and now it's like light dancer.

Not even nakedness, not even a wisp of a song clothes what has no weight.

Yet my feets still know how to dance, there are simply no footprints.

Made in the USA
San Bernardino, CA
07 October 2017